Carin Edwards,
Cambridge, Oct. 1965.

The Muses' Library

★

COLLECTED POEMS
OF JONATHAN SWIFT

This 'English' Swift, in the National Portrait Gallery, London, is one of several painted by Charles Jervas, showing him as he appeared in about his 45th year, before the physical decline that marks his most creative period.

COLLECTED POEMS

OF

JONATHAN SWIFT

edited
with an introduction
and critical comments
by

JOSEPH HORRELL
M.Litt., M.A. (Cantab.)

VOLUME ONE

LONDON
ROUTLEDGE AND KEGAN PAUL LTD

First published in 1958
by Routledge and Kegan Paul Limited
Broadway House
68–74 Carter Lane
London E.C.4
Printed in Great Britain
by Butler and Tanner Limited
Frome and London

To

CAMBRIDGE FRIENDS

AT JESUS AND QUEENS'

AND IN THE TOWN

CONTENTS

THE POEMS

CONTENTS

CONTENTS

CONTENTS

CONTENTS

CONTENTS

LIST OF PLATES

INTRODUCTION

INTRODUCTION

By

JOSEPH HORRELL

SWIFT'S LIFE

THE forces in Swift's life that hold our interest are those he struggled against in vain: his Anglo-Irish birth (or split nationality), his disease, and his exile.

Jonathan Swift was born in Dublin of English parents on November 30th, 1667, some months after the death of his father, a young attorney who rode the circuit. His mother, left also with a two-year-old daughter, Jane, felt no strong tie to the country of her in-laws, and returned to her native Leicestershire some time while her son was being bred at Kilkenny School and Trinity College through the generosity of well-to-do uncles, one of whom appears to have reared the daughter.

Swift grew up without any particular allegiance to the land of his birth. In his lifetime it was impossible to define Irish patriotism: the inhabitants were Irish and enjoyed a kind of national character by identifying themselves with one or another of the passions that tore the country apart. 'The English' were the ruling class, reinforced by viceroy and garrison, a dominant minority based on the Anglican establishment and the law that preserved order and guaranteed their land titles. Pressing from two sides were Irish Catholics and Scotch Presbyterians. No one lived apart from these divisions, and their mark is so indelible in Swift's life that we can imagine Ireland taking possession of him at an early age. As a schoolboy at Kilkenny he could witness in the ruins of St. Canice the violent extremes of Irish history, the stained glass shattered by Cromwell's soldiers in the wake of the papal nuncio who had made his seat there, all this not many years before. We can hear accentuated in the *Tale of a Tub* the opposing voices of superstition and fanaticism that rail in Hobbes's 'kingdom of darkness'. Swift's scoffing about such things had the misfortune to fall on English ears attuned to more pleasing sounds than came from Ireland or Hobbes. His background provided him no accurate gauge of the English mood, and he sometimes vexed the people he really meant to divert, at a time in his life when the distinction was important.

Swift intended to shed his Irish background as soon as he could because he regarded it as an inconvenience and an unhappy accident of birth. Moving to England gave him an opportunity to set about recovering his English birthright, which was the only debt he acknowledged to his family. This desire took shape at Moor Park, Sir William Temple's seat, where during the Revolution he sheltered as the retired diplomatist's secretary, dragging out his stay over the better part of a decade. Oxford gave him the M.A. she still grants Trinity graduates under the academic rite of 'incorporation'; and he took extraordinary pride in this English stamp obtained after a residence at Hart Hall (now Hertford College) of only a few weeks, probably the length of time his residence at Trinity College had been cut short. His career there had been undistinguished except for his rebellion against the scholastic dry-rot which Bacon, Milton, and Hobbes scorned at Oxford or Cambridge, and for which Temple, a Cambridge man of indifferent record, had no sympathy.

The picture of Swift and Temple is a fascinating

one. (Macaulay may overcolour it, but he does not misjudge the interest of a situation.) Possibly the most interesting thing about Temple in Swift's eyes was the fact that here was a man whose family had been identified with the English in Ireland since the Elizabethan Conquest, but who had moved to England young and carved out a handsome career for himself. The analogy was not too far-fetched for a young man having a poor boy's ambition and a rapidly maturing genius with now a patron who was a personal acquaintance of William III. Unfortunately the 'barren court' Temple shunned did not respond to diffident overtures for preferment of someone else, remembering that Temple's answer to the broil of politics had been complete retirement. Swift probably could not fathom Temple's inbred discretion, a political necessity in a statesman one of whose brothers, now dead and no longer mentioned, had served the Cromwellian general Venables as secretary, and whose father had sat in the Long Parliament. Swift was content, after copying all of Temple's writings for the Press, to defer to his advice against publishing the *Tale of a Tub* and the *Battle of the Books*. Meanwhile he had taken orders in the Church of Ireland, the right church but the wrong pew, because he could not lay his hands on anything in England. He must have known he was forging another link in the chain he was determined to break.

Swift awoke from dreams of preferment to find himself, at thirty-two, vicar of Laracor, an obscure Irish parish of half a score rustic souls. Temple was dead, having left him a number of introductions to great men, the care of his unpublished writings, and £100. Now began his years of shuttling between Ireland and England seeking a place 'a little above contempt'.

The accounts of these years, inspired by Swift's own writings, generally stress the political aspect. But such

an exterior view of Swift fails to expose the psychological bars to his 'rising', the bedrock of frustration
and despair on which his great achievement in Ireland
stands. Nor can we accept his estimate of the Tory
years as the noontide of his life, when in fact such an
estimate testifies better to his subaltern colonial outlook. The provincialism that clung to every English
growth in Ireland throve on Swift's divided and
uncertain nationality. No Oxford or Cambridge college could boast a brighter array of graduates than
Trinity College in Swift's lifetime. And yet in literature
alone we have the spectacle of Congreve, Farquhar,
Southerne, and Parnell—let Swift and Berkeley be
exceptions—shedding their lustre in England as
happily as Irish absentees bled their estates. From his
Moor Park days Swift's distaste for Ireland never
abated. Not expecting to stay there, he carelessly
alienated the Irish bishops, who take the view when
he needs them that he is too well connected with
English ministers for their benevolence to be of any
use. 'I had as live be a Beau in Dublin', Swift told
Ford, 'as a Politician, nay, I had as lieve be an Author
there; and if ever I have any thoughts of making a
figure in that Kingdom, it shall be at Laracor. I will
talk Politicks to the Farmers, and publish my Works
at Trim.' He read Molyneux, 'the friend of Locke and
Liberty', without any visible response to his argument
that Ireland was an independent kingdom. It was to
be years before he would say to the English viceroy,
'My lord, cultivate the Grattans, for the Grattans, my
lord, can raise 10,000 men.' This was provincialism of
harder stuff, but it came too late to further his own
ambitions, for when based on Ireland, he had neglected
to muster forces there. 'We were determined to have
you,' Bolingbroke told him; 'you were the only one
we were afraid of.' But the strength Bolingbroke
sought was Swift's pen, which after he had been a

priest for twenty years was still his principal resource and not one, considering his 'sin of wit', calculated to put a mitre on his head.

The highest Tory in Ireland would make a tolerable Whig in England, Swift told William III. This geopolitical dilemma teased him for the better part of his life, though it contained little to interest an Englishman. Crossing St. George's Channel confounded Swift's politics because he was never sure whether he was on a visit or had come to stay, or which interest he should identify himself with. Issues like repeal of the test or occasional conformity (which Defoe called 'playing Bo-peep with God Almighty') changed political hue depending on the shore from which they were viewed. Williamite high churchmen passed without notice in Ireland, because that was a kingdom in which the ruling class being exposed to revolutionary pressures, could not risk debilitating itself in political sport and cared little for partisan consistency. But in England there was a growing fondness for politics along simple partisan lines of Whig and Tory. High church Irish Whigs introduced complications that made the game unnecessarily difficult to play. Swift never found a receptive audience for his explanation how he could be at once a Tory and an 'old Whig'.

Swift's abandoning the Whigs for the Tories is less a matter of political apostasy, as Jeffrey and Macaulay describe it, than a drastic attempt to reorient himself in accordance with English standards. Likewise the failure of his political schemes, envisaging an English benefice for himself and possibly even a seat in the House of Lords, cannot be explained merely as bad politics even though the political sphere is the one in which we see it revealed. His failure is personal, and we suspect Steele (another Dubliner by birth) of recognizing this from his taunt, 'the English would laugh at us, should we argue in so Irish a manner'.

The 'moderating' schemes of the Tories left Swift cold because he unconsciously regarded the Tories as a ruling class rather than a party, and this Irish outlook accounts for his party violence and extremism. His background leaves him as innocent of Jacobitism as Berkeley, to whom 'it is inconceivable what shadow of advantage an Irish Protestant can fancy to himself from such a revolution'; and yet we must think him naïve in not seeing, or in being unable to believe if he did see, the consistent drift of Tory policy towards St. Germain. His great prestige as the unofficial adviser and mouthpiece of the Tory government only heightened the shock of being 'thrown into' the deanery of St. Patrick's, or shoved back on Ireland. It took him years of ruminating on his native land as a place of exile to discover that it was the only sure footing he had. He became a Dublin politician after all.

When Swift was twenty-one, at Moor Park, he suffered his first attack of 'giddiness', later accompanied by deafness, which for the remainder of his life overpowered him at unexpected moments, making his head swim and his ears fill with the 'sound of a thousand oceans'. This affliction was not described until long after his death as labyrinthine vertigo, or Meunière's disease, of which the symptoms are dizziness, nausea, depression, and faintness. Swift's doctors were as ignorant of what ailed him as he was, and the 'fits' that brought him down for weeks at a time filled him with shame and loathing. He could not bear for anyone unfamiliar with his attacks, not even his friend Pope, to witness his suffering, but entrusted himself to an impoverished cousin in London or Stella in Ireland, both prepared to hear him cry out above the 'windmills' in his ears. During respites he prepared for the next attack. On the advice of physician friends—and there was always one in his inner circle—he swallowed bitter draughts and stuffed his ears with garlic. Constantly testing his own theories he abstained from fruit, gave up snuff, and watered down his wine, as he increased the anxiety symptomatic of his disease in his desperate search for some rational cause to allay his apprehension as to its proper name, nature, and course. The fear and disgust he felt at Bedlam are the emotions that drew him there, fascinated by its horrifying spectacle which he felt compelled to witness. His world was undermined like the epileptic's, all his plans and movements subject to cancellation by attacks that left him helpless as a child.

Between attacks he required the distraction of mental and physical activity, and his writings are often an escape from worse apprehensions than they express. He writes his 'Holyhead Journal' ('What can I do but write everything that comes into my head') during 'unwalkable hours' or when he is exhausted from climbing over the barren Welsh scene, struggling to keep awake against the nightmare of the mind. He exercised incessantly, scouring Irish bogs and fens on horseback, racing up and down the deanery stairs when impossible weather kept him indoors. On the night of Stella's funeral he sits in a secluded room of the deanery where he cannot see the burial torches, writing his factual and prosaic memoir of the woman who devoted her life to him.

Like any bachelor jealous of his freedom, Swift always had reasons not to take a wife. In his younger years he lived in suspense, ready to break camp at any time; and his settlement in St. Patrick's found him nearing fifty, sick and profoundly depressed in spirit. By this time physical infirmities had become one of the bonds between Swift and Stella, who talked more of 'spectacles and pills' and 'such mortifying stuff' than romancers care to allow. He had known Esther

Johnson since her childhood at Moor Park, where she was brought up in the service of Lady Giffard, Temple's sister, to whom her mother was a servant. He took her away to Ireland after Temple's death hoping to dissociate her from the dependent relationship in which her mother still lived; but this was impossible. She was indebted to Temple for the living he bequeathed her; Lady Giffard continued to manage her money; and concealment of her position in the Temple household (Swift does not mention the family in his memoir) left a vacuum for the rumour that she was Temple's illegitimate daughter. Swift himself spoke too soon when he told Stella, 'I am glad I have wholly shaken off that family.' For when Stella's mother left Lady Giffard's service to marry again, Swift's sister, 'poor Jenny', who had made an unfortunate marriage against his wishes, came over from Ireland to replace her with 'that old beast'.[1] This arrangement, estranging Swift for ever from his sister, probably owed something to their mother, who had claims on the Temple family that have not been explained except by conjectures as adventitious as those attaching to Stella's mother. Moor Park was a long shadow in the lives of Swift and Stella. As for their alleged secret marriage in 1716, documentary evidence is lacking, but there is ample evidence that their friends believed them married. Since they did not live together, the ceremony at most gave Stella the security she needed against a rival, which she had in Vanessa.

As far as our knowledge of Stella is concerned she is Swift's creation, and he did not allow the letters she

[1] The date of the second marriage of Stella's mother, Bridget Johnson, which was to Ralph Mose, Temple's steward, has been guessed at quite needlessly. The marriage is recorded in the Farnham register under October 25th, 1711. The *Journal to Stella* is silent on the subject, though Swift's anger at his sister's substitution with Lady Giffard breaks out.

wrote him to survive. But Vanessa, as he called Esther Vanhomrigh, possessed a fortune which obtains for her a skeletal existence in legal records, and she forestalled the oblivion of her love by keeping copies of the letters she wrote Swift, a painful, living record contrasting with the cold pastoral in which he enshrines her in *Cadenus and Vanessa*. She desired not just to be his devoted slave, but his mistress, his wife, and in her desperate pursuit she shipwrecked on the relationship Stella had habituated Swift to, if not on the marriage itself. The death of both women within a few years of each other released Swift from the bondage of their love.

The 'great dean' is an ancestral figure in the genealogy of Irish liberty as Lecky traces it, from Molyneux to Swift, from Swift to Lucas, from Lucas to Flood, a line crowned by the illustrious Grattan. Molyneux is a philosopher whose coldly reasoned 'case' for Ireland not being bound by acts of the English parliament lay dormant for twenty-five years after the House of Commons burned his book. Grattan is a parliamentary statesman and patriot rather than a revolutionist, an orator like Burke, of fiery but not inflammatory eloquence. Swift on the other hand is an agitator trading on what Lecky calls the Irish 'appetite for political excitement'. His pamphlets against English rule appeared politically dangerous because he arouses men to particular courses of action without providing them enough general ideas to mark their drift or goal. He blasphemes kings without advocating republics. Implicit in his thought is his belief, derived from Polybius, in the inevitability of decay, which disposes him to seek amelioration since there is no cure.

Swift became the hero of Ireland in the Drapier affair writing under a pseudonym as transparent as 'Junius' is impenetrable. Opposition to measures of the Walpole government for issuing copper coins in Ireland by private patent had already congealed before Swift moved in on the controversy. He waited to see which way the crowd was going before he made himself its leader. His thinly disguised Drapier letters stirred the agitation until the disparate elements of Ireland found themselves for a moment united on a single issue in opposition to English rule. This had never happened before, and the potentialities of Irish unity proved more frightening than those of division. Swift played on these fears by abruptly reviving Molyneux's arguments amongst less important ones about the coinage, which was a short-lived issue. His tactic was possibly only a diversion, but it reveals for the first time his consciousness of the latent strength of his Irish background. The crowd at Swift's back forced the English government to compound at a lower rate by withdrawing the patent, and he recognized that his personal triumph was a hollow political victory.

Swift's conduct in Irish affairs quite as much as his attitude towards women reveals extremes of compassion and hatred without the mediation of love. His misanthropy was at first (in *Gulliver*) a rational attempt to bridge this emotional gulf. He hates mankind for producing the objects of his pity. But he immersed his misanthropy in darker feelings induced by his tireless survey of the miserable scenes of his exile, by feasting his eyes on the face of Ireland wherein he saw reflected his own 'age of sourness and morosity'. His sensibility was one requiring constant physical stimulus, and he appears to soak up the data of politics and economics as features of the landscape, not out of books. *A Modest Proposal* resembles dozens of other 'proposals', but is the product of his ironic humour playing upon three terrible years of famine. Exile in a land of beggars and slaves became the ideal garment of his spiritual desolation: so much so that

he once considered breaking the harmony by be-
queathing his body to Wales, a bleaker shore with
which he had no connection at all.

This 'stranger in a strange land' devoted himself to
Irish affairs from his personal triumph in 1725 until
his powers failed a few years before his death in 1745.
The incredible energy that distinguishes his old age
made these his most productive years, spurred by his
increasing rage, frustration, and despair, his hopeless
view of human destiny, as he resigned himself to
dying in Ireland 'like a poisoned rat in a hole'. With
such feelings, if not because of them, he produced
pamphlet after pamphlet setting forth in everyday
language practical measures for remedying the economic condition of the country, for improving tillage,
native manufactures, and trade, in the belief 'that
whoever could make two Ears of Corn, or two Blades
of Grass to grow upon a Spot of Ground where only
one grew before; would deserve better of Mankind,
and do more essential Service to his Country, than
the whole Race of Politicians put together'. The Irish
themselves possessed the means of improving their
economic lot, whereas the political issue was (in his
stoic phrase) 'without our power'. Grattan had already
introduced and spoken for his first independence bill
when Dr. Johnson gave his just estimate of Swift's
work: 'It was from the time when he first began to
patronize the Irish, that they may date their riches and
prosperity. He taught them first to know their own
interest, their weight, and their strength, and gave
them spirit to assert that equality with their fellow-
subjects to which they have ever since been making
vigorous advances, and to claim those rights which
they have at last established.'

But it was Swift's fate to struggle against forces out-
side his power, and he angrily flailed at the benefici-
aries of English rule because the servility of its victims

was more offensive to him than the rule itself. His protests eventually sank to impotent demonstrations as when on the King's birthday he hung the deanery windows in black and rang muffled peals on his cathedral bells. He had long since despaired of arousing the conscience of a ruling class devoted to its perquisites, or shaming a populace that exhibited a brute-like contentment in its degradation. Thus his role as patriot-hero of Ireland left him unmoved except as duty to one's country was a Roman virtue. While the Dublin crowds were burning bonfires on his birthday, he remained in the deanery house reading, as was his custom, the third chapter of Job: 'Let the day perish wherein I was born, and the night in which it was said, "There is a man child conceived." '

Especially in his later years Swift personifies the miseries that are Ireland's national treasure, and his heroic stature owes something to the Irish folk memory. Like Oedipus at Colonus his body blesses the soil, resting 'where savage indignation no longer lacerates his heart': an eighteenth-century apotheosis hard to imagine anywhere except in Ireland. But at the same time he is the greatest representative of England's classical age. The English form embodies the Irish substance.

This was in Swift's mind a predicament, and we are perhaps entitled to view his life and work as expressions of it. His churchly, political, and literary ideals are essentially uninteresting except as they are harnessed to Irish actualities. The *Tale of a Tub* and the *Battle of the Books* are bookish, unsociable works conceived like his early poems in the loneliness of Moor Park. (The *Tale* does not show Swift 'beside himself', as Dr. Johnson claimed to believe, but rather not yet himself.) What is lacking might appear to be what he found in the friendship of Addison, Prior, Pope, and Gay; but he preserves nothing vital of them.

It is the 'middling' friends of his Irish acquaintance who come alive in his hands. The substance may (at least in Swift's opinion) have changed for the worse, but that also was its challenge: it possessed only the interest that he would lend it. 'Those black corrosive vapours which he exhaled so profusely formerly in the open air', Bolingbroke wrote Pope in 1724, 'have been long pent up in a cloister, and he is become the martyr of that humour which was given him for the punishment of others.' This did not come to pass for a long time because, among other reasons, the conversation of Sheridan, the Grattan brothers, Dan Jackson, and the servants at Market Hill was more congenial to him than he would admit or Bolingbroke could suppose. The humour that makes his misanthropy so contemptuous and withering also makes it significant and tolerable. It makes material of the ugly incongruities that are the despair of a rational mind. He is unhappy with the world, but it is his oyster. His poetry rather more than his prose signifies his resolution to live on whatever terms with the problems he could not solve.

SWIFT'S POETRY

English poets are expected to write good prose, if only with their left hand, but it is uncommon to find major prose writers giving us distinguished verse. Hardy is one, though poetry or prose was an exclusive interest at any particular time. Swift is unusual among the great prose writers because of the extent to which his poetry and prose are mutual and supporting interests. The sheer bulk of his poetry is surprising, for we hardly expect a public person taken up as he was with ecclesiastical and political affairs to write as much poetry as Pope (excepting his Homer) and more than Prior, Parnell, Gay, or Young. The 'several occasions' of his poems are nearly always fresh and revealing because he has no highfalutin' notions of 'poetry' or literary reputation to restrain him. He gets in and out of verse as easily as he changes his gown, and his poems open like windows on persons and places, on his darkest and most joyous moods. They celebrate no exalted moods only because he acknowledged none. They are attractive because we feel in them Swift's compulsion, like Horace's, to write whatever the colour of life may be. His verse is a social activity like conversation, which it owes much to. 'There are no sciences', Saint Evremond said, 'that particularly deserve the care of a Gentleman, but *Morality*, *Politicks*, and *polite Learning*. The first has a relation to Reason; the second to Society; the third to Conversation.' Swift was less preoccupied with poetry than Dryden and Pope, but closer than they to the civic ideal of his time.

The greatest part of his poetry he wrote late in life. We have to adjust ourselves to the fact that Swift flourished alongside Pope, who was young enough to be his son. Steele addressed him in an early *Tatler* as 'the Janus of his times, whom by his years and wit, you would take to be of the last age; but by his dress and morals, of this'. Congreve and Prior were his true contemporaries, but Congreve remains a Restoration figure, and Prior appears lonely and isolated after Queen Anne's time. In the Georgian age Swift represented the older generation of Queen Anne wits, the rest of whom had stopped writing, sunk into mediocrity, or died.

He suppressed the odes and heroic verse that we now read of his first period, 1689–1698, best known for the *Tale of a Tub*. These poems are 'interesting' but little else, respectable baroque, Cowley and Waller in turn giving us our one chance to see him writing derivative styles.

The poems of his second period, 1698–1718, are

'characteristic', which means that they are familiar, satirical, or in eight-syllable couplets. During these years he gave himself over to pamphleteering and English interests, and his poetical output seems relatively small if we consider that he reached his fiftieth birthday having written only one-fifth the poetry he was to write. His biographers shun the conclusion that if he had died with Queen Anne—and he told Pope his 'death' began then—he would now be known as a minor literary figure a grade or two below Addison and Steele, his fame resting on a single piece of prose. The 'English' Swift is a reference point of his exile, and even the face that Jervas gives him, with its healthy rubicund complexion, serves as the 'original' for the lowering Irish portraits of Bindon and Slaughter. For nearly everything of enduring significance that Swift wrote or did belongs to his 'death' in Ireland.

There his working up was tantalizingly slow. The poetry of his third period, 1718–1727, during which he wrote *Gulliver's Travels*, is devoted mainly to 'private' subjects: familiar epistles to friends, poems to Stella, and trifles exchanged with Sheridan. His longest poem, *Cadenus and Vanessa*, an elegant piece of persiflage, was probably completed at this time, while Vanessa and Stella are offset by the Chloes of his impersonal satires on love, beauty, and marriage. These poems remained for the time in manuscript, and he gave the Press only a few verse squibs on the Drapier affair.

In his productive final period, 1727–1738, Swift was free from many restraints. Vanessa and Stella were dead; his role of Drapier made him the voice of the Anglo-Irish who had regarded him as another Englishman beneficed on Ireland; and the new reign defeated his lingering hope of a political reconciliation that would permit his resettlement in England. Now, not earlier, he 'commenced Irishman for life'.

Now there was nothing to lose, and he wrote and published with an outspokenness that is itself one of his chief literary characteristics. At one extreme are his lampoons, their victims ranging from George II and Walpole to the shoals of Irish officialdom and small fry whose names (contrary to the advice he gave Pope) he transmits to posterity. The lampoons on English subjects culminate in *On Poetry: A Rapsody*; on Irish subjects, in *The Legion Club*. At the other extreme are his impersonal satires on the sexual relationship, revealing his innermost thoughts in the self-immolation of publicity, indifferent to the 'common forms' by which his frankness would be judged. 'I don't care', he used to write to Stella; now he says it publicly. He is determined to make a controversial issue of his character, of which his poems are memorials like his epitaph and madhouse.

On Poetry: A Rapsody has often been admired as Swift's best poem, and it is true that no other shows both his wit and humour to better advantage. The poem is his most complicated and difficult to follow, and some of the 'rapidity' of his thought is due to the variety of subjects he traverses, like converging spokes of a wheel, so as to reach his goal from several different directions. For his critical essay is really a lampoon on Walpole and George II, in which the indirection of irony was a desirable precaution. Swift's major poems usually bring together all his interests of the moment. *On Poetry* draws upon his unpublished *Directions for Making a Birthday Song*, a much more direct assault in the 'instructions' fashion started by Marvell's parody of Waller. It takes its ostensible theme from *The Beasts Confession*, though Swift treats half a dozen other subjects than how men mistake their talents. Its political satire relates it to *A Libel on Dr. Delany*, *A Panegyric on Dean Swift* ('I chose to abuse myself with the direct reverse of my character'), and other recent poems, and the reference to Horace's Epistle to Augustus in the rejected passages suggests where Swift, like Pope a little later, got the idea of an ironical panegyric on the King. The passage laden with regal imagery in which Swift cuts George II to ribbons, marked by an abrupt turn in the thought,

> *Tho' Peace with Olive bind his Hands,*
> *Confest the Conqu'ring Hero stands,*

is one of the most brilliant he ever wrote. The publishers were arrested.

Both Swift and Pope proceed to their *apologiae* via imitations of Horace's Satire I Book II, the classical prototype, though the *Verses on the Death of Dr. Swift* and the *Epistle to Dr. Arbuthnot* are as different as their authors. Pope's poem is still an 'imitation', an essay in wit as that word had come to be understood, though one of the more original parts of his Horatian 'system'. Swift's fragmentary imitation of Satire I Book II suggests that he originally intended to write an *apologia pro sua satura* along Horatian lines, and the 'counterfeit' version of the *Verses* called the *Life and Genuine Character of Dr. Swift* accordingly dwells more than its successor on his works. But 'a certain uncommon way of thinking' that Steele observed in him draws him far afield from Horace to La Rochefoucauld's maxim about the secret pleasure we take in the misfortunes of our friends; and Swift exemplifies the maxim in scenes that he imagines as following his death, posthumous scenes revealed with the mirth of an Irish wake. He prefers originality and humour to imitation and wit. To this fooling he appends a serious *apologia pro sua vita*, acknowledging the stronger claim of life than literature, of character than 'works', while Pope was asking:

> *This subtle Thief of life, this paltry Time,*
> *What will it leave me, if it snatch my rhyme?*

As Swift's grip on reality loosens in his later years his poems take on an imaginative hue lacking before. *On the Death of Dr. Swift* distorts facts as it displays his character, and his lampoons occasionally fall on persons innocent of any wrong. These are misreadings of fact, but the imagination is not bound by fact. Against the verifiable character in the *Furniture of a Woman's Mind* and 'annals of a female day' in the *Journal of a Modern Lady*, we have the 'gaudy tulips rais'd from dung' in *A Beautiful Young Nymph Going to Bed*, *The Lady's Dressing Room*, and *Strephon and Chloe*, which are works of the imagination. He has seen none of this; he has induced himself to imagine it. The usual moral on decency in these demi-fables only makes Swift's imaginings more oppressive, until he loses whatever laughs he intended from the nymph who on her wedding night must unburden herself of a dozen cups of tea. Yet this imagination has great power. The visionary eschatology of *The Day of Judgement* is as terrifying as Lear's 'As flies to wanton boys'; Swift's Jove damns the race of human kind merely to please his wit. The sights and sounds and smells of *The Legion Club* with its Vergilian other-world machinery applied to Irish subjects, inspire the revulsion that we feel in the *Inferno*, where we condemn sinners on the evidence of our senses before we are told the nature of their crimes. But Swift's vision has a personal note, for the 'dire infectious crew' of the Irish Senate is pictured at home in Dr. Swift's madhouse, condemned to the same hell he feared for himself.

The elements of Swift's poetry are picture and dialogue, held in humorous suspense by his style. These displace the steady narrative-like progression of topics that is the tedious aspect of Butler and Dryden, who rely more on their styles for our interest. Butler's 'acrobatism' is so conspicuous and irresistible that he abandons his subject for a canto at a time. Dryden, who confessed his lack of gifts for conversation, writes with Juvenal's declamatory grandeur, his characters talking at uniform 'height', their talk almost indistinguishable from the rest of the poem and difficult to punctuate. Only late in life and after he had stopped writing satires did Dryden take the laurel from Juvenal and give it to Horace, whose *sermo pedestris* is an influence on Pope's 'plain prose' as well as Swift's bare style, an influence allied to the art of conversation. It was Rochester, an imitator of Horace, not Butler and Dryden, who used his eyes and ears and a talking style to escape from the 'rimed chronicle' and 'leading article' manner (as Previté-Orton describes it) of Restoration satire. A comparison of Swift and Pope on the one hand with Dryden and Butler on the other is not so violent as may at first appear. Pope wrote two imitations of Horace 'in the manner of Dr. Swift'—an honour he paid no other contemporary.

The *Journal to Stella* has few literary merits to put beside the easy, unaffected way in which it talks, sounding like an overheard conversation between two friends. The charm of many of Swift's poems—*Stella at Wood Park*, *An Apology to Lady Carteret*, *The Journal of a Modern Lady*—lies in nuances of speech which we unhesitatingly accept as authentic without other evidence than they provide. Saintsbury says that only piecemeal in older comedies and more recent novels can we find dialogue of the freshness and perennial charm that Swift brought into English prose with his *Polite Conversation*. It is more remarkable that he should have so often caught the accents of real speech in his short lines.

What Yeats said of Mr. Eliot's early poems with their scraps of newspapers in vacant lots applies equally well to Swift's: they exhibit 'an unexaggerated plainness that has the effect of novelty'. One of his poems, Steele says, is a description of the morning, 'but of the morning in town; nay, of the morning at this end of the town'. Swift's sensibility was alive to the grey nostalgic world of familiar sights and sounds and smells: 'All Christian vittals stink of fish', 'The Winter-Sky began to frown', 'The smutty Wainscot full of Cracks', 'The Dean is dead, (and what is Trumps?)'. No one ever yoked poetry so mercilessly to life. He feels so little reverence for the sacred precincts of poetry that he brings inside all the interests normally identified with prose. In other words, his subject-matter no less than his bare style is the profanation underlying the finical accusation that he wrote rhymed prose. But one of his problems was to find a decorous style for 'the Deal, the Shuffle, and the Cut', for the stink of fish and smutty wainscots. He wrote his 'description' of the *Morning* and the *City Shower* (Pope called these poems his 'georgic' style) to ridicule the high baroque treatment that it was fashionable to lavish on all subjects impartially, the writhing within the bonds of heroic couplets devoted to landscape or husbandry to find a suitable posture for the 'turn':

> *Such is the Sprinkling which some careless Quean*
> *Flirts on you from her Mop, but not so clean.*
> *You fly, invoke the Gods; then turning, stop*
> *To rail; she singing, still whirls on her Mop.*

Swift's chief literary interest is style, and like his own style this interest is an aspect of his pessimism. It was a conviction with him, not a mere matter of literary taste, that an age of Georges could not furnish subjects to be taken seriously in the great forms of poetry over which the muses preside. The age deserved satire, which has no muse. The 'kinds' were useful as familiar habitations inside which he could go about his work, and we often find him writing in one or another: fables, epistles, odes, imitations of Horace, ballads, epigrams, topographical essays. Conventional elements usually mark one of the limits of his humorous distortion. In the Court of Venus of *Cadenus and Vanessa* he has the rose-tinted props of a French painter's studio, and the air rattles with lawyer's jargon.

Swift has his own uses for the baroque decoration of regal pictures 'seen o'er many an Alehouse fire', but his favourite and characteristic rhetorical device is bareness. His 'types', or analogies, emphasize the point at issue by paralleling it, like the witty series on poetical vacuity in *On Poetry* ending with:

> *So Geographers in Afric-maps*
> *With Savage-Pictures fill their Gaps;*
> *And o'er unhabitable Downs*
> *Place Elephants for want of Towns.*

His meagre lines have a music attributable to his keen ear:

> *Where Folly, Pride, and Faction sway,*
> *Remote from St. John, Pope, and Gay.*

Their effects range from great tension ('Not Beggar's Brat, on Bulk begot') to an utter prose-like relaxation of deceptive simplicity. Anyone can versify

> *Suppose me dead, and then suppose*
> *A Club assembled at the Rose,*

but the difficulty is not to lose readers after a page of this. The mystery of Swift's bare style is the secret energy that keeps it going. Pope identified the 'manner of Dr. Swift' with Swift's 'odd way', and this odd way is humour, 'a singular and unavoidable manner', in Congreve's words, 'of doing, or saying any thing, Peculiar and Natural to one Man only'.

Humour was the quality Swift was proudest of:

What Humor is, not all the Tribe
Of Logick-mongers can describe;
Here, onely Nature acts her Part,
Unhelpt by Practice, Books, or Art.
For Wit and Humor differ quite,
That gives Surprise, and this Delight:
Humor is odd, grotesque, and wild,
Onely by Affectation spoild,
Tis never by Invention got,
Men have it when they know it not.

We 'taste' Swift in his trifles and society verse because in these 'private things' (as he described the Market Hill poems) his humour exists in a pure state without the 'satiric itch' and chafings of wit that public issues provoked. He is free, disengaged, as frothy and delightful as his two-line 'Satyr on an Inconstant Lover':

You are as faithless as a Carthaginian,
To love at once, Kate, Nell, Doll, Martha, Jenny,
Anne.

In such things Swift is a prankster, a lover of 'bites', but his trifles contain the essence of much else that he wrote. Remove the 'biting' humour (and 'bite' means to 'take in' a person, not to sting him) from his works and the secret attraction of their form and substance disappears. In the Fourth Book of *Gulliver* (if it is conceivable that we could have this book without its humour) we should lack the Houyhnhnm threading a needle, Gulliver's troubled uncertainty whether he should claim for the Crown the countries he has discovered, above all his final protestations of truthfulness buttressed by an abrupt quotation from the *Aeneid* of the mendacious words of Sion, who also told a story about a horse. In his *Epistle to Augustus* Pope 'bites' George II with ironic wit; but the corresponding leg of Swift's irony (even in the anguish of *A Modest Proposal*) is humour.

The impressive thing about Swift's poetry is its precise gauge of his experience—a palpable reality that can never be ignored; just as the literary quality that he possesses in the highest degree is that of being able to intercept always at an intelligible point the mysterious communication between sensation and thought. The beautiful and moving poem that he wrote to Stella on her last birthday, a poem of restrained grief in the tradition of King's *Exequy*, contains a simple idea of 'remembrance' which, given some complication, furnished Wordsworth with matter for hundreds of lines. But Swift, with his 'undeviating attention to the point at issue', disciplines thought to expression.

> *For Virtue in her daily Race,*
> *Like* Janus, *bears a double Face;*
> *Looks back with Joy where she has gone,*
> *And therefore goes with Courage on.*

The point is arguable that in requiring a rational translation of feeling into thought for literary expression, Swift was left more than others of his age with a large untranslatable residue, in his case a frustrating deadweight. This is less easy to verify than the testimony of his poems that in his most savage as in his lighter moments he expresses himself with glaring clarity.

CANON AND TEXT

Despite their being unsigned Swift's best-known poems were always unmistakably his, but the canon of his poetry remained indefinite until 1937, when Sir Harold Williams published his definitive edition relieving him of responsibility for more than 150 poems, none of much merit, which had at various times been attributed to him. The present edition adopts the Williams canon with few exceptions, the chief being the inclusion here of *A Description of Mother Ludwell's Cave*, which Williams rejects.

Within the canon there is still the problem of authorization. Swift's canon is as large as it is and contains as much inferior work as it does because his control over it was indecisive during his lifetime and non-existent after his death. By and large the poems of Pope's that we read are those he meant for us to read, and scholars have returned surprisingly few 'wild fowl' to his roost. But Swift took poor care of his literary estate. A significant part of his canon consists of (i) poems he published singly but did not collect, apparently desiring their suppression, and (ii) poems left in manuscript, often unfinished or imperfect: both classes found their way into his works after his death and even before. It is mainly to help in distinguishing the second class that I have placed after all poems their dates of composition and first publication respectively.[1]

Faulkner, 'the prince of Dublin printers', published Swift's *Works* in four volumes, 1735, six volumes, 1738, and eight volumes, 1746, giving over the second volume to the 'poetical works' and making substantial additions to these in the eighth. This eight-volume set grew to twenty volumes by 1769, making further additions to the verse in 1763. For the present edition I have drawn texts from Faulkner's eight-volume set, and I have only drawn on other collections, single issues, and manuscripts as necessary, with the intention of assembling reliable texts of reasonably uniform spelling and typographical appearance. This edition puts the reader on the modern side of Swift's

---

[1] A recent biographer compares Swift to an animal 'who relieves itself upon the carcass of a despised adversary' for reason of *The Discovery* and *The Problem*, without specifying that these poems were published from manuscript after he was dead, which is about fifty years after they were written.

spelling, which reflects the changes that took place in his lifetime; and to some extent spares him the distracting typographical vagaries of the many printers who set Swift's writings. This is perhaps sufficient reason for preferring 'folio' to 'quarto', if any is needed.

The arrangement of poems in this edition is not the chronological order which, with minor concessions to subject, all past editions have followed. I have grouped the poems by 'kind' or subject (following chronology within the group), except for the longer and more important pieces which stand alone. Disadvantages in this arrangement are obvious. Swift is not the systematic poet who writes fables in one period of his life and epistles in another, and his disregard for form as an end in itself is apparent from the way in which he subverts form to his own purpose, often satirical. Even so, there are certain impregnable groups (odes, trifles, Stella, Market Hill); there are definite advantages in reading his long series (1719–1731) of impersonal satires on love, beauty, and marriage as a single group, side by side with the Stella poems; the Market Hill poems take up where the Stella poems leave off; the imitations of Horace are related to the *Verses*; the familiar epistle is a favourite medium which he used with polish and skill; his lampoons (despite much poor stuff) are a characteristic achievement of which *On Poetry* and *The Legion Club* are a part; his personal poems are a testament of central interest; and it may be of value to hold in single view his spotty and erratic performance in fable, epigram, and the like. If the price of this arrangement is a certain number of catchalls, I hope it is justified by a demonstration of the range and diversity of Swift's poems, many deserving a better fate than to be ordered like footnotes to his biography.

This edition faithfully follows the sources from

which the texts of poems were taken except that: I have silently corrected obvious misprints; I have ignored ornate initials and other typographical flourishes; I have not hesitated to close a quotation left open; I have filled up hiatuses that dashes signify, supplying within brackets the word or name known to be meant if it is not clear; and I have revised the typography and in a few cases the text of titles of poems when this was necessary to give the significant part due emphasis. The unsigned notes appearing on the same pages as the poems are those there is reason to believe (from their style and appearance in the early Faulkner volumes) Swift himself wrote or inspired.

The size of these volumes dictated that the notes (placed at the end of each volume) be kept brief. They indicate sources of texts and contain biographical and other references, but set forth only a few textual variants that appreciably alter the meaning of poems.

Takoma Park, Maryland

ACKNOWLEDGEMENTS

A NUMBER of persons have been so generous in helping me with this task that I should like to express my appreciation to them without implicating them unduly: to Mr. Geoffrey Grigson, who assisted in arranging for the publication of these volumes; to the Master of Jesus College (Dr. E. M. W. Tillyard), and Mr. A. P. Rossiter, Fellow of Jesus College, Cambridge, for friendly advice and encouragement; to Mr. L. J. Potts, Fellow of Queens' College, Cambridge, who gave much time to my questions; and to Dr. Mary Claire Randolph, Chapel Hill, North Carolina, who answered calls for help.

My thanks are due to several library staffs for personal attention or for supplying photostats: the University Library, Cambridge; the British Museum Library; the Victoria and Albert Museum Library; the Bodleian Library; the Library of the Royal Irish Academy, Dublin; the Pierpont Morgan Library, New York; the Harvard College Library; the Library of Congress; and the Library of the University of Texas.

I gratefully acknowledge permission of the Trustees of the National Portrait Gallery, London, to reproduce the Jervas portrait as the frontispiece of Volume I, and of the Governors and Guardians of the National Gallery of Ireland for similar use of the Bindon portrait in Volume II. I am indebted to Miss Fannie Ratchford, Director of Rare Book Collections, Library of the University of Texas, for obtaining a photograph of an annotated copy of the *Verses on the Death of Dr. Swift*, and to the Library for permission to reproduce a page here. I am indebted to my associate, Mr. William A. Floyd, for photographing books in my possession and for other assistance with the plates.

ACKNOWLEDGEMENTS

A popular edition like the present one is apt to mask the difficult textual and bibliographical problems that other persons have had to solve. Students of Swift will recognize my debt to the published work of Sir Harold Williams, whose definitive edition of the *Poems* in 1937 rescued Swift from a chaos of false and doubtful attributions. I gladly acknowledge this debt.

I am solely responsible for the use made of any assistance acknowledged here.

SELECT BIBLIOGRAPHY

COLLECTED EDITIONS

THE authorized collections of Swift's writings were his unsigned *Miscellanies in Prose and Verse*, 1711, the Pope-Swift *Miscellanies in Prose and Verse*, four volumes, 1727–1732, and Faulkner's Dublin edition of the *Works*, four volumes, 1735 (with additions in Swift's lifetime). The Hawkesworth edition of the *Works*, 1755, supplanted the *Miscellanies* after that set had grown from four to fourteen volumes without further help from Swift. The Faulkner and Hawkesworth collections flourished in competition, making fresh additions and borrowing freely from each other. The principal collected editions that followed them are:

Works, ed Thomas Sheridan, 17 vols., 1784

Works, ed. John Nichols, 19 vols., 1801. (Another edn., 24 vols., 1803)

Works, ed. Walter Scott, 19 vols., 1814. (Second edn., 19 vols., 1824)

Poetical Works, Aldine Edition, 3 vols., 1833–1834. (From Scott's second edn.)

Prose Works, ed. Temple Scott, Bohn's Library, 10 vols., 1897–1908

Poems, ed. W. E. Browning, Bohn's Library, 2 vols., 1910

Poems, ed. Harold Williams, 3 vols., 1937. (Definitive edn.)

Prose Writings, ed. Herbert Davis, 14 vols., 1939–. (Definitive edn., nearing completion)

CORRESPONDENCE

The handsomest exhibit among Swift studies is the magisterial edition of his *Correspondence* by the late F. Elrington Ball (6 vols., 1910–1914). *Vanessa and her Correspondence with Jonathan Swift*, edited by A. Martin Freeman (1921), is based on her drafts of her own letters and her originals of Swift's (earlier editors relied on transcripts). *The Letters of Jonathan Swift and Charles Ford*, edited by D. Nichol Smith (1935), filled an important gap long known to exist in the correspondence. The authoritative edition of the *Journal to Stella* is by Harold Williams (2 vols., 1948).

BIBLIOGRAPHIES

Lists of writings by or about Swift are contained in the following:

W. Spencer Jackson, *Bibliography of the Writings of Jonathan Swift* (in Vol. xii of Temple Scott's edn. of *Works*)

H. Teerink, *A Bibliography of the Writings in Prose and Verse of Jonathan Swift* (The Hague, 1937)

Cambridge Bibliography of English Literature (1943), ii. 581–96

L. A. Landa and J. E. Tobin, *Jonathan Swift: A List of Critical Studies published from 1895 to 1945* (New York, 1945)

BIOGRAPHY AND CRITICISM

There are several memoirs of Swift by persons who boasted of his acquaintance. Mrs. Letitia Pilkington in her own *Memoirs* (3 vols., 1748–54) supplied anecdotes about the Dean as often as she could. The first book devoted to him was the Earl of Orrery's *Remarks on the Life and Writings of Jonathan Swift* (1752), written in the form of letters to his son. To the unkind and ungrateful reflections in Orrery's book, Patrick Delany (signing himself 'J. R.') replied briefly in *Observations on Lord Orrery's Remarks* (1754). Deane Swift (grandson of Swift's uncle Godwin) wrote the first full-dress biography, *Essay upon the Life, Writings, and Character of Dr. Jonathan Swift* (1755). Despite mutual suspicion and animosity, these early writers were unanimous in believing Swift and Stella married, and their opinion prevailed until the next century.

The biographies by John Hawkesworth and Thomas Sheridan prefaced their editions of Swift's works. Dr. Johnson's *Life of Swift* (1781) was written for his *Lives of the Poets*, to preface Swift's poems.

W. Monck Mason's account of Swift in his *History of the Cathedral Church of St. Patrick's* (1819) is distinguished for first marshalling the arguments against the marriage. Scott's *Memoirs of Jonathan Swift*, written for his edition of the works, compresses a mass of detail into an interesting narrative. The reaction to Scott's sympathetic treatment of the Tory dean came from the two Whig lords whose contumely reverberates in later estimates of Swift's character. Jeffrey (reviewing Scott's edition in the *Edinburgh Review*, 1816) attacked Swift in what seemed his weakest quarter—he was a heartless philanderer who changed political parties in the wrong direction; and Macaulay reached a large audience with his portrait of 'the apostate politician, the ribald priest, the perjured lover, the heart burning with hatred against the whole human race'. Thackeray added the melodramatic note in the *English Humourists* (1851), elaborating around Stella the theme of injured innocence. The defence of Swift was to be the work of John Forster, though his *Life* (1875), lumbering along like Masson's *Milton*, never got beyond its first volume (or the year

1711). Henry Craik's voluminous *Life* (1882) represented all that was known about Swift at the time. Leslie Stephen wrote the essay for the 'English Men of Letters' (1882). Churton Collins wrote a 'biographical and critical essay' (1893).

In this century there are biographies by Sophie Shilleto Smith (1910), Shane Leslie (1929), Carl Van Doren (New York, 1930), and Stephen Gwynn (1933). Of Emile Pons' ambitious study only the first volume, *Swift: les Années de Jeunesse et le 'Conte du Tonneau'* (Strasbourg, 1925), has appeared. M. M. Rossi and J. M. Hone have written a psychological study, *Swift, or the Egotist* (1934). John Middleton Murry's *Jonathan Swift: A Critical Biography* (1954) is the best account of Swift's life and work, besides being the most readable biography since Scott.

Certain books of special interest should be mentioned. After reviewing all the evidence M. B. Gold finds in favour of the marriage in *Swift's Marriage to Stella* (Cambridge, Mass., 1937). The relationship with Stella and Vanessa is analysed by Evelyn Hardy in *The Conjured Spirit* (1949). Herbert Davis has written *Stella: A Gentlewoman of the Eighteenth Century* (New York, 1942) and *The Satire of Jonathan Swift* (New York, 1947). The important critical studies are by W. D. Taylor, *Jonathan Swift: A Critical Essay* (1933), and Ricardo Quintana, *The Mind and Art of Jonathan Swift* (1936).

These volumes deal with the poetry: F. Elrington Ball, *Swift's Verse: An Essay* (1928), and M. O. Johnson, *The Sin of Wit: Jonathan Swift as a Poet* (Syracuse, N.Y., 1950).

CRITICAL COMMENTS

JONATHAN SWIFT

I WONDER you will doubt of your genius. The world is wider to a poet than to any other man, and new follies and vices will never be wanting, any more than new fashions. *Je donne au diable* the wrong notion that matter is exhausted; for as poets in their Greek names are called creators, so in one circumstance they resemble the great Creator by having an infinity of space to work in.

Letter to Gay, 1729

I have been only a man of rhymes, and that upon trifles, never having written serious couplets in my life, yet never any without a moral view....

As I am conjectured to have generally dealt in raillery and satire, both in prose and verse, if that conjecture be right, although such an opinion has been an absolute bar to my rising in the world, yet that very world must suppose that I followed what I thought to be my talent, and charitable people will suppose I had a design to laugh the follies of mankind out of countenance, and as often to lash the vices out of practice....

Dr. Young is the gravest among us, and yet his satires have many mixtures of sharp raillery....

As to your blank verse, it has too often fallen into the same vile hands of late. One Thomson, a Scotchman, has succeeded the best in that way, in four poems he has writ on the four seasons, yet I am not over fond of them, because they are all description, and nothing is doing, whereas Milton engages me in actions of the highest importance, *modo me Romae, modo ponit Athenis*....

You see Pope, Gay, and I, use all our endeavours

to make folks merry and wise, and profess to have no enemies, except knaves and fools. . . .

Letter to Charles Wogan, 1732

The following Poems chiefly consist either of Humour or Satyr, and very often of both together. What Merit they may have, we confess ourselves to be no Judges of in the least; but, out of due Regard to a Writer, from whose Works we hope to receive some Benefit, we cannot conceal what we have heard from several Persons of great Judgment; that the Author never was known either in Verse or Prose to borrow any Thought, Simile, Epithet, or particular manner of Style; but whatever he writ, whether good, bad, or indifferent, is an Original in itself.

Advertisement, *Works*, Vol. II, 1735

ALEXANDER POPE

I have not the courage. . .to be such a satirist as you, but I would be as much, or more, a philosopher. You call your satires, libels; I would rather call my satires, epistles. They will consist more of morality than of wit, and grow graver, which you will call duller.

Letter to Swift, 1733

My sincere love for this valuable, indeed incomparable man, will accompany him through life, and pursue his memory, were I to live a hundred lives, as many as his works will live, which are absolutely original, unequalled, unexampled. His humanity, his charity, his condescension, his candour are equal to his wit; and require as good and as true a taste to be equally valued.

Letter to Orrery, 1737

Let Ireland tell, how Wit upheld her cause,
Her Trade supported, and supply'd her Laws;

And leave on Swift this grateful verse ingrav'd,
The Rights a Court attack'd, a Poet sav'd.

Epistle to Augustus, 1737

VOLTAIRE

M. Swift est Rabelais dans son bon sens et vivant en
bonne compagnie. Il n'a pas à la vérité la gaieté du
premier, mais il a toute la finesse, la raison, le choix,
le bon goût, qui manquent à notre curé de Meudon.
Ses vers sont d'un goût singulier et presque inimitable;
la bonne plaisanterie est son partage en vers et en
prose; mais, pour le bien entendre, il faut faire un
petit voyage dans son pays.

Lettres sur les Anglais, 1734

ADAM SMITH

In our own language, Mr. Pope and Dr. Swift have
each of them introduced a manner different from
what was practised before, into all works that are
written in Rhyme, the one in long verses, the other
in short. The quaintness of Butler has given place to
the plainness of Swift. The rambling freedom of
Dryden and the correct but often tedious and prosaic
languor of Addison are no longer the objects of imitation, but all long verses are now written after the manner of the nervous precision of Mr. Pope.

Theory of Moral Sentiments, 1759

WILLIAM SHENSTONE

Swift in poetry deserves a place, somewhere between Butler and Horace. He has the wit of the former,

and the graceful negligence which we find in the latter's epistles and satires.

Essays on Men, Manners, and Things, 1764

GOLDSMITH

Dean Swift ... perceived that there was a spirit of romance mixed with all the works of the poets who preceded him; or, in other words, that they had drawn nature on the most pleasing side. There still therefore was a place for him, who, careless of censure, should describe it just as it was, with all its deformities; he therefore owes much of his fame, not so much to the greatness of his genius, as to the boldness of it. He was dry, sarcastic, and severe; and suited his style exactly to the turn of his thought, being concise and nervous.

An History of England, 1764

ON POETRY. A RHAPSODY.—Here follows one of the best versified poems in our language, and the most masterly production of its author....

BAUCIS AND PHILEMON. From Swift.—This poem is very fine; and, though in the same strain with the preceding [Prior's *Hans Carvel*], is yet superior.

CADENUS AND VANESSA.—This is thought one of Dr. Swift's correctest pieces; its chief merit, indeed, is the elegant ease with which a story, but ill-conceived in itself, is told.

The Beauties of English Poetry, 1767

DR. JOHNSON

His style was well suited to his thoughts, which are never subtilised by nice disquisitions, decorated by sparkling conceits, elevated by ambitious sentences, or variegated by far-sought learning. He pays no court to the passions; he excites neither surprise nor admiration; he always understands himself, and his readers always understand him: the peruser of Swift wants little previous knowledge; it will be sufficient that he is acquainted with common words and common things; he is neither required to mount elevations nor to explore profundities; his passage is always on a level, along solid ground, without asperities, without obstruction....

In the poetical works of Dr. Swift there is not much upon which the critic can exercise his powers. They are often humorous, almost always light, and have the qualities which recommend such compositions, easiness and gaiety. They are, for the most part, what their author intended. The diction is correct, the numbers are smooth, and the rhymes exact. There seldom occurs a hard-laboured expression, or a redundant epithet; all his verses exemplify his own definition of a good style—they consist of 'proper words in proper places'.

Life of Swift, 1781

SIR WALTER SCOTT

As a poet, Swift's post is pre-eminent in the sort of poetry which he cultivated. He never attempted any species of composition, in which either the sublime or the pathetic were required of him. But in every department of poetry where wit is necessary, he displayed, as the subject chanced to require, either the blasting lightning of satire, or the lambent and meteor-like coruscations of frolicsome humour. His powers of versification are admirably adapted to his favourite subjects. Rhyme, which is a handcuff to an inferior poet, he who is master of his art wears as a bracelet. Swift was of the latter description; his lines fall as easily into the best grammatical arrangement, and the most simple and forcible expression, as if he had been writing in prose. The numbers and the coincidence of rhymes, always correct and natural, though often unexpected, distinguish the current of his poetical composition, which exhibits, otherwise, no mark of the difficulty with which these graces are attained. In respect of matter, Swift seldom elevates his tone above a satirical diatribe, a moral lesson, or a poem on manners; but the former are unrivalled in severity, and the latter in ease. Sometimes, however, the intensity of his satire gives to his poetry a character of emphatic violence, which borders upon grandeur. This is peculiarly distinguishable in the Rhapsody on Poetry, which, according to Dr. King, he accounted his best satire, and surely with great justice. Yet this grandeur is founded, not on sublimity either of conception or expression, but upon the energy of both; and indicates rather ardour of temper, than power of imagination. *Facit indignatio versus....*

Swift has the more easily attained this perfection of fictitious narrative, because in all his works of whatever description, he has maintained the most undeviating attention to the point at issue.

Memoirs of Jonathan Swift, 1814

FRANCIS JEFFREY

He was, without exception, the greatest and most efficient *libeller* that ever exercised the trade; and possessed, in an eminent degree, all the qualifications which it requires:—a clear head—a cold heart—a vindictive temper—no admiration of noble qualities—no sympathy with suffering—not much conscience

—not much consistency—a ready wit—a sarcastic humour—a thorough knowledge of the baser parts of human nature—and a complete familiarity with every thing that is low, homely, and familiar in language. These were his gifts;—and he soon felt for what ends they were given. Almost all his works are libels; generally upon individuals, sometimes upon sects and parties, sometimes upon human nature.... Disregarding all the laws of polished hostility, he uses, at one and the same moment, his sword and his poisoned dagger—his hands, and his teeth, and his envenomed breath,—and does not even scruple, upon occasion, to imitate his own yahoos, by discharging on his unhappy victims a shower of filth, from which neither courage nor dexterity can afford any protection.—Against such an antagonist, it was, of course, at no time very easy to make head; and accordingly his invective seems, for the most part, to have been as much dreaded, and as tremendous as the personal ridicule of Voltaire. Both were inexhaustible, well directed, and unsparing; but even when Voltaire drew blood, he did not mangle the victim, and was only mischievous when Swift was brutal.... Of his Poetry, we do not think there is much to be said;—for we cannot persuade ourselves that Swift was in any respect a poet.

Edinburgh Review, 1816

WILLIAM HAZLITT

Swift's reputation as a poet has been in a manner obscured by the greater splendour, by the natural force and inventive genius of his prose writings; but if he had never written either the Tale of a Tub or Gulliver's Travels, his name merely as a poet would have come down to us, and have gone down to posterity with well-earned honours. His Imitations of Horace, and still more his Verses on his own Death, place him in the first rank of agreeable moralists in verse. There is not only a dry humour, an exquisite tone of irony, in these productions of his pen; but there is a touching, unpretending pathos, mixed up with the most whimsical and eccentric strokes of pleasantry and satire. His Description of the Morning in London, and of a City Shower, which were first published in the Tatler, are among the most delightful of the contents of that very delightful work. Swift shone as one of the most sensible of the poets; he is also distinguished as one of the most nonsensical of them. No man has written so many lack-a-daisical, slip-shod, tedious, trifling, foolish, fantastical verses as he, which are so little an imputation of the wisdom of the writer, and which in fact only show his readiness to oblige others, and to forget himself. He has gone so far as to invent a new stanza of fourteen and sixteen syllable lines for Mary the cookmaid to vent her budget of nothings, and for Mrs. Harris to gossip with the deaf old housekeeper. Oh, when shall we have such another Rector of Laracor!

Lectures on the English Poets, 1818

COLERIDGE

Swift's style is, in its line, perfect; the manner is a complete expression of the matter, the terms appropriate, and the artifice concealed. It is simplicity in the true sense of the word.

Lecture on Style, 1818

Swift was *anima Rabelaisii habitans in sicco*,—the soul of Rabelais dwelling in a dry place.

Table Talk, 1830

THACKERAY

Would you have liked to be a friend of the great Dean? ... If you had been his inferior in parts (and that, with a great respect for all persons present, I fear is only very likely), his equal in mere social station, he would have bullied, scorned, and insulted you; if, undeterred by his great reputation, you had met him like a man, he would have quailed before you, and not had the pluck to reply, and gone home, and years after written a foul epigram about you—watched for you in a sewer, and come out to assail you with a coward's blow and a dirty bludgeon. If you had been a lord with a blue riband, who flattered his vanity, or could help his ambition, he would have been the most delightful company in the world.... His laugh jars on one's ear after seven score years. He was always alone—alone and gnashing in the darkness, except when Stella's sweet smile came and shone upon him. When that went, silence and utter night closed over him. An immense genius: an awful downfall and ruin. So great a man he seems to me, that thinking of him is like thinking of an empire falling.

Lectures on the English Humourists, 1853

SIR HENRY CRAIK

Was there not, in the original bent of that genius [in his early poems], something which the accomplished work of Swift does not contain? We cannot claim for any of his verses the qualities of real poetry. We find in them no flights of imagination: no grandeur either of emotion or of form: and even the deftness of his rhythmical skill never attains to the harmony of poetic utterance. But when we search through the tangled mazes of the Pindaric odes: when we watch their tensity and earnestness in the light of these early confidences: when we place side by side with them the fierce energy of the later verses,—evident as is the severe repression therein of any poetic fancy,—we feel that Swift, though he never attained to true poetic utterance, had a temperament, which in his own words was 'blasted with poetic fire'. The fire was indeed checked by untoward experiences, smothered under a burden of contending faculties, and done to death. But how much of Swift's cynicism, how much of his apparent indifference to fame, was due to the withering of those early aspirations, and to the repression of a temperament of surpassing keenness, forced to utter itself only in the language of satire, and not of poetry?

We must not forget this early impulse in judging of Swift's later work, with its union of contrasting qualities. By nothing did he affect men more than by his marvellous combination of the grimmest earnestness with the most mocking humour. The two are ever at combat, but the combat is maintained on almost equal terms. The mocking laugh never sounds without telling of the earnestness behind; the fury of denunciation never speaks but as the humour rules it, and with such sense of repression as doubles its effect....

Besides his strength of idiom, besides his combined earnestness and humour, Swift has another power as rare. It is that of presenting thought in lucid metaphor or allegory sustained by a long train of implicit reasoning. It is by such travesty of metaphysics that he avenged himself on what seemed to him the wordy triflings of philosophy; and it is this which gives at once its chief subtlety, and much of its interest, to his most characteristic work.

Life of Swift, 1882

GEORGE SAINTSBURY

As in Johnson's case later, though in a different manner and degree, the special character of Augustanism shows itself in what we may call the cohabitation of gravity and gaiety. In Swift's case the gravity undoubtedly turns not seldom to actual grimness, if not to positive horror; and the gaiety, by a sort of concatenation, to extravagant burlesque and even sheer nonsense. But this is only the strongest testimony to the virtue of that Augustanism itself, though of course we must add something or allow something for the extraordinary greatness of Swift's own genius. Never, except in Shakespeare, the eternal exception, has such lightness consisted with such strength ...

Swift may be claimed as a whole—work and man—as one of the greatest, one of the completest, sources of interest ... in the whole range of literature. His actual work would—supposing that we knew nothing of the man at all but only a little about the public circumstances in which he wrote—supply an immensely wide and varied range of such interest ... But the least curious of readers about personality, the most sluggish in hunting for biographic or autobiographic detail, can hardly refuse to acknowledge that, in Swift's case, the nature of the man does add enormously to the interest of the work. The vast amount of talk over this nature and the light thrown upon it by internal evidence and external gossip, have, it has been admitted, ... 'made his memory a little confused'.... But this very mystery is a bait to many, and can hardly be denied to be a seasoning to the most austere. And, setting it aside, Swift's remains perhaps the most interesting study of literary character that we have.

The Peace of the Augustans, 1916

IRVING BABBITT

The tender misanthropy of the Rousseauist is at the opposite pole from that of a Swift, which is the misanthropy of the naked intellect. Instead of seeing human nature through an Arcadian haze he saw it without any illusion at all. His irony is like that of Socrates, the irony of intellect. Its bitterness and cruelty arise from the fact that his intellect does not, like the intellect of Socrates, have the support of insight. Pascal would have said that Swift saw man's misery without at the same time seeing his grandeur. For man's grandeur is due to his infinitude and this infinitude cannot be perceived directly, but only through a veil of illusion; only, that is, through a right use of the imagination.

Rousseau and Romanticism, 1919

F. ELRINGTON BALL

Without knowledge of his verse a true picture of Swift cannot be drawn. In his verse he sets forth his life as a panorama, he shows more clearly than in his prose his peculiar turn of thought, and he reveals his character in all its phases from the most attractive to the most repellent. Before the testimony of his verse the work of many of his biographers cannot stand.

No exact prototype is to be found for Swift's style of versification. It has been described as Hudibrastic, but the influence of Samuel Butler was only partial. In its construction Swift laid under contribution all classes of metrical composition from the Elizabethan age to his own, ephemeral songs and ballads no less than the standard writings of poets and dramatists.

Swift's Verse: An Essay, 1929

T. S. ELIOT

Tourneur's 'suffering, cynicism, and despair', to use Collins' words, are static; they might be prior to experience, or be the fruit of but little; Swift's is the progressive cynicism of the mature and disappointed man of the world. As an objective comment on the world, Swift's is by far the more terrible. For Swift had himself enough pettiness, as well as enough sin of pride, and lust of dominion, to be able to expose and condemn mankind in its universal pettiness and pride and vanity and ambition; and his poetry, as well as his prose, attests that he hated the very smell of the human animal. We may think as we read Swift, 'how loathesome human beings are'; in reading Tourneur we can only think, 'how terrible to loathe human beings so much as that'.

Selected Essays, 1932

W. B. YEATS

I turned from Goldsmith and from Burke because they had come to seem a part of the English system, from Swift because I acknowledged, being a romantic, no verse between Cowley and Smart's *Song to David*, no prose between Sir Thomas Browne and the *Conversations* of Landor. But now I read Swift for months together, Burke and Berkeley less often but always with excitement, and Goldsmith lures and waits.... Swift haunts me; he is always just round the next corner.

Wheels and Butterflies, 1934

SIR HAROLD WILLIAMS

The poems of Jonathan Swift have been undeservedly overshadowed. The perfection of his prose, the satirical and imaginative genius of *A Tale of a Tub*, *Gulliver's Travels*, and *Polite Conversation*, the incisive mastery of his political pamphlets have screened off his pages of verse. Nevertheless it must be recognized that his standing was within the circle of the Augustan poets; and in prose his range was far beyond their compass. In verse Pope was his superior. ... Gay and Prior had a more lyrical gift. Swift's genius lay in the succession of Samuel Butler. *Hudibras* he knew by heart. But Butler's stream lay in a narrow channel through a monotonous country. His antipathies and sympathies were limited by a confined experience and limited responsiveness. Swift's powers of mind were far greater than Butler's; his experience of life was more complex; he knew more intimately the extremes of joy and pain, love and hate. The content of his verse shows a diversity Butler's lacks, his variations of theme and metre are frequent. *Cadenus and Vanessa* may want the porcelain elegance of *The Rape of the Lock*, but it is a definite achievement of sustained artifice and fancy. The metrical accomplishment and vigour of *On Poetry: A Rapsody*, which moved the admiration of contemporaries, are not less apparent to-day. No verse satire in English, or in any language, pierces, wounds, and scarifies like that of Swift.... And here there is all the wide range from a squib or lampoon of a few lines to lengthy and polished pieces like the *Libel on Dr. Delany*, or *Epistle to Mr. Gay*, or the typical social satire of *The Journal of a Modern Lady*, or, finally, the uncontrollable outburst of *The Legion Club*. Again, there is the everyday friendliness of his familiar verse, the addresses to Stella, to the Rochforts, Achesons, Sheridan, Delany, and other Irish friends, and the great *Verses on the Death of Dr. Swift*, which are also of this order, if with a difference. And, yet again, is not *Mrs. Harris's Petition* one of the best of all colloquial pieces? Add to these the nonsense poems and frolics in rhyme, and we have not exhausted a variety which rarely falters or fails.

Swift's Poems, 1937

SIR HERBERT READ

There is a general difficulty in any critical approach to Swift's work . . . : the temerity of any purely literary judgement. . . .

Swift could write quizzically of Dr. George Berkeley, as he did in an otherwise kindly letter of recommendation to Lord Carteret; but if he had had more of Berkeley's humility he might have had some of his success. Berkeley is one of the contrasts that best illuminate Swift; for Berkeley had qualities of imagination and speculative intelligence which were totally wanting in the genius of Swift. . . . Whether we consider him as a writer or as a prospective bishop, this is a drastic limitation. It is not that it implies a lack of intellectual energy (Swift was inventive enough), but it does qualify the nature of that energy, making it operative on a lower plane and with a narrower range. The poet, who in this sense is not confined to verse, sees beyond his 'separate fantasy'; he perceives the 'clear universe of things around', and from this perception he derives a sense of sublimity and an eloquence to which Swift was a total stranger. . . .

Mrs. Harris is as vivid as the Wife of Bath, and the verses in which she lives are a miracle of humorous invention. It must be admitted that we never find in Swift that 'rude sweetness of a Scotch tune' which

Dryden rather grudgingly allowed to Chaucer, but in the poems which we would make the basis of an apology for him, the very accents of human speech are imposed upon the rhythm, giving it an actuality in which mere sweetness is transcended.

Collected Essays, 1938

JOHN MIDDLETON MURRY

With all the perverted passion of his egotism he repudiated the idea that he had offended. Nature and God were wrong; and Jonathan Swift was right. Four years before Stella died his unconscious genius had contrived his own complete vindication by granting him the vision of the Yahoo: the special revelation that men and women, in their physical reality, were utterly abominable. They were not a little, or a good deal, lower than the angels; they were infinitely below the brute creation, separated from them by an impassable gulf in which animal innocence and animal cleanliness together were swallowed up. Man, and above all woman, in their animal nature were unclean and untouchable. Love shrank, because it must, in a paroxysm of horror from the physical relation of sex; and, in so far as woman did not, she was incapable of love. To the extent that love begat desire in a woman's nature she relapsed into the Yahoo.

Jonathan Swift: A Critical Biography, 1954

PINDARIC ODES AND
HEROIC VERSE

Ode to the King

On his Irish Expedition
and the Success of his Arms in general

I

SURE there's some Wondrous Joy in *Doing Good*;
Immortal Joy, that suffers no Allay from Fears,
  Nor dreads the Tyranny of Years,
By none but its Possessors to be understood:
    Else where's the Gain in being *Great?*
  Kings would indeed be Victims of the State;
  What can the Poet's humble Praise?
  What can the Poet's humble Bays?
  (We Poets oft our Bays allow,
    Transplanted to the Hero's Brow)   10
  Add to the Victor's Happiness?
  What do the Scepter, Crown and Ball,
Rattles for Infant Royalty to play withal,
  But serve t' adorn the Baby-dress
  Of one poor Coronation-day,
    To make the Pageant gay:
  A three Hours Scene of empty Pride,
And then the Toys are thrown aside.

II

But the Delight of *Doing Good*
Is fix't like Fate among the Stars,   20
    And Deifi'd in Verse;
'Tis the best Gemm in Royalty,
The Great Distinguisher of Blood,
Parent of Valour and of Fame,
  Which makes a Godhead of a Name,
And is Contemporary to Eternity.

3

This made the Ancient Romans to afford
To *Valour* and to *Virtue* the *same Word*:
To shew the Paths of both must be together trod,
   Before the *Hero* can commence *a God*.   30

III

   These are the Ways
By which our happy Prince carves out his Bays;
      Thus he has fix'd His Name
   First, in the mighty List of Fame,
And thus He did the Airy Goddess Court,
      He sought Her out in Fight,
      And like a Bold Romantick Knight
   Rescu'd Her from the Giant's Fort:
   The Tyrant Death lay crouching down,
      Waiting for Orders at his Feet,   40
         Spoil'd of his Leaden Crown;
      He trampled on this Haughty *Bajazet*,
         Made him his Footstool in the War,
   And a Grim Slave to wait on his Triumphal Car.

IV

      And now I in the Spirit see
      (The Spirit of Exalted Poetry)
      I see the *Fatal Fight* begin;
And, lo! where a Destroying Angel stands,
      (By all but Heaven and Me unseen,)
With Lightning in his Eyes, and Thunder in his
         Hands;   50
   In vain, said He, *does* [1]Utmost Thule *boast
      No poys'nous Beast will in Her breed,
         Or no Infectious Weed,
   When she sends forth such a malignant Birth,
   When Man himself's the* Vermin *of her Earth;*

[1] *Ireland.*

4

When Treason *there in* Person *seems to stand,*
And Rebel *is the* growth *and* manufacture *of the Land.*
  He spake, and a dark Cloud flung o're his light,
        And hid him from Poetick sight,
  And (I believe) began himself the Fight,   60
        For strait I saw the Field maintain'd,
  And what I us'd to laugh at in *Romance*,
  And thought too great ev'n for effects of Chance,
The Battel almost by *Great William*'s single Valour
        gain'd;
  The *Angel* (doubtless) kept th' Eternal Gate,
        And stood 'twixt Him and every Fate;
And all those flying Deaths that aim'd him from the
        Field,
        (Th' impartial Deaths which come
        Like Love, wrapt up in Fire;
  And like that too, make every breast their home) 70
        Broke on his everlasting Shield.

                    V

  The *Giddy Brittish Populace*,
        That *Tyrant-Guard* on *Peace*,
        Who watch Her like a Prey,
        And keep Her for a Sacrifice,
  And must be sung, like *Argus*, into *ease*
Before this *Milk-white Heifer* can be stole away,
    Our *Prince* has charm'd its many hundred Eyes;
        Has lull'd the Monster in a Deep
        And (I hope) an Eternal Sleep,   80
  And has at last redeem'd the *Mighty Prize*
  The *Scots* themselves, that Discontented Brood,
  Who always loudest for *Religion* bawl,
        (*As those still do wh' have none at all*)
  Who claim so many Titles to be *Jews*,
  (But, surely such whom God did never for *his*
        People chuse)

                    5

Still murmuring in *their Wilderness* for *Food*,
Who pine us like a *Chronical Disease*;
And one would think 'twere past Omnipotence to
please;
Your Presence all their *Native Stubborness*
controuls, 90
And for a while unbends their contradicting Souls:
As in old Fabulous Hell,
When some *Patrician* God wou'd visit the Immortal
Jayl,
The very Brightness of His Face
Suspended every Horror of the Place,
The Gyants under *Ætna* ceas'd to groan,
And *Sisiphus* lay sleeping on his Stone.
Thus has our Prince compleated every Victory,
And glad *Iërne* now may see
Her Sister Isles are *Conquered* too as well as She. 100

VI

How vainly (Sir) did Your fond *Enemy* try
Upon *a rubbish Heap of broken Laws*
To climb at Victory
Without the Footing of a *Cause;*
His Lawrel now must only be a *Cypress* Wreath,
And His best Victory a Noble Death;
His scrap of Life is but a Heap of Miseries,
The Remnant of a falling Snuff,
Which hardly wants another puff,
And needs must *stink* when e're it dies; 110
Whilst at Your Victorious Light
All lesser ones expire,
Consume, and perish from our sight,
Just as the Sun puts out a Fire;
And every foolish *Flye* that dares to aim
To buzz about the might Flame;

6

The wretched Insects singe their Wings, and fall,
  And humbly at the bottom crawl.

VII

    That *Restless Tyrant*, who of late
    Is grown so impudently Great,   120
        That Tennis-Ball of Fate;
    This Gilded Meteor which flyes
    As if it meant to touch the Skies;
        For all its boasted height,
        For all its Plagiary Light,
        Took its first Growth and Birth
    From the worst [1]Excrements of Earth;
Stay but a little while and down again 'twill come,
And end as it began, in Vapour, Stink, and Scum.
        Or has he like some fearful Star appear'd?   130
Long dreaded for his *Bloody Tail* and *Fiery Beard*,
    Transcending Nature's ordinary Laws,
        Sent by just Heaven to threaten Earth
        With War, and Pestilence, and Dearth,
Of which it is at once the Prophet and the Cause.
        Howe're it be, the Pride of *France*
        Has finish'd its short Race of Chance,
    And all Her boasted Influences are
    Rapt in the *Vortex* of the *Brittish* Star;
Her *Tyrant* too an unexpected Wound shall feel   140
    In the last wretched Remnant of his Days;
Our Prince has hit Him, like *Achilles*, in the *Heel*,
    The poys'nous Darts has made him reel,
    Giddy he grows, and down is hurl'd,
And as a Mortal to his [2]*Vile Disease*,
Falls sick in the *Posteriors* of the World.
                1691/1735

[1] *The* French *King suppos'd a Bastard.*
[2] *Fistula in Ano.*

Ode to the Athenian Society

Moor-Park, Feb. 14, 1691–2

As when the Deluge first began to fall,
    That mighty Ebb never to flow again,
(When this huge Body's Moisture was so great,
    It quite o'ercame the vital Heat)
That Mountain which was highest first of all
Appear'd above the universal Main,
To bless the primitive Sailor's weary Sight;
And 'twas perhaps *Parnassus*, if in Height
    It be as great as 'tis in Fame,
    And nigh to Heaven as is its Name: 10
So after th' Inundation of a War,
When Learning's little Houshold did embark
With her World's fruitful System in her sacred Ark,
    At the first Ebb of Noise and Fears,
    Philosophy's exalted Head appears:
And the Dove-Muse will now no longer stay,
But plumes her silver Wings, and flies away;
    And now a Laurel Wreath she brings from far,
    To crown the happy Conqueror,
    To shew the Flood begins to cease,   20
And brings the dear Reward of Victory and Peace.

II

The eager Muse took Wing upon the Waves decline,
    When War her cloudy Aspect just withdrew,
    When the bright Sun of Peace began to shine,
And for a while in heav'nly Contemplation sat
    On the high Top of peaceful *Ararat;*
And pluck'd a Laurel Branch (for Laurel was the
        first that grew,
The first of Plants after the Thunder, Storm, and
        Rain)

    And thence with joyful, nimble Wing,
    Flew dutifully back again,   30
And made an humble ¹Chaplet for the King,
    And the Dove-Muse is fled once more
(Glad of the Victory, yet frighted at the War)
    And now discovers from afar
    A peaceful and a flourishing Shore:
        No sooner did she land
        On the delightful Strand,
    Than strait she sees the Country all around,
    Where fatal *Neptune* rul'd e'erwhile,
Scatter'd with flow'ry Vales, with fruitful Gardens
        crown'd,   40
        And many a pleasant Wood;
        As if the universal *Nile*
        Had rather water'd it than drown'd:
    It seems some floating piece of Paradise,
        Preserv'd by wonder from the Flood,
    Long wand'ring thro' the Deep, as we are told
        Fam'd *Delos* did of old,
        And the transported Muse imagin'd it
To be a fitter Birth-place for the God of Wit,
        Or the much-talk'd Oracular Grove;   50
        When with amazing Joy she hears
        An unknown Musick all around,
        Charming her greedy Ears
        With many a heavenly Song
Of Nature and of Art, of deep Philosophy and Love,
Whilst Angels tune the Voice, and God inspires the
        Tongue.
    In vain she catches at the empty Sound,
In vain pursues the Musick with her longing Eye,
    And courts the wanton Echoes as they fly.

¹ *The Ode I writ to the King in* Ireland.

9

III

Pardon, ye great Unknown, and far-exalted Men, 60
The wild Excursions of a youthful Pen;
  Forgive a young, and (almost) Virgin-Muse,
  Whom blind and eager Curiosity
     (Yet Curiosity they say,
  Is in her Sex a Crime needs no Excuse)
       Has forc'd to grope her uncouth Way
After a mighty Light that leads her wand'ring Eye:
No wonder then she quits the narrow Path of Sense
    For a dear Ramble thro' Impertinence;
    Impertinence, the Scurvy of Mankind. 70
And all we Fools, who are the greater Part of it,
    Tho' we be of two different Factions still,
      Both the Good-natur'd and the Ill,
    Yet wheresoe'er you look, you'll always find
We join like Flies, and Wasps, in buzzing about Wit.
    In me, who am of the first Sect of these,
    All Merit that transcends the humble Rules
      Of my own dazzled scanty Sense,
Begets a kinder Folly and Impertinence
      Of Admiration and of Praise. 80
    And our good Brethren of the Surly Sect
    Must e'en all herd us with their Kindred Fools:
    For tho' possess'd of present Vogue they've made
Railing a Rule of Wit, and Obloquy a Trade;
Yet the same Want of Brains produces each Effect
    And you whom *Pluto*'s Helm does wisely shroud
      From us the blind and thoughtless Croud,
    Like the fam'd Hero in his Mother's Cloud,
Who both our Follies and Impertinencies see,
Do laugh perhaps at theirs, and pity mine and me. 90

IV

But Censure's to be understood
    Th' authentic Mark of the Elect,
The publick Stamp Heav'n sets on all that's Great and
        Good;
    Our shallow Search and Judgment to direct.
        The War methinks has made
Our Wit and Learning narrow as our Trade;
Instead of boldly sailing far to buy
A Stock of Wisdom and Philosophy,
        We fondly stay at home in fear
        Of ev'ry censuring Privateer;   100
Forcing a wretched Trade by beating down the Sale,
        And selling basely by Retail.
    The Wits, I mean the Atheists of the Age,
Who fain would rule the Pulpit, as they do the Stage;
    Wond'rous Refiners of Philosophy,
        Of Morals and Divinity,
By the new Modish System of reducing all to Sense,
    Against all Logick and concluding Laws,
        Do own th' Effects of Providence,
        And yet deny the Cause.   110

V

This hopeful Sect, now it begins to see
    How little, very little do prevail
        Their first and chiefest Force,
    To censure, to cry down, and rail,
    Not knowing What, or Where, or Who you be,
        Will quickly take another Course:
        And by their never-failing Ways
Of solving all Appearances they please,
We soon shall see them to their ancient Methods fall,
And straight deny you to be Men, or any thing at all.
    I laugh at the grave Answer they will make,   121

Which they have always ready, general and cheap:
    'Tis but to say, that what we daily meet,
        And by a fond Mistake
Perhaps imagine to be wond'rous Wit,
And think, alas, to be by Mortals writ,
Is but a Croud of Atoms justling in a Heap,
        Which from eternal Seeds begun,
Justling some thousand Years till ripen'd by the Sun;
    They're now, just now, as naturally born,   130
    As from the Womb of Earth a Field of Corn.

VI

    But as for poor contented me,
Who must my Weakness and my Ignorance confess,
That I believe in much, I ne'er can hope to see;
    Methinks I'm satisfy'd to guess
    That this new, noble and delightful Scene
Is wonderfully mov'd by some exalted Men,
    Who have well studied in the World's Disease,
(That Epidemick Error and Depravity,
    Or in our Judgment or our Eye)   140
    That what surprizes us can only please:
We often search contentedly the whole World round,
    To make some great Discovery,
        And scorn it when 'tis found.
Just so the mighty *Nile* has suffer'd in its Fame,
    Because 'tis said (and perhaps only said)
We've found a little inconsiderable Head
    That feeds the huge unequal Stream.
Consider Human Folly, and you'll quickly own,
    That all the Praises it can give,   150
By which some fondly boast they shall for ever live,
    Won't pay th' Impertinence of being known:
    Else why shou'd the fam'd *Lydian* King,
Whom all the Charms of an usurped Wife and State,

With all that Power unfelt, courts Mankind to be
        Great,
    Did with new unexperienc'd Glories wait,
Still wear, still doat on his invisible Ring?

VII

    Were I to form a regular Thought of Fame,
      Which is perhaps as hard t'imagine right
        As to paint *Echo* to the Sight;   160
I would not draw th' Idea from an empty Name:
        Because, alas, when we all die,
      Careless and ignorant Posterity,
    Altho' they praise the Learning and the Wit,
      And tho' the Title seems to show
    The Name and Man by whom the Book was writ,
      Yet how shall they be brought to know
Whether that very Name was He, or You, or I?
Less should I dawb it o'er with transitory Praise,
      And Water-Colours of these Days: 170
These Days! where e'en th' Extravagance of Poetry
    Is at a Loss for Figures to express
    Mens Folly, Whimsies, and Inconstancy,
    And by a faint Description makes them less.
Then tell us what is Fame, where shall we search for
        it?
Look where exalted Virtue and Religion sit
      Enthron'd with Heav'nly Wit,
      Look where you see
    The greatest Scorn of Learned Vanity,
  (And then how much a Nothing is Mankind! 180
Whose Reason is weigh'd down by popular Air,
  Who by that, vainly talks of baffling Death;
  And hopes to lengthen Life by a Transfusion of
        Breath,
    Which yet whoe'er examines right will find
  To be an Art as vain as bottling up of Wind:)

And when you find out these, believe true Fame is
there,
Far above all Reward, yet to which all is due;
And this, ye great Unknown, is only known in you.

VIII

The juggling Sea-God, when by Chance trepan'd
By some instructed Querist sleeping on the Sand,   190
Impatient of all Answers, strait became
A stealing Brook, and strove to creep away
Into his native Sea,
Vext at their Follies, murmur'd in his Stream;
But disappointed of his fond Desire,
Would vanish in a Pyramid of Fire.
This surly, slipp'ry God, when he design'd
To furnish his Escapes,
Ne'er borrow'd more Variety of Shapes
Than you to please and satisfy Mankind,   200
And seem (almost) transform'd to Water, Flame, and
Air,
So well you answer all Phenomena's there:
Tho' Madmen and the Wits, Philosophers and Fools,
With all that factious, or enthusiastick Dotards
dream,
And all the incoherent Jargon of the Schools;
Tho' all the Fumes of Fear, Hope, Love, and
Shame,
Contrive to shock your Minds with many a senseless
Doubt;
Doubts where the *Delphick* God would grope in
Ignorance and Night,
The God of Learning and of Light,
Would want a [1]God himself to help him out. 210

[1] Θεὸς ἀπὸ μήχανῆς.

14

IX

Philosophy, as it before us lies,
Seems to have borrow'd some ungrateful Taste
Of Doubts, Impertinence, and Niceties,
From every Age thro' which it pass'd,
But always with a stronger Relish of the last.
This beauteous Queen, by Heav'n design'd
To be the great Original
For Man to dress and polish his uncourtly Mind,
In what Mock Habits have they put her since the
Fall!
More oft in Fools and Madmens Hands than
Sages,   220
She seems a Medley of all Ages,
With a huge Fardingal to swell her fustian Stuff,
A new Commode, a Top-knot and a Ruff,
Her Face patch'd o'er with modern Pedantry,
With a long sweeping Train
Of Comments and Disputes, ridiculous and vain,
All of old Cut with a new Die:
How soon have you restor'd her Charms
And rid her of her Lumber and her Books,
Drest her again genteel and neat,   230
And rather tight than great,
How fond we are to court her to our Arms!
How much of Heav'n is in her naked Looks!

X

Thus the deluding Muse oft blinds me to her Ways,
And ev'n my very Thoughts transfers
And changes all to Beauty, and the Praise
Of that proud Tyrant Sex of Hers.
The Rebel Muse, alas, takes part
But with my own rebellious Heart,

And you with fatal and immortal Wit conspire   240
       To fan th' unhappy Fire.
     Cruel unknown! what is it you intend?
Ah could you, could you hope a Poet for your Friend!
     Rather forgive what my first Transport said:
May all the Blood, which shall by Woman's Scorn
          be shed,
     Lie upon you, and on your Childrens Head;
For you (Ah, did I think I e'er should live to see
     The fatal Time when that could be!)
     Have e'en increas'd their Pride and Cruelty.
   Woman seems now above all Vanity grown,   250
     Still boasting of her great Unknown
Platonick Champions, gain'd without one female
          Wile,
     Or the vast Charges of a Smile;
     Which 'tis a Shame how much of late
     You've taught the cov'tous Wretches to o'er-
          rate,
And which they've now the Conscience to weigh
     In the same Balance with our Tears,
     And with such scanty Wages pay
     The Bondage and Slavery of Years.
Let the vain Sex dream on, their Empire comes from
          us,   260
     And had they common Generosity
     They would not use us thus.
  Well—tho' you've rais'd her to this high Degree,
     Ourselves are rais'd as well as she;
   And spight of all that they or you can do,
  'Tis Pride and Happiness enough to me
Still to be of the same exalted Sex with you.

XI

     Alas, how fleeting and how vain,
If even the nobler Man, our Learning and our Wit!
16

I sigh when'er I think of it: 270
   As at the closing of an unhappy Scene
      Of some great King and Conqu'ror's Death,
      When the sad melancholy Muse
Stays but to catch his utmost Breath.
I grieve, this nobler Work most happily begun,
So quickly and so wonderfully carry'd on,
May fall at last to Interest, Folly and Abuse.
      There is a Noon-Tide in our Lives,
        Which still the sooner it arrives,
   Altho' we boast our Winter-Sun looks bright, 280
And foolishly are glad to see it at its Height,
Yet so much sooner comes the long and gloomy
           Night.
      No Conquest ever yet begun,
And by one mighty Hero carried to its Height,
E'er flourish'd under a Successor or a Son;
It lost some mighty Pieces thro' all Hands it past,
And vanish'd to an empty Title in the last.
   For when the animating Mind is fled,
      (Which Nature never can retain,
        Nor e'er call back again) 290
The Body, tho' Gigantick, lies all cold and dead.

XII

     And thus undoubtedly 'twill fare,
     With what unhappy Men shall dare
    To be Successors to these Great Unknown,
     On Learning's high-establish'd Throne.
   Censure, and Pedantry, and Pride,
  Numberless Nations, stretching far and wide,
Shall (I foresee it) soon with *Gothick* Swarms come
         forth
From Ignorance's universal North,
And with blind Rage break all this peaceful
      Government: 300

Yet shall these Traces of your Wit remain,
   Like a just Map, to tell the vast Extent
   Of Conquest in your short and happy Reign;
     And to all future Mankind shew
     How strange a Paradox is true,
  That Men, who liv'd and dy'd without a Name,
Are the chief Heroes in the sacred List of Fame.

               1692/1692

Ode to Dr. William Sancroft
Late Lord Archbishop of Canterbury

Written in May 1689, at the Desire of the
Late Lord Bishop of Ely

I

TRUTH is eternal, and the Son of Heav'n,
Bright effluence of th' immortal ray,
Chief cherub, and chief lamp, of that high sacred
              Seven,
Which guard the throne by night, and are its light by
              day:
    First of God's darling attributes,
    Thou daily seest Him face to face,
Nor does thy essence fix'd depend on giddy circum-
              stance
      Of time or place,
Two foolish guides in ev'ry sublunary dance:
  How shall we find Thee then in dark disputes?   10
  How shall we search Thee in a battle gain'd, .
  Or a weak argument by force maintain'd?
In dagger contests, and th' artillery of words,
(For swords are madmen's tongues, and tongues are
            madmen's swords)
    Contriv'd to tire all patience out,
    And not to satisfy the doubt?

18

II

But where is ev'n thy Image on our earth?
    For of the person much I fear,
Since Heaven will claim its residence as well as birth,
And God himself has said, He shall not find it here, 20
For this inferior world is but Heaven's dusky shade,
By dark reverted rays from its reflection made;
    Whence the weak shapes wild and imperfect pass,
Like sunbeams shot at too far distance from a glass:
        Which all the mimick forms express,
Though in strange uncouth postures, and uncomely
                dress;
        So when Cartesian artists try
        To solve appearances of sight
        In its reception to the eye,
And catch the living landscape through a scanty
                light,   30
        The figures all inverted shew,
        And colours of a faded hue;
    Here a pale shape with upward footstep treads,
        And men seem walking on their heads;
        There whole herds suspended lie
    Ready to tumble down into the sky;
    Such are the ways ill-guided mortals go
    To judge of things above by things below.
Disjointing shapes as in the fairy land of dreams,
        Or images that sink in streams;   40
        No wonder, then, we talk amiss
        Of truth, and what, or where it is:
        Say, Muse, for thou, if any, know'st
Since the bright essence fled, where haunts the
                reverend ghost?

III

If all that our weak knowledge titles virtue, be
(High Truth) the best resemblance of exalted Thee,
  If a mind fix'd to combat fate
With those two pow'rful swords, submission and
    humility,
  Sounds truly good, or truly great;
Ill may I live, if the good Sancroft in his holy rest, 50
  In the divin'ty of retreat,
 Be not the brightest pattern earth can show
  Of heav'n-born Truth below:
 But foolish man still judges what is best
  In his own balance, false and light,
  Foll'wing opinion, dark, and blind,
  That vagrant leader of the mind,
Till honesty and conscience are clear out of sight.

IV

And some, to be large ciphers in a state,
Pleas'd with an empty swelling to be counted great;
Make their minds travel o'er infinity of space, 61
  Rapp'd through the wide expanse of thought,
 And oft in contradiction's vortex caught,
To keep that worthless clod, the body, in one place:
Errors like this did old astronomers misguide,
Led blindly on by gross philosophy and pride,
  Who, like hard masters, taught the sun
  Through many a needless sphere to run,
Many an eccentrick and unthrifty motion make,
 And thousand incoherent journies take, 70
  Whilst all th' advantage by it got,
 Was but to light earth's inconsiderable spot.
The herd beneath, who see the weathercock of state
  Hung loosely on the church's pinnacle,

Believe it firm, because perhaps the day is mild and
        still;
But when they find it turn with the first blast of fate,
   By gazing upward giddy grow,
   And think the church itself does so;
  Thus fools, for being strong and num'rous known,
  Suppose the truth, like all the world, their own;   80
And holy Sancroft's motion quite irregular appears,
   Because 'tis opposite to theirs.

V

In vain then would the Muse the multitude advise,
  Whose peevish knowledge thus perversely lies
   In gath'ring follies from the wise;
  Rather put on thy anger and thy spight,
   And some kind pow'r for once dispense
  Through the dark mass, the dawn of so much
        sense,
To make them understand, and feel me when I write;
  The Muse and I no more revenge desire,   90
Each line shall stab, shall blast, like daggers and like
       fire;
  Ah, Britain, land of angels! which of all thy sins,
   (Say hapless isle, although
   It is a bloody list we know)
Has given thee up a dwelling place to fiends?
   Sin and the plague ever abound
In governments too easy, and too fruitful ground;
   Evils which a too gentle king,
   Too flourishing a spring,
   And too warm summers bring: 100
  Our British soil is over rank, and breeds
Among the noblest flow'rs a thousand pois'nous
       weeds,
   And ev'ry stinking weed so lofty grows,
   As if 'twould overshade the Royal Rose,

The Royal Rose the glory of our morn,
  But, ah, too much without a thorn.

VI

Forgive (original mildness) this ill govern'd zeal,
  'Tis all the angry slighted Muse can do
    In the pollution of these days;
  No province now is left her but to rail,   110
    And poetry has lost the art to praise,
      Alas, the occasions are so few:
      None e'er but you,
      And your Almighty Master, knew
      With heavenly peace of mind to bear
(Free from our tyrant passions, anger, scorn, or fear)
      The giddy turns of pop'lar rage,
And all the contradictions of a poison'd age;
    The son of God pronounc'd by the same breath
      Which straight pronounc'd his death;   120
    And though I should but ill be understood
    In wholly equalling our sin and theirs,
    And measuring by the scanty thread of wit
    What we call holy, and great, and just, and good,
(Methods in talk whereof our pride and ignorance
              make use)
    And which our wild ambition foolishly compares
      With endless and with infinite;
    Yet pardon native Albion, when I say,
Among thy stubborn sons there haunts that spirit of
              the Jews,
    That those forsaken wretches who to day   130
      Revile His great ambassador,
    Seem to discover what they would have done
    (Were his humanity on earth once more)
To his undoubted Master, Heaven's Almighty Son.

22

VII

But zeal is weak and ignorant, though wond'rous
        proud,
  Though very turbulent and very loud;
    The crazy composition shows,
Like that fantastick medley in the idols toes,
    Made up of iron mixt with clay,
    This crumbles into dust,   140
    That, moulders into rust,
    Or melts by the first show'r away.
Nothing is fix'd that mortals see or know,
Unless, perhaps, some stars above be so;
    And those, alas, do show
Like all transcendent excellence below;
    In both, false mediums cheat our sight,
And far exalted objects lessen by their height:
    Thus, primitive Sancroft moves too high
    To be observ'd by vulgar eye,   150
    And rolls the silent year
    On his own secret regular sphere,
And sheds, though all unseen, his sacred influence
        here.

VIII

Kind star, still may'st thou shed thy sacred influence
      here,
  Or from thy private peaceful orb appear;
  For, sure, we want some guide from Heav'n to
      show
The way which ev'ry wand'ring fool below
    Pretends so perfectly to know;
And which for aught I see, and much I fear,
    The world has wholly miss'd;   160
  I mean the way which leads to Christ:
Mistaken ideots! see how giddily they run,

Led blindly on by avarice and pride,
　What mighty numbers follow them;
　Each fond of erring with his guide:
Some whom ambition drives, seek Heaven's high
　　　Son
　In Cæsar's court, or in Jerusalem:
　　Others, ignorantly wise,
Among proud doctors and disputing pharisees:
What could the sages gain but unbelieving scorn;　170
　Their faith was so uncourtly when they said
That Heaven's high Son was in a village born;
　　That the world's Saviour had been
　　In a vile manger laid,
　And foster'd in a wretched inn?

IX

Necessity, thou tyrant conscience of the great,
Say, why the church is still led blindfold by the state;
　Why should the first be ruin'd and laid waste,
　To mend dilapidations in the last?
And yet the world, whose eyes are on our mighty
　　　Prince,　　　　　　　　　　180
　　Thinks Heav'n has cancell'd all our sins,
And that his subjects share his happy influence;
Follow the model close, for so I'm sure they should,
But wicked kings draw more examples than the good;
　And divine Sancroft, weary with the weight
Of a declining church, by faction her worst foe
　　　oppress'd,
　　Finding the mitre almost grown
　　A load as heavy as the crown,
　Wisely retreated to his heavenly rest.

24

X

Ah, may no unkind earthquake of the state,   190
    Nor hurricano from the crown,
Disturb the present mitre, as that fearful storm of late,
  Which in its dusky march along the plain,
    Swept up whole churches as it list,
    Wrapp'd in a whirlwind and a mist;
Like that prophetick tempest in the virgin reign,
  And swallow'd them at last, or flung them down.
  Such were the storms good Sancroft long has born;
  The mitre, which his sacred head has worn,
Was, like his Master's Crown, inwreath'd with thorn.
Death's sting is swallow'd up in victory at last,   201
    The bitter cup is from him past:
    Fortune in both extremes
  Though blasts from contrariety of winds,
    Yet to firm heavenly minds,
  Is but one thing under two different names;
And even the sharpest eye that has the prospect seen,
  Confesses ignorance to judge between;
And must to human reasoning opposite conclude, 209
To point out which is moderation, which is fortitude.

XI

Thus Sancroft, in the exaltation of retreat,
  Shows lustre that was shaded in his seat;
    Short glimm'rings of the prelate glorified;
Which the disguise of greatness only served to hide.
    Why should the Sun, alas, be proud
    To lodge behind a golden cloud;
Though fringed with ev'ning gold the cloud appears
        so gay,
'Tis but a lowborn vapour kindled by a ray;
    At length 'tis overblown and past,
    Puff'd by the people's spightful blast,   220

The dazzling glory dimms their prostituted sight,
   No deflowered eye can face the naked light:
   Yet does this high perfection well proceed
    From strength of its own native seed,
This wilderness the world, like that poetick wood of
        old,
   Bears one, and but one branch of gold,
  Where the bless'd spirit lodges like the dove,
And which (to heavenly soil transplanted) will
     improve,
To be, as 'twas below, the brightest plant above;
  For, whate'er theologick lev'llers dream,   230
   There are degrees above I know
   As well as here below,
 (The goddess Muse herself has told me so)
  Where high patrician souls dress'd heavenly gay,
  Sit clad in lawn of purer woven day,
There some high-spirited throne to Sancroft shall be
       given,
   In the metropolis of Heaven;
Chief of the mitred saints, and from archprelate here,
   Translated to archangel there.

XII

  Since, happy saint, since it has been of late   240
   Either our blindness or our fate,
   To lose the providence of thy cares,
  Pity a miserable church's tears,
  That begs the pow'rful blessing of thy pray'rs.
  Some angel say, what were the nation's crimes,
  That sent these wild reformers to our times:
   Say what their senseless malice meant,
   To tear religion's lovely face;
  Strip her of ev'ry ornament and grace:
In striving to wash off th' imaginary paint: 250
   Religion now does on her deathbed lie,

Heart-sick of a high fever and consuming atrophy;
How the physicians swarm to show their mortal skill,
And by their college arts methodically kill:
Reformers and physicians differ but in name,
  One end in both, and the design the same;
  Cordials are in their talk, while all they mean
    Is but the patient's death, and gain—
    Check in thy satire, angry Muse,
    Or a more worthy subject choose: 260
  Let not the outcasts of this outcast age
Provoke the honour of my Muse's rage,
   Nor be thy mighty spirit rais'd,
   Since Heaven and Cato both are pleas'd—

[The rest of the poem is lost.]

1692/1789

Ode to Sir William Temple

VIRTUE, the greatest of all Monarchies,
    Till its first Emperor rebellious Man
      Depos'd from off his Seat
  It fell, and broke with its own Weight
Into small States and Principalities,
    By many a petty Lord possess'd,
But ne'er since seated in one single Breast.
      'Tis you who must this Land subdue,
      The might Conquest's left for you,
      The Conquest and Discovery too: 10
    Search out this *Utopian* Ground,
    Virtue's *Terra Incognita*,
    Where none ever led the Way,
Nor ever since but in Descriptions found,
    Like the Philosopher's Stone,
With Rules to search it, yet obtain'd by none.

27

II

We have too long been led astray,
Too long have our misguided Souls been taught
   With Rules from musty Morals brought,
   'Tis you must put us in the Way;   20
   Let us (for shame) no more be fed
   With antique Reliques of the Dead,
   The Gleanings of Philosophy,
   Philosophy, the Lumber of the Schools,
   The Roguery of Alchymy,
      And we the bubbled Fools
Spend all our present [Stock] in hopes of golden
      Rules.

III

But what does our proud Ign'rance Learning call
   We odly *Plato*'s Paradox make good,
Our Knowledge is but mere Remembrance all,   30
   Remembrance is our Treasure and our Food;
Nature's fair Table-book our tender Souls
We scrawl all o'er with old and empty Rules,
    Stale Memorandums of the Schools;
    For Learning's mighty Treasures look
      In that deep Grave a Book,
   Think she there does all her Treasures hide,
And that her troubled Ghost still haunts there since
      she dy'd;
Confine her Walks to Colleges and Schools,
   Her Priests, her Train and Followers show   40
   As if they all were Spectres too,
   They purchase Knowledge at the Expence
   Of common Breeding, common Sense,
   And at once grow Scholars and Fools;
   Affect ill-manner'd Pedantry,
Rudeness, Ill-nature, Incivility,

And sick with Dregs of Knowledge grown,
Which greedily they swallow down,
Still cast it up and nauseate Company.

IV

Curst be the Wretch, nay doubly curst,   50
    (If it may lawful be
To curse our greatest Enemy)
Who learnt himself that Heresy first
    (Which since has seiz'd on all the rest)
That Knowledge forfeits all Humanity;
Taught us, like *Spaniards*, to be proud and poor,
    And fling our Scraps before our Door.
Thrice happy you have 'scap't this gen'ral Pest;
Those mighty Epithets, Learn'd, Good, and Great,
Which we ne'er join'd before, but in Romances meet,
    We find in you at last united grown.   61
      You cannot be compar'd to one,
    I must, like him that painted *Venus'* Face,
    Borrow from every one a Grace;
Virgil and *Epicurus* will not do,
    Their courting a Retreat like you,
Unless I put in *Cæsar*'s Learning too,
      Your happy Frame at once controuls
      This great Triumvirate of Souls.

V

Let not old *Rome* boast *Fabius'* Fate,   70
    He sav'd his Country by Delays,
      But you by Peace,
    You bought it at a cheaper Rate;
Nor has it left the usual bloody Scar,
    To shew it cost its Price in War,
War! that mad Game, the World so loves to play,
    And for it does so dearly pay;

For though with Loss or Victory awhile
  Fortune the Gamesters does beguile,
Yet at the last the Box sweeps all away.   80

VI

  Only the Laurel got by Peace
    No Thunder e'er can blast,
  Th' Artillery of the Skies
    Shoots to the Earth and dies;
For ever green and flourishing 'twill last,
Nor dipt in Blood, nor Widows Tears nor Orphans
           Cries;
  About the Head crown'd with these Bays,
  Like lambent Fire the Lightning plays;
Nor its triumphal Cavalcade to grace
  Make up its solemn Train with Death;   90
It melts the Sword of War, yet keeps it in the Sheath.

VII

The wily Shafts of State, those Juggler's Tricks
Which we call deep Design and Politicks,
(As in a Theatre the Ignorant Fry,
  Because the Cords escape their Eye,
  Wonder to see the Motions fly)
  Methinks, when you expose the Scene,
  Down the ill-organ'd Engines fall;
Off fly the Vizards and discover all,
  How plain I see thro' the Deceit!   100
  How shallow! and how gross the Cheat!
  Look where the Pully's ty'd above!
  Great God! (said I) what have I seen!
    On what poor Engines move
The Thoughts of Monarchs, and Designs of States,
  What petty Motives rule their Fates!
How the Mouse makes the mighty Mountain shake!

The mighty Mountain labours with its Birth,
   Away the frighted Peasants fly,
     Scar'd at th' unheard-of Prodigy,   110
Expect some great gigantick Son of Earth;
       Lo it appears!
   See how they tremble! how they quake!
Out starts the little Beast and mocks their idle Fears.

VIII

   Then tell (dear fav'rite Muse)
  What Serpent's that which still resorts,
  Still lurks in Palaces and Courts,
     Take thy unwonted Flight,
     And on the Terras light.
       See where she lies!   120
     See how she rears her Head,
  And rolls about her dreadful Eyes,
To drive all Virtue out, or look it dead!
'Twas sure this Basilisk sent *Temple* thence,
And tho' as some ('tis said) for their Defence
  Have worn a Casement o'er their Skin,
    So he wore his within,
Made up of Virtue and transparent Innocence:
   And tho' he oft renew'd the Fight,
And almost got priority of Sight,   130
   He ne'er could overcome her quite,
(In pieces cut, the Viper still did reunite)
   Till at last tir'd with loss of Time and Ease,
Resolv'd to give himself, as well as Country, Peace.

IX

Sing (belov'd Muse) the Pleasures of Retreat,
  And in some untouch'd Virgin Strain
Shew the Delights thy Sister Nature yields,

Sing of thy Vales, sing of thy Woods, sing of thy
           Fields;
    Go publish o'er the Plain
    How mighty a Proselyte you gain!   140
How noble a Reprisal on the Great!
    How is the Muse luxuriant grown,
        Whene'er she takes this Flight
        She soars clear out of sight,
These are the Paradises of her own;
(The Pegasus, like an unruly Horse,
    Tho' ne'er so gently led
To the lov'd Pasture where he us'd to feed,
Runs violently o'er his usual Course.)
    Wake from thy wanton Dreams,   150
    Come from thy dear-lov'd Streams,
The crooked Paths of wandering *Thames*.
    Fain the fair Nymph would stay,
    Oft she looks back in vain,
Oft 'gainst her Fountain does complain,
And softly steals in many Windings down,
As loth to see the hated Court and Town,
    And murmurs as she glides away.

X

    In this new happy Scene
    Are nobler Subjects for your learned Pen;   160
    Here we expect from you
More than your Predecessor, *Adam*, knew;
Whatever moves our Wonder, or our Sport,
Whatever serves for innocent Emblems of the Court;
    (How that which we a Kernel see,
Whose well-compacted Forms escape the Light,
    Unpierc'd by the blunt Rays of Sight)
    Shall ere long grow into a Tree,
Whence takes it its Increase, and whence its Birth,
Or from the Sun, or from the Air, or from the Earth,

Where all the fruitful Atoms lie,   171
   How some go downward to the Root,
  Some more ambitiously upwards fly,
And form the Leaves, the Branches, and the Fruit.
You strove to cultivate a barren Court in vain,
Your Garden's better worth your noble Pain,
Here Mankind fell, and hence must rise again.

XI

Shall I believe a Spirit so divine
   Was cast in the same Mold with mine?
Why then does Nature so unjustly share   180
Among her Elder Sons the whole Estate?
   And all her Jewels and her Plate,
Poor we *Cadets* of Heav'n, not worth her Care,
Take up at best with Lumber and the Leavings of a
        Fate:
   Some she binds 'Prentice to the Spade,
   Some to the Drudgery of a Trade,
Some she does to *Egyptian* Bondage draw,
Bids us make Bricks, yet sends us to look out for
        Straw;
   Some she condemns for Life to try
To dig the leaden Mines of deep Philosophy: 190
Me she has to the Muse's Gallies ty'd,
In vain I strive to cross this spacious Main,
   In vain I tug and pull the Oar,
   And when I almost reach the Shore,
Strait the Muse turns the Helm, and I launch out
        again;
     And yet to feed my Pride,
Whene'er I mourn, stops my complaining Breath,
With Promise of a mad Reversion after Death.

XII

Then (Sir,) accept this worthless Verse,
  The Tribute of an humble Muse,   200
'Tis all the Portion of my niggard Stars;
Nature the hidden Spark did at my Birth infuse,
And kindled first with Indolence and Ease,
And since too oft debauch'd by Praise,
'Tis now grown an incurable Disease:
In vain to quench this foolish Fire I try
  In Wisdom and Philosophy;
  In vain all wholesome Herbs I sow,
    Where nought but Weeds will grow.
Whate'er I plant (like Corn on barren Earth)   210
    By an equivocal Birth
  Seeds and runs up to Poetry.

                    1692/1745

A Description of Mother Ludwell's Cave

Hæ latebræ dulces, et si mihi credis, amœnæ

Lett others with Parnassus swell their theam,
Drinke inspiration from th' Aonian stream:
Lett them draw Phœbus down to patch a line,
Invoke, that hackney fry, the tunefull nine:
I that of Ludwell sing, to Ludwell run,
Her self my muse, her spring my Helicon.
The neighbouring park its friendly aid allows;
Perfum'd with thyme, o'erspread with shadie boughs;
Its leafie canopys new thoughts instill,
And Crooksberry supplies the cloven hill.   10
Pomona does Minerva's stores dispence,
And Flora sheds her balmie influence;
All things conspire to press my modest Muse,
The morning herbs adorn'd with pearly dews,

The meadows interlaced with silver flouds,
The frizled thickets, and the taller woods.
The whisp'ring Zephyrs my more silent tongue
Correct, and Philomela chirps a song.
Is there a bird of all the blooming year,
That has not sung his early Mattins here?   20
That has not sip'd the Fairy Matron's spring,
Or hover'd o'er her cave with wishfull wing?
An awfull Fabrick build by Nature's hand
Does raise our wonder, our respect command.
Three lucky trees to wilder art unknown
Seem on the front a growing triple crown.
At first the arched room is high and wide,
The naked walls with mossie hangings hid;
The cieling sandy: as you forward press
The roof is still declining into less;   30
Despair to reach the end—a little arch
Narrow and low forbids your utmost search.
So to her lover the chaste, beauteous lass
Without a blush vouchsafes to shew her face,
Her neck of Ivory, her snowy breast,
These shown, she modestly conceals the rest.
A shallow brook, that restless under ground
Strugled with earth, here a moist passage found.
Down thro' a stony vein the waters rowl
O'erflowing the capacious iron bowl: 40
Oh! happy bowl, that gladness can infuse,
And yet was never stain'd with heady juice.
Here thirsty souls carouse with innocence,
Nor owe their pleasure to their loss of sence.
Here a smooth floor had many a figure shown,
Had Virgin footsteps made impression,
That soft and swift Camilla-like advance,
While even movements seem to fly a dance.
No quilted couch, the sickman's daily bed,
No seats to lull asleep diseases made,   50
Are seen; but such as healthy persons please

Of wood or stone, such as the wearied ease.
O might I still enjoy this peacefull gloom!
The truest entrance to Elizium.
Who would to the Cumæan den repaire?
A better Sybil, wiser power is here.
Methinks I see him from his palace come,
And with his presence grace the balefull room:
Consider, Ludwell, what to him you owe,
Who does for you the noisy court forego;   60
Nay he a rich and gaudy silence leaves,
You share the honour, sweet Moorparke receives.
You with your wrinkles admiration move,
That with its beauty better merits love.
Here's careless Nature in her ancient dress,
There she's more modish, & consults the glass.
Here she's an old, but yet a pleasant dame;
There she'l a fair, not painted Virgin seem.
Here the rich Mettal hath through no fire pass'd,
There, tho refin'd, by no allay debas'd.   70
Thus nature is preserv'd in every part,
Sometimes adorn'd, but nere debauch'd by art.
When scatter'd locks, that dangle on the brow,
Into more decent hairy circles grow,
After enquiry made, tho no man love
The curling iron, all the comb approve.

1693?/1911

To Mr. Congreve

THRICE, with a prophet's voice and prophet's
    pow'r,
The Muse was called in a poetick hour,
And insolently thrice, the slighted maid
Dared to suspend her unregarded aid;
Then with that grief we form in spirits divine

Pleads for her own neglect, and thus reproaches mine:
    Once highly honour'd! False is the pretence
You make to truth, retreat, and innocence;
Who, to pollute my shades, bring'st with thee down
The most ungen'rous vices of the town;   10
Ne'er sprung a youth from out this isle before
I once esteem'd, and lov'd, and favour'd more,
Nor ever maid endured such courtlike scorn,
So much in mode, so very city-born;
'Tis with a foul design the muse you send,
Like a cast mistress to your wicked friend;
But find some new address, some fresh deceit,
Nor practise such an antiquated cheat;
These are the beaten methods of the stews,
Stale forms of course, all mean deceivers use,   20
Who barbarously think to 'scape reproach,
By prostituting her they first debauch.
    Thus did the Muse severe unkindly blame
This off'ring long design'd to Congreve's fame;
First chid the zeal as unpoetick fire,
Which soon his merit forced her to inspire;
Then call this verse, that speaks her largest aid,
The greatest compliment she ever made,
And wisely judge, no pow'r beneath divine
Could leap the bounds which part your world and
      mine;   30
For, youth, believe, to you unseen, is fix'd
A mighty gulf unpassable betwixt.
    Nor tax the goddess of a mean design
To praise your parts by publishing of mine;
That be my thought when some large bulky writ
Shows in the front the ambition of my wit;
There to surmount what bears me up, and sing
Like the victorious wren perch'd on the eagle's wing;
This could I do, and proudly o'er him tower,
Were my desires but heighten'd to my power.   40
    Godlike the force of my young Congreve's bays,

Soft'ning the muse's thunder into praise;
Sent to assist an old unvanquish'd pride
That looks with scorn on half mankind beside;
A pride that well suspends poor mortals fate,
Gets between them and my resentment's weight,
Stands in the gap 'twixt me and wretched men,
T'avert th'impending judgments of my pen.

    Thus I look down with mercy on the age,
By hopes my Congreve will reform the stage;   50
For never did poetick mine before
Produce a richer vein or cleaner ore;
The bullion stamp'd in your refining mind
Serves by retail to furnish half mankind.
With indignation I behold your wit
Forc'd on me, crack'd, and clipp'd, and counterfeit,
By vile pretenders, who a stock maintain
From broken scraps and filings of your brain.
Through native dross your share is hardly known,
And by short views mistook for all their own;   60
So small the gain those from your wit do reap,
Who blend it into folly's larger heap,
Like the sun's scatter'd beams which loosely pass,
When some rough hand breaks the assembling glass.

    Yet want your criticks no just cause to rail,
Since knaves are ne'er obliged for what they steal.
These pad on wit's high road, and suits maintain
With those they rob, by what their trade does gain.
Thus censure seems that fiery froth which breeds
O'er the sun's face, and from his heat proceeds,   70
Crusts o'er the day, shadowing its parent beam
As ancient nature's modern masters dream;
This bids some curious praters here below
Call Titan sick, because their sight is so;
And well, methinks, does this allusion fit
To scribblers, and the god of light and wit;
Those who by wild delusions entertain
A lust of rhyming for a poet's vein,

Raise envy's clouds to leave themselves in night,
But can no more obscure my Congreve's light   80
Than swarms of gnats, that wanton in a ray
Which gave them birth, can rob the world of day.
    What northern hive pour'd out these foes to wit?
Whence came these Goths to overrun the pit?
How would you blush the shameful birth to hear
Of those you so ignobly stoop to fear;
For, ill to them, long have I travell'd since
Round all the circles of impertinence,
Search'd in the nest where every worm did lie
Before it grew a city butterfly;   90
I'm sure I found them other kind of things
Than those with backs of silk and golden wings;
A search, no doubt, as curious and as wise
As virtuosoes' in dissecting flies;
For, could you think? the fiercest foes you dread,
And court in prologues, all are country bred;
Bred in my scene, and for the poet's sins
Adjourn'd from tops and grammar to the inns;
Those beds of dung, where schoolboys sprout up
    beaus
Far sooner than the nobler mushroom grows: 100
These are the lords of the poetick schools,
Who preach the saucy pedantry of rules;
Those pow'rs the criticks, who may boast the odds
O'er Nile, with all its wilderness of gods;
Nor could the nations kneel to viler shapes,
Which worship'd cats, and sacrificed to apes;
And can you think the wise forbear to laugh
At the warm zeal that breeds this golden calf?
    Haply you judge these lines severely writ
Against the proud usurpers of the pit;   110
Stay while I tell my story, short, and true;
To draw conclusions shall be left to you;
Nor need I ramble far to force a rule,
But lay the scene just here at Farnham school.

Last year, a lad hence by his parent sent
With other cattle to the city went;
Where having cast his coat, and well pursued
The methods most in fashion to be lewd,
Return'd a finish'd spark this summer down,
Stock'd with the freshest gibberish of the town; 120
A jargon form'd from the lost language, wit,
Confounded in that Babel of the pit;
Form'd by diseased conceptions, weak, and wild,
Sick lust of souls, and an abortive child;
Born between whores and fops, by lewd compacts,
Before the play, or else between the acts:
Nor wonder, if from such polluted minds
Should spring such short and transitory kinds,
Or crazy rules to make us wits by rote
Last just as long as ev'ry cuckoo's note: 130
What bungling, rusty tools, are us'd by fate!
'Twas in an evil hour to urge my hate,
My hate, whose lash just Heaven has long decreed
Shall on a day make sin and folly bleed;
When man's ill genius to my presence sent
This wretch, to rouse my wrath, for ruin meant;
Who in his idiom vile, with Gray's inn grace,
Squander'd his noisy talents to my face;
Named ev'ry player on his fingers ends,
Swore all the wits were his peculiar friends; 140
Talk'd with that saucy and familiar ease
Of Wycherley, and you, and Mr. Bays;
Said, how a late report your friends had vex'd,
Who heard you meant to write heroicks next;
For, tragedy, he knew, would lose you quite,
And told you so at Will's but t'other night.

Thus are the lives of fools a sort of dreams,
Rend'ring shades, things, and substances of names;
Such high companions may delusion keep,
Lords are a footboy's cronies in his sleep. 150
As a fresh miss, by fancy, face, and gown,

40

Render'd the topping beauty of the town,
Draws ev'ry rhyming, prating, dressing sot,
To boast of favours that he never got;
Of which, whoe'er lacks confidence to prate,
Brings his good parts and breeding in debate;
And not the meanest coxcomb you can find,
But thanks his stars, that Phillis has been kind;
Thus prostitute my Congreve's name is grown
To ev'ry lewd pretender of the town.   160
'Troth I could pity you; but this is it,
You find, to be the fashionable wit;
These are the slaves whom reputation chains,
Whose maintenance requires no help from brains.
For, should the vilest scribbler to the pit,
Whom sin and want e'er furnish'd out a wit;
Whose name must not within my lines be shown,
Lest here it live, when perish'd with his own;
Should such a wretch usurp my Congreve's place,
And choose out wits who ne'er have seen his face;
I'll be my life but the dull cheat would pass,   171
Nor need the lion's skin conceal the ass;
Yes, that beau's look, that vice, those critick ears,
Must needs be right, so well resembling theirs.

    Perish the Muse's hour, thus vainly spent
In satire, to my Congreve's praises meant;
In how ill season her resentments rule,
What's that to her if mankind be a fool?
Happy beyond a private muse's fate,
In pleasing all that's good among the great,   180
Where though her elder sisters crowding throng,
She still is welcome with her inn'cent song;
Whom were my Congreve blest to see and know,
What poor regards would merit all below!
How proudly would he haste the joy to meet,
And drop his laurel at Apollo's feet.

    Here by a mountain's side, a reverend cave
Gives murmuring passage to a lasting wave;

'Tis the world's wat'ry hourglass streaming fast,
Time is no more when th' utmost drop is past;   190
Here, on a better day, some druid dwelt,
And the young Muse's early favour felt;
Druid, a name she does with pride repeat,
Confessing Albion once her darling seat;
Far in this primitive cell might we pursue
Our predecessors footsteps, still in view;
Here would we sing—But, ah! you think I dream,
And the bad world may well believe the same;
Yes; you are all malicious standers by,
While two fond lovers prate, the Muse, and I.   200
   Since thus I wander from my first intent,
Nor am that grave adviser which I meant;
Take this short lesson from the god of bays,
And let my friend apply it as he please:
Beat not the dirty paths where vulgar feet have trod,
    But give the vigorous fancy room.
  For when like stupid alchymists you try
     To fix this nimble god,
     This volatile mercury,
  The subtil spirit all flies up in fume;   210
  Nor shall the bubbled virtuoso find
More than a fade insipid mixture left behind.[1]

  While thus I write, vast shoals of criticks come,
And on my verse pronounce their saucy doom;
The Muse, like some bright country virgin, shows,
Fall'n by mishap among a knot of beaux;
They, in their lewd and fashionable prate,
Rally her dress, her language, and her gait;
Spend their base coin before the bashful maid,
Current like copper, and as often paid: 220
She, who on shady banks has joy'd to sleep
Near better animals, her father's sheep;

[1] Out of an Ode I writ, inscribed 'The Poet'. The rest of it is lost.

Shamed and amazed, beholds the chatt'ring throng,
To think what cattle she has got among;
But with the odious smell and sight annoy'd,
In haste she does th' offensive herd avoid.
'Tis time to bid my friend a long farewell,
The Muse retreats far in yon crystal cell;
Faint inspiration sickens as she flies,
Like distant echo spent, the spirit dies.   230
   In this descending sheet you'll haply find
Some short refreshment for your weary mind,
Nought it contains is common or unclean,
And once drawn up, is ne'er let down again.
                                                       1693/1789

Occasioned by Sir William Temple's Late Illness and Recovery

STRANGE to conceive, how the same objects strike
At distant hours the mind with forms so like!
Whether in time, Deduction's broken chain
Meets, and salutes her sister link again;
Or hunted Fancy, by a circling flight,
Comes back with joy to its own seat at night;
Or whether dead Imagination's ghost
Oft hovers where alive it haunted most;
Or if Thought's rolling globe, her circle run,
Turns up old objects to the soul her sun;   10
Or loves the muse to walk with conscious pride
O'er the glad scene whence first she rose a bride:
   Be what it will; late near yon whisp'ring stream,
Where her own Temple was her darling theme;
There first the visionary sound was heard,
When to poetick view the Muse appear'd.
Such seem'd her eyes, as when an evening ray
Gives glad farewell to a tempestuous day;

43

Weak is the beam to dry up nature's tears,
Still ev'ry tree the pendent sorrow wears;   20
Such are the smiles where drops of crystal show
Approaching joy at strife with parting woe.
　　As when to scare th' ungrateful or the proud
Tempests long frown, and thunder threatens loud,
Till the blest sun to give kind dawn of grace
Darts weeping beams across Heaven's wat'ry face;
When soon the peaceful bow unstring'd is shown,
A sign God's dart is shot, and wrath o'erblown;
Such to unhallowed sight the Muse divine
Might seem, when first she rais'd her eyes to mine. 30
　　What mortal change does in thy face appear,
Lost youth, she cried, since first I met thee here!
With how undecent clouds are overcast
Thy looks, when every cause of grief is past!
Unworthy the glad tidings which I bring,
Listen while the Muse thus teaches thee to sing:
　　As parent earth, burst by imprison'd winds,
Scatters strange agues o'er men's sickly minds,
And shakes the atheist's knees; such ghastly fear
Late I beheld on every face appear;   40
Mild Dorothea, peaceful, wise, and great,
Trembling beheld the doubtful hand of fate;
Mild Dorothea, whom we both have long
Not dared to injure with our lowly song;
Sprung from a better world, and chosen then
The best companion for the best of men:
As some fair pile, yet spared by zeal and rage,
Lives pious witness of a better age;
So men may see what once was womankind,
In the fair shrine of Dorothea's mind.   50
　　You that would grief describe, come here and trace
Its wat'ry footsteps in Dorinda's face:
Grief from Dorinda's face does ne'er depart
Farther than its own palace in her heart:
Ah, since our fears are fled, this insolent expel,

At least confine the tyrant to his cell.
And if so black the cloud, that Heaven's bright queen
Shrouds her still beams; how should the stars be seen?
Thus, when Dorinda wept, joy ev'ry face forsook,
And grief flung sables on each menial look;   60
The humble tribe mourn'd for the quick'ning soul,
That furnish'd spirit and motion through the whole;
So would earth's face turn pale, and life decay,
Should Heaven suspend to act but for a day;
So nature's crazed convulsions make us dread
That time is sick, or the world's mind is dead.—
Take, youth, these thoughts, large matter to employ
The fancy furnish'd by returning joy;
And to mistaken man these truths rehearse,
Who dare revile the integrity of verse: 70
Ah fav'rite youth, how happy is thy lot!—
But I'm deceiv'd, or thou regard'st me not;
Speak, for I wait thy answer, and expect
Thy just submission for his bold neglect.
    Unknown the forms we the high-priesthood use
At the divine appearance of the Muse,
Which to divulge might shake profane belief,
And tell the irreligion of my grief;
Grief that excused the tribute of my knees,
And shaped my passion in such words as these.   80
    Malignant goddess! bane to my repose,
Thou universal cause of all my woes;
Say, whence it comes that thou art grown of late
A poor amusement for my scorn and hate;
The malice thou inspir'st I never fail
On thee to wreak the tribute when I rail;
Fools commonplace thou art, their weak ensconcing
    fort,
Th' appeal of dullness in the last resort:
Heaven with a parent's eye regarding earth,
Deals out to man the planet of his birth: 90
But sees thy meteor blaze about me shine,

And passing o'er, mistakes thee still for mine:
Ah, should I tell a secret yet unknown,
That thou ne'er hadst a being of thy own,
But a wild form dependent on the brain,
Scatt'ring loose features o'er the optick vein;
Troubling the crystal fountain of the sight,
Which darts on poets eyes a trembling light;
Kindled while reason sleeps, but quickly flies,
Like antick shapes in dreams, from waking eyes: 100
In sum, a glitt'ring voice, a painted name,
A walking vapour, like thy sister fame.
But if thou be'st what thy mad vot'ries prate,
A female pow'r, loose govern'd thoughts create;
Why near the dregs of youth perversely wilt thou stay,
So highly courted by the brisk and gay?
Wert thou right woman, thou shouldst scorn to look
On an abandon'd wretch by hopes forsook;
Forsook by hopes, ill fortune's last relief,
Assign'd for life to unremitting grief;   110
For, let Heaven's wrath enlarge these weary days,
If hope e'er dawns the smallest of its rays.
Time o'er the happy takes so swift a flight,
And treads so soft, so easy, and so light,
That we the wretched, creeping far behind,
Can scarce th' impression of his footsteps find;
Smooth as that airy nymph so subtly born
With inoffensive feet o'er standing corn;
Which bow'd by evening breeze with bending stalks,
Salutes the weary trav'ller as he walks;   120
But o'er th' afflicted with a heavy pace
Sweeps the broad sithe, and tramples on his face.
Down falls the summer's pride, and sadly shows
Nature's bare visage furrowed as he mows:
See Muse, what havock in these looks appear,
These are the tyrant's trophies of a year;
Since hope his last and greatest foe is fled,
Despair and he lodge ever in its stead;

March o'er the ruin'd plain with motion slow,
Still scatt'ring desolation where they go.   130
To thee I owe that fatal bent of mind,
Still to unhappy restless thoughts inclin'd;
To thee, what oft I vainly strive to hide,
That scorn of fools, by fools mistook for pride;
From thee whatever virtue takes its rise,
Grows a misfortune, or becomes a vice;
Such were thy rules to be poetically great,
'Stoop not to int'rest, flattery, or deceit;
Nor with hired thoughts be thy devotion paid;
Learn to disdain their mercenary aid;   140
Be this thy sure defence, thy brazen wall,
Know no base action, at no guilt turn pale;
And since unhappy distance thus denies
T'expose thy soul, clad in this poor disguise;
Since thy few ill presented graces seem
To breed contempt where thou hast hoped esteem.'—
     Madness like this no fancy ever seized,
Still to be cheated, never to be pleased;
Since one false beam of joy in sickly minds
Is all the poor content delusion finds.—   150
There thy enchantment broke, and from this hour
I here renounce thy visionary pow'r;
And since thy essence on my breath depends,
Thus with a puff the whole delusion ends.
                                        1693/1789

MISCELLANY POEMS

Verses wrote in a Lady's Ivory Table-Book

PERUSE my Leaves thro' ev'ry Part,
And think thou seest my Owner's Heart;
Scrawl'd o'er with Trifles thus; and quite
As hard, as senseless, and as light,
Expos'd to ev'ry Coxcomb's Eyes,
But hid with Caution from the Wise.
Here you may read, (*Dear charming Saint*)
Beneath, (*A new Receipt for Paint.*)
Here in Beau-spelling, (*tru tel Deth.*)
There, in her own (*far an el Breth.*)   10
Here, (*lovely Nymph pronounce my Doom.*)
There, (*a safe Way to use Perfume.*)
Here, a Page fill'd with Billet-Doux;
On t'other Side, (*laid out for Shoes.*)
(*Madam, I die without your Grace*)
(Item, *for half a Yard of Lace.*)
Who, that had Wit would place it here,
For ev'ry peeping Fop to jeer?
In Power of Spittle, and a Clout,
Whene'er he please, to blot it out;   20
And then to heighten the Disgrace,
Clap his own Nonsense in the Place.
Whoe'er expects to hold his Part
In such a Book, and such a Heart;
If he be wealthy, and a Fool,
Is in all Points the fittest Tool;
Of whom it may be justly said,
He's a *Gold* Pencil tipt with *Lead.*

1698/1711

To their [1]Excellencies
the Lords Justices of Ireland
The Humble Petition of Frances Harris

Who must starve, and die a Maid if it miscarries

Humbly Sheweth,　　　　　　　•

That I went to warm my self in Lady *Betty*'s Cham-
　　　ber, because I was cold;

And I had in a Purse Seven Pounds, Four Shillings
　　　and Six Pence, (besides Farthings,) in Money
　　　and Gold;

So, because I had been buying Things for my *Lady*
　　　last Night,

I was resolv'd to tell my Money, to see if it was right.

Now you must know, because my Trunk has a very
　　　bad Lock,

Therefore all the Money I have, (which, GOD
　　　knows, is a very small Stock,)

I keep in my Pocket, ty'd about my Middle, next my
　　　Smock,

So, when I went to put up my Purse, as GOD would
　　　have it, my Smock was unript;

And instead of putting it into my Pocket, down it
　　　slipt:

Then the Bell rung, and I went down to put my *Lady*
　　　to Bed;　　　　　　　　　　　　　　　　10

And, GOD knows, I thought my Money was as safe as
　　　my Maïdenhead.

So, when I came up again, I found my Pocket feel
　　　very light,

But when I search'd and miss'd my Purse, *Lord!* I
　　　thought, I should have sunk outright:

Lord! Madam, says *Mary*, how d'ye do? Indeed, said
　　　I, never worse.

---

[1] *Earl of* BERKELEY, *and the Earl of* GALWAY.

52

To their * Excellencies the

LORDS JUSTICES

OF

IRELAND.

The humble Petition of FRANCES HARRIS,
Who must starve, and die a Maid if it miscarries.

WRITTEN in the YEAR, 1701.

Humbly Sheweth,

 HAT I went to warm my self in Lady
Betty's Chamber, because I was cold;
And I had in a Purse Seven Pounds,
Four Shillings and Six Pence, (besides
Farthings,) in Money and Gold;

* *Earl of* BERKELEY, *and the Earl of* GALWAY.

VOL. II.　　　　B　　　　So

This is the first page of Faulkner's Volume II,
the 'Poetical Works', showing the typographical
flourishes that the 'prince of Dublin printers',
as Swift called George Faulkner, devoted to his
most esteemed author and publication.

[face page 52

STELLA.
From an Original Drawing by the Revd George Parnel, Archdeacon of Clogher, in the Possession of G. Faulkner.

This engraving, which appeared in Faulkner's Volume XVII, is the best authenticated likeness of Stella, shown in about her 35th year. The original drawing by Thomas Parnell (not George as stated), Archdeacon of Clogher, is lost.

[*face page 53*

But pray, *Mary*, can you tell what I have done with
    my Purse:

Lord help me, said *Mary*, I never stirr'd out of this
    Place:

Nay, said I, I had it in Lady *Betty*'s Chamber, that's a
    plain Case.

So, *Mary* got me to Bed, and cover'd me up warm:

However, she stole away my Garters that I might do
    my self no Harm.

So, I tumbled and toss'd all Night, as you may very
    well think;   20

But hardly ever set my Eyes together, or slept a Wink.

So, I was adream'd, methought, that we went and
    search'd the Folks round:

And in a Corner of Mrs. *Duke*'s Box, ty'd in a Rag,
    the Money was found.

So, next Morning we told [1]*Whittle*, and he fell a
    swearing:

Then my Dame [2]*Wadgar* came, and she, you know,
    is thick of Hearing:

Dame, said I, as loud as I could bawl, do you know
    what a Loss I have had?

Nay, said she, my Lord [3]*Collway*'s Folks are all very
    sad:

For my Lord [4]*Dromedary* comes a *Tuesday* without
    fail:

Pugh; said I, but that's not the Business that I ail.

Says [5]*Cary*, says he, I have been a Servant this Five
    and Twenty Years come Spring;   30

And in all the Places I liv'd, I never heard of such a
    Thing.

Yes, says the Steward, I remember, when I was at my
    Lady *Shrewsbury*'s,

---

[1] *Earl of* BERKELEY'S *Valet.*   [2] *The old deaf House-Keeper.*
[3] GALWAY.
[4] DROGHEDA, *who with the Primate were to succeed the two Earls.*
[5] *Clerk of the Kitchen.*

53

Such a Thing as this happen'd, just about the Time of
    Gooseberries.

So I went to the Party suspected, and I found her full
    of Grief;

(Now you must know, of all Things in the World I
    hate a Thief.)

However, I was resolv'd to bring the Discourse slily
    about;

Mrs. [1]*Dukes*, said I, here's an ugly Accident has
    happen'd out:

'Tis not that I value the Money [2]three Skips of a
    Louse;

But the Thing I stand upon is, the Credit of the
    House:

'Tis true, Seven Pounds, Four Shilling, and Six Pence,
    makes a great Hole in my Wages;   40

Besides, as they say, Service is no Inheritance in
    these Ages.

Now, Mrs. *Dukes*, you know, and every Body
    understands,

That tho' 'tis hard to judge, yet Money can't go
    without Hands.

The *Devil* take me, said she, (blessing her self,) if ever
    I saw't!

So she roar'd like a *Bedlam*, as tho' I had call'd her
    all to naught:

So you know, what could I say to her any more?

I e'en left her, and came away as wise as I was before.

Well: But then they would have had me gone to the
    Cunning-Man:

No, said I, 'tis the same Thing, the *Chaplain* will be
    here anon.

So the *Chaplain* came in. Now the Servants say he is
    my Sweet-heart,   50

---

[1] *A Servant, one of the Footmen's Wives.*
[2] *An usual Saying of hers.*

Because he's always in my Chamber, and I always
    take his Part;

So, as the *Devil* would have it, before I was aware,
    out I blunder'd,

Parson, said I, can you cast a *Nativity*, when a Body's
    plunder'd?

(Now you must know, he hates to be call'd *Parson*
    like the *Devil.*)

Truly, says he, Mrs. *Nab*, it might become you to be
    more civil:

If your Money be gone, as a learned *Divine* says,
    d'ye see,

You are no *Text* for my handling, so take that from
    me:

I was never taken for a *Conjurer* before, I'd have you
    know:

Lord, said I, don't be angry, I am sure I never thought
    you so:

You know, I honour the Cloth; I design to be a
    Parson's Wife;   60

I never took one in *your Coat* for a *Conjurer* in all my
    Life.

With that, he twisted his Girdle at me like a Rope;
    as who should say,

Now you may go hang your self for me; and so went
    away.

Well; I thought, I should have swoon'd: *Lord*, said I,
    what shall I do?

I have lost my *Money*; and I shall lose my *True-love*
    too.

So, my *Lord* call'd me, [1]*Harry*, said my *Lord*, don't
    cry,

I'll give something towards thy Loss: And says my
    Lady, so will I.

Oh! but said I; what if after all, the Chaplain won't
    come to?

[1] *A Cant Word of my Lord and Lady to Mrs.* HARRIS.

For that, he said, (an't please your *Excellencies*,) I
    must petition You.

The Premisses tenderly consider'd, I desire your
    Excellencies Protection: 70
And that I may have a Share in next *Sunday*'s
    Collection:
And over and above, that I may have your *Excellen-*
    cies Letter,
With an Order for the *Chaplain* aforesaid; or instead
    of him a better.
And then your poor *Petitioner*, both Night and Day,
Of the *Chaplain* (for 'tis his *Trade*,) as in Duty bound,
    shall ever *pray*.

                                  1701/1711

A Ballad
On the Game of Traffick

MY [1]*Lord* to find out who must deal
    Delivers Cards about,
But the first Knave does seldom fail
    To find the *Doctor* out.

But then his *Honour* cry'd, Godzooks!
    And seem'd to knit his Brow;
For on a Knave he never looks
    But H' thinks upon *Jack How.*

My *Lady* tho' she is no Player
    Some bungling Partner takes,   10
And wedg'd in Corner of a Chair
    Takes Snuff, and holds the Stakes.

[1] The Earl of Berkeley.

Dame *Floyd* looks out in grave Suspence
    For Pair-royals and Sequents;
But wisely cautious of her Pence,
    The Castle seldom frequents.

Quoth *Herries*, fairly putting Cases,
    I'd won it on my Word,
If I had put a Pair of Aces,
    And could pick up a Third.   **20**

But *Weston* has a new-cast Gown
    On *Sundays* to be fine in,
And if she can but win a *Crown*,
    'Twill just new dye the Lining.

'With these is Parson *Swift*,
    'Not knowing how to spend his Time,
'Does make a wretched Shift,
    'To deafen 'em with Puns and Rhime.'
                           1702/1746

Lady Betty Berkeley *finding this Ballad in the Author's Room unfinished, she underwrit the last Stanza, and left the Paper where she had found it; which occasioned the following Song, that the Author wrote in a counterfeit Hand, as if a third Person had done it.*

A Ballad
to the Tune of 'The Cut-purse'

I

ONCE on a time, as old Stories rehearse,
    A Friar would needs shew his Talent in *Latin*,
But was sorely put to't in the Midst of a Verse,

Because he could find out no Word to come pat in.
       Then all in the Place
       He left a void Space;
And so went to Bed in a desperate Case.
When behold, the next Morning a wonderful Riddle!
He found it was strangely fill'd up in the Middle.
   CHO. *Let censuring Criticks then think what they*
      list on't,   10
Who would not write Verses with such an Assistant?

II

This put me the Friar into an Amazement;
   For he wisely consider'd it must be a Sprite,
That came thro' the Key-Hole, or in at the Casement;
   And it needs must be one, that could both read and
              write:
       Yet he did not know
       If it were Friend or Foe,
Or whether it came from above or below.
Howe'er, it was civil in Angel or Elf;
For he ne'er could have fill'd it so well of himself. 20
   CHO. *Let censuring, &c.*

III

Even so Master Doctor had puzzled his Brains
   In making a Ballad, but was at a stand;
He had mix'd little Wit with a great deal of Pains;
   When he found a new Help from invisible Hand.
       Then good Dr. *S[wift]*,
       Pay thanks for the Gift,
For you freely must own you were at a dead Lift:
And tho' some malicious young Spirit did do't,
You may see by the *Hand* it had no cloven *Foot*. 30
   CHO. *Let censuring, &c.*

                        1702/1711

The Description of a Salamander

Out of Pliny's Nat. Hist. lib. 10, cap.
67. & lib. cap. 4

As Mastiff Dogs in modern Phrase are
Call'd *Pompey*, *Scipio*, and *Cæsar*;
As *Pies* and *Daws* are often styl'd
With Christian Nick-names, like a Child;
As we say *Monsieur* to an *Ape*,
Without Offence to human Shape:
So Men have got from Bird and Brute
Names that will best their Natures suit.
The *Lion*, *Eagle*, *Fox*, and *Boar*
Were Heroes Titles heretofore,   10
Bestow'd as Hi'roglyphicks fit
To shew their Valour, Strength, or Wit,
For what is understood by *Fame*,
Besides the getting of a *Name?*
But e'er since Men invented Guns,
A diff'rent Way their Fancy runs;
To paint a Hero, we enquire
For something that will conquer *Fire*.
Would you describe *Turenne* or *Trump*,
Think of a Bucket, or a Pump.   20
Are these too low?—then find out grander,
Call my Lord *Cutts*, a *Salamander*.
'Tis well:—But since we live among
Detractors with an evil Tongue,
Who may object against the Term:
Pliny shall prove what we affirm:
Pliny shall prove, and we'll apply,
And I'll be judg'd by Standers-by.

First then, our Author has defin'd
This Reptile of the Serpent Kind,   30
With gaudy Coat and shining Train,
But loathsome Spots his Body stain:

59

Out from some Hole obscure he flies,
When Rains descend, and Tempests rise,
Till the Sun clears the Air, and then
Crawls back, neglected, to his Den.

So when the War has rais'd a Storm:
I've seen a Snake in human Form,
All stain'd with Infamy and Vice,
Leap from the Dunghill in a Trice;   40
Burnish and make a gaudy Show,
Become a General, Peer, and Beau;
Till Peace hath made the Sky serene,
Then shrink into its Hole again.

All this we grant—why then look yonder,
Sure that must be a SALAMANDER.

Farther we are by *Pliny* told,
This *Serpent* is extremely cold;
So cold, that put it in the Fire,
'Twill make the very Flames expire: 50
Besides it spues a filthy Froth,
(Whether thro' Rage, or Lust, or both,)
Of Matter purulent and white,
Which, happening on the Skin to light,
And there corrupting to a Wound,
Spreads Leprosy and Baldness round.

So have I seen a batter'd Beau,
By Age and Claps grown cold as Snow,
Whose Breath, or Touch, where'er he came,
Blew out Love's Torch, or chill'd the Flame: 60
And should some Nymph, who ne'er was cruel,
Like *Carleton* cheap, or fam'd *Du-Ruel*,
Receive the Filth, which he ejects;
She soon wou'd find the same Effects
Her tainted Carcass to pursue,

As from the *Salamander*'s Spue:
A dismal Shedding of her Locks,
And, if no Leprosy, a Pox.

> *Then I'll appeal to each By-stander*
> *If this be not a* SALAMANDER?　　**70**
>
> 　　　1705/1711

The History of Vanbrug's House

WHEN Mother *Clud* had rose from Play;
And call'd to take the Cards away;
Van saw, but seem'd not to regard,
How *Miss* pick'd ev'ry painted Card;
And busy both with Hand and Eye,
Soon rear'd a House two Stories high:
Van's *Genius*, without Thought or Lecture,
Is hugely turn'd on *Architecture:*
He view'd the Edifice, and smil'd,
Vow'd it was pretty for a Child:　　10
It was so perfect in its Kind,
He kept the Model in his Mind.

But, when he found the Boys at Play,
And saw them dabbling in their Clay;
He stood behind a Stall to lurk,
And mark the Progress of their Work:
With true Delight observ'd 'em all
Raking up *Mud*, to build a Wall:
The Plan he much admir'd, and took
The *Model* in his Table-Book;　　20
Thought himself now exactly skill'd,
And so resolv'd a *House* to build;
A *real House*, with *Rooms* and *Stairs*,
Five times at least as big as theirs,

Taller than *Miss*'s by two Yards;
Not a sham Thing of Clay or Cards.
And so he did; for in a while
He built up such a monstrous Pile,
That no two Chairmen could be found
Able to lift it from the Ground: 30
Still at *Whitehall* it stands in View,
Just in the Place, where first it grew:
There all the little School-boys run,
Envying to see themselves out-done.

    From such deep Rudiments as these,
Van is become by due Degrees,
For Building fam'd; and justly reckon'd
At Court, *Vitruvius* the *Second*.
No Wonder; since wise *Authors* show,
That *best Foundations* must be *low*.   40
And now the *Duke* has wisely ta'en him
To be his *Architect* at *Blenheim*.
But Raillery for once apart,
If this Rule holds in ev'ry Art;
Or if his *Grace* were no more skill'd in
The Art of battering Walls than Building;
We might expect to see next Year
A *Mouse-trap* Man chief Engineer.
                   1706/1711

An Elegy on the supposed Death of Partrige the Almanack-maker

    WELL; 'tis as *Bickerstaff* has guess't,
Tho' we all took it for a Jest:
Partrige is dead; nay more, he dy'd,
E'er he could prove the good '*Squire* ly'd.
Strange, an Astrologer should die,

Without one Wonder in the Sky!
Not one of all his *Crony* Stars
To pay their Duty at his Herse?
No Meteor, no Eclipse appear'd?
No Comet with a flaming Beard?   10
The Sun has rose, and gone to Bed,
Just as if *Partrige* were not dead:
Nor hid himself behind the Moon,
To make a dreadful Night at Noon.
He at fit Periods walks through *Aries*,
Howe'er our earthly Motions varies;
And twice a Year he'll cut th' *Equator*,
As if there had been no such Matter.

Some Wits have wonder'd what Analogy
There is 'twixt [1]*Cobling* and *Astrology*:   20
How *Partrige* made his *Opticks* rise
From a *Shoe-Sole*, to reach the Skies.

A List the Cobler's Temples ties,
To keep the Hair out of their Eyes;
From whence 'tis plain, the *Diadem*
That Princes wear, derives from them;
And therefore *Crowns* are now a-days
Adorn'd with *golden Stars* and *Rays*:
Which clearly shews the near Alliance,
'Twixt *Cobling* and the *Planets Science*.   30

Besides, that slow-pac'd Sign *Boötes*,
As 'tis miscall'd, we know not who 'tis:
But *Partrige* ended all Disputes;
He knew his Trade, and call'd it [2]*Boots*.

The *horned Moon*, which heretofore
Upon their Shoes the *Romans* wore,
Whose Wideness kept their Toes from Corns,

[1] Partrige *was a* Cobler.   [2] *See his Almanack.*

And whence we claim our *Shoeing-Horns*;
Shews how the Art of *Cobling* bears
A near Resemblance to the *Spheres*.   40

  A Scrap of *Parchment* hung by *Geometry*,
(A great Refinement in *Barometry*)
Can like the Stars foretel the Weather;
And what is *Parchment* else but *Leather*?
Which an Astrologer might use,
Either for *Almanacks* or *Shoes*.

  Thus *Partrige* by his Wit and Parts,
At once did practise both these Arts:
And as the boading Owl (or rather
The Bat, because her Wings are *Leather*)   50
Steals from her private Cell by Night,
And flies about the Candle-Light;
So learned *Partrige* could as well
Creep in the Dark from *Leathern* Cell,
And in his Fancy fly as far,
To peep upon a twinkling Star.

  Besides, he could confound the *Spheres*,
And set the *Planets* by the Ears:
To shew his Skill, he *Mars* could join
To *Venus* in *Aspect Mali'n*;   60
Then call in *Mercury* for Aid,
And cure the Wounds, that *Venus* made.

  Great Scholars have in *Lucian* read,
When *Philip* King of *Greece* was dead,
His *Soul* and *Spirit* did divide,
And each Part took a different Side;
One rose a Star; the other fell
Beneath, and mended Shoes in Hell.

Thus *Partrige* still shines in each Art,
The *Cobling* and *Star-gazing* Part;   70
And is install'd as good a Star,
As any of the *Cæsars* are.

Triumphant *Star!* some Pity shew
On *Coblers militant* below,
Whom roguish Boys in stormy Nights
Torment, by pissing out their Lights;
Or thro' a Chink convey their Smoke,
Inclos'd *Artificers* to choke.

Thou, high-exalted in thy Sphere,
May'st follow still thy calling there.   80
To thee the *Bull* will lend his *Hide*,
By *Phœbus* newly tann'd and dry'd.
For thee they *Argo*'s Hulk will tax,
And scrape her pitchy Sides for *Wax*.
Then, *Ariadne* kindly lends
Her braided Hair, to make thee *Ends*.
The Point of *Sagitarius*' Dart
Turns to an *Awl*, by heavenly Art:
And *Vulcan*, wheedled by his Wife,
Will forge for thee a *Paring-Knife*.   90
For want of Room, by *Virgo*'s Side,
She'll strain a Point, and sit ¹astride,
To take thee kindly in *between*,
And then the *Signs* will be *Thirteen*.

The EPITAPH

Here, five Feet deep, lies on his Back
A Cobler, Star-monger, *and* Quack;
Who, to the Stars in pure Good-Will,
Does to his best look upward still.
Weep all you Customers, that use

¹ *Tibi brachia contrahet ingens Scorpius,* &c.

65

His Pills, *his* Almanacks, *or* Shoes: 100
And you, that did your Fortunes seek,
Step to his Grave but once a Week:
This Earth, which bears his Body's Print,
You'll find has so much Virtue in't,
That I durst pawn my Ears, 'twill tell
Whate'er concerns you full as well,
In Physick, stolen Goods, *or* Love,
As he himself could, when above.

1708/1711

Vanbrug's House

**Built from the Ruins of Whitehall,
that was Burnt**

In Times of *Old*, when Time was *young*,
And Poets their own Verses sung,
A Verse could draw a Stone or Beam,
That now would over-load a Team;
Lead 'em a Dance of many a Mile,
Then rear 'em to a goodly Pile.
Each Number had its diff'rent Pow'r;
Heroick Strains could build a Tow'r;
Sonnets, or Elegies to *Chloris*,
Might raise a House about two Stories;   10
A Lyrick Ode would slate; a Catch
Would tile; an Epigram would thatch.

But to their own, or Landlord's Cost,
Now Poets feel this Art is lost;
Not one of all our tuneful Throng
Can raise a Lodging *for a Song*.
For *Jove* consider'd well the Case;
Observ'd they grew a num'rous Race,
And should they *build* as fast as *write*,

'Twould ruin Undertakers quite.   20
This Evil therefore to prevent,
He wisely chang'd their Element:
On Earth, the God of Wealth was made,
Sole Patron of the Building Trade;
Leaving the Wits the spacious Air,
With Licence to *build Castles* there:
And 'tis conceiv'd their old Pretence
To lodge in Garrets, comes from thence.

Premising thus in modern Way
The better Half we have to say;   30
Sing *Muse*, the House of Poet *Van*
In higher Strains than we began.

Van, (for 'tis fit the Reader know it,)
Is both a Herald and a Poet;
No Wonder then, if nicely skill'd
In both Capacities to build.
As Herald, he can in a Day,
Repair a *House* gone to Decay;
Or, by *Atchievement*, *Arms*, *Device*,
Erect a new one in a Trice.   40
And, as a Poet, he has Skill
To build in Speculation still.
Great *Jove!* he cry'd, the Art restore,
To build by Verse, as heretofore;
And make my Muse the Architect;
What Palaces shall we erect!
No longer shall forsaken *Thames*
Lament his old *Whitehall* in Flames:
A Pile shall from its Ashes rise,
Fit to invade, or prop the Skies.   50

Jove smil'd, and like a gentle God,
Consenting with his usual Nod:
Told *Van* he knew his Talent best,

And left the Choice to his own Breast.
So *Van* resolv'd to write a Farce;
But well perceiving Wit was scarce,
With Cunning that Defect supplies;
Takes a *French* Play as lawful Prize;
Steals thence his Plot, and ev'ry Joke,
Not once suspecting *Jove* would *smoke*;   60
And (like a Wag) sat down to write,
Would whisper to himself; *A Bite*.
Then from this motly mingl'd Style
Proceeded to erect his Pile.
So Men of old, to gain Renown, did
Build *Babel* with their Tongues confounded.
Jove saw the Cheat, but thought it best
To turn the Matter to a Jest:
Down from *Olympus*' Top he slides,
Laughing as if he'd burst his Sides;   70
Ay, thought the God, are these your Tricks?
Why then *old* Plays deserve *old Bricks*;
And since you're sparing of your Stuff,
Your Building shall be small enough.
He spake, and grudging lent his Aid:
Th' experienc'd Bricks that knew their Trade,
(As being Bricks at second Hand,)
Now move, and now in Order stand.

    The Building, as the Poet writ,
Rose in Proportion to his Wit: 80
And first the Prologue built a Wall,
So wide as to encompass all.
The Scene a Wood, produc'd no more
Than a few scrubby Trees before.
The Plot as yet lay deep, and so
A Cellar next was dug below:
But this a Work so hard was found,
Two Acts it cost him under Ground.
Two other Acts we may presume

Were spent, in building each a Room: 90
Thus far advanc'd, he made a Shift
To raise a Roof with Act the Fift.
The Epilogue behind, did frame
A Place, not decent here to name.

Now Poets from all Quarters ran
To see the House of Brother *Van*:
Look'd high and low, walk'd often round,
But no such House was to be found:
One asks the Watermen hard by,
Where may the Poet's Palace lie?   100
Another, of the *Thames* enquires,
If he has seen its gilded Spires!
At length they in the Rubbish spy
A Thing resembling a Goose-Pye:
Thither in haste the Poets throng,
And gaze in silent Wonder long:
Till one in Raptures thus began
To praise the Pile, and Builder *Van*.

Thrice happy Poet, who may trail
Thy House about thee, like a Snail;   110
Or harness'd to a Nag, at Ease,
Take Journeys in it like a Chaise;
Or, in a Boat, whene'er thou wilt,
Can'st make it serve thee for a Tilt.
Capacious House! 'Tis own'd by all,
Thou'rt well contriv'd, tho' thou art small;
For ev'ry Wit in *Britain*'s Isle
May lodge within thy spacious Pile.
Like *Bacchus* thou, as Poet's feign,
Thy Mother burnt, are born again;   120
Born like a *Phœnix* from the Flame;
But neither *Bulk* nor *Shape* the same;
As Animals of largest Size
Corrupt to Maggots, Worms, and Flies.

A Type of *Modern* Wit and Style,
The Rubbish of an ancient Pile.
So *Chymists* boast, they have a Pow'r
From the dead Ashes of a Flow'r,
Some faint Resemblance to produce;
But not the Virtue, Taste, or Juice.   130
So modern Rhymers wisely *blast*
The Poetry of Ages past,
Which after they have overthrown,
They from its Ruins build their own.

                                        1709/1711

Baucis and Philemon

Imitated from the Eighth Book of Ovid

IN ancient Times, as Story tells,
The Saints would often leave their Cells,
And strole about, but hide their Quality,
To try good People's Hospitality.

It happen'd on a *Winter*-Night,
(As Authors of the *Legend* write,)
Two Brother-Hermits, Saints by Trade,
Taking their *Tour* in Masquerade,
Disguis'd in tatter'd Habits, went
To a small Village down in *Kent*;   10
Where, in the Strolers canting Strain,
They begg'd from Door to Door in vain;
Try'd ev'ry Tone might Pity win,
But not a Soul would let them in.

Our wand'ring Saints in woful State,
Treated at this ungodly Rate,
Having thro' all the Village pass't,
To a small Cottage came at last;

Where dwelt a good old honest Ye'man,
Call'd in the Neighbourhood, *Philemon*.   20
Who kindly did the Saints invite
In his poor Hut to pass the Night:
And then the hospitable Sire
Bid Goody *Baucis* mend the Fire;
While he from out the Chimney took
A Flitch of Bacon off the Hook;
And freely from the fattest Side,
Cut out large Slices to be fry'd:
Then stepp'd aside to fetch 'em Drink,
Fill'd a large Jug up to the Brink;   30
And saw it fairly twice go round;
Yet (what was wonderful) they found
'Twas still replenish'd to the Top,
As if they ne'er had touch'd a Drop.
The good old Couple were amaz'd,
And often on each other gaz'd:
For both were frighted to the Heart,
And just began to cry,—What *art* !
Then softly turn'd aside to view,
Whether the Lights were burning blue.   40
The gentle *Pilgrims* soon aware on't,
Told 'em their Calling, and their Errant:
Good Folks, you need not be afraid,
We are but *Saints*, the Hermits said:
No Hurt shall come to you or yours;
But, for that Pack of churlish Boors,
Not fit to live on Christian Ground,
They and their Houses shall be drown'd:
While you shall see your Cottage rise,
And grow a Church before your Eyes.   50

They scarce had spoke; when fair and soft,
The Roof began to mount aloft;
Aloft rose ev'ry Beam and Rafter;
The heavy Wall climb'd slowly after.

The Chimney widen'd and grew higher,
Became a Steeple with a Spire.

The Kettle to the Top was hoist,
And there stood fasten'd to a Joist;
But with the Up-side down, to show
Its Inclination for below: 60
In vain; for some superior Force,
Apply'd at Bottom, stops its Course;
Doom'd ever in Suspense to dwell;
'Tis now no Kettle, but a Bell.

A wooden Jack, which had almost
Lost, by Disuse, the Art to roast,
A sudden Alteration feels,
Increas'd by new intestine Wheels:
And what exalts the Wonder more,
The Number made the Motion flow'r,   70
The Flyer, which, tho't had Leaden Feet,
Turn'd round so quick, you scarce could see't;
Now slacken'd by some secret Pow'r,
Can hardly move an Inch an Hour.
The Jack and Chimney, near ally'd,
Had never left each other's Side;
The Chimney to a Steeple grown,
The Jack would not be left alone;
But, up against the Steeple rear'd,
Became a Clock, and still adher'd: 80
And still its Love to Houshold Cares,
By a shrill Voice at Noon declares;
Warning the Cook-Maid not to burn
That roast Meat, which it cannot turn.

The groaning Chair was seen to crawl,
Like an huge Snail half up the Wall;
There stuck aloft in publick View;
And with small Change, a Pulpit grew.

The Porringers, that in a Row
Hung high, and made a glitt'ring Show, 90
To a less noble Substance chang'd,
Were now but Leathern Buckets, rang'd.

The Ballads pasted on the Wall,
Of *Joan* of *France*, and *English Moll*,
Fair *Rosamond*, and *Robin Hood*,
The *Little Children in the Wood*;
Now seem'd to look abundance better,
Improv'd in Picture, Size, and Letter;
And high, in Order plac'd describe
The Heraldry of ev'ry *Tribe*. 100

A Bedstead of the antique Mode,
Compact of Timber many a Load;
Such as our Grandsires wont to use,
Was metamorphos'd into Pews;
Which still their ancient Nature keep,
By lodging Folks dispos'd to sleep.

The Cottage, by such Feats as these,
Grown to a Church by just Degrees;
The Hermits then desire their Host
To ask for what he fancy'd most. 110
Philemon, having paus'd a while,
Return'd them Thanks in homely Style;
Then said; My House is grown so fine,
Methinks I still would call it mine:
I'm old, and fain would live at Ease,
Make me the *Parson*, if you please.

He spoke, and presently he feels
His Grazier's Coat fall down his Heels:
He sees, yet hardly can believe,
About each Arm a Pudding-Sleeve: 120
His Waistcoat to a Cassock grew,

And both assum'd a sable Hue;
But being old, continu'd just
As thread-bare, and as full of Dust.
His Talk was now of *Tythes* and *Dues*:
Could smoke his Pipe, and read the News,
Knew how to preach old Sermons next,
Vamp'd in the Preface, and the Text;
At Christ'nings well could act his Part,
And had the Service all by Heart: 130
Wish'd Women might have Children fast,
And thought whose *Sow* had farrow'd last:
Against *Dissenters* would repine,
And stood up firm for *Right Divine*:
Found his Head fill'd with many a System,
But Classick Authors,—he ne'er mist 'em.

Thus having furbish'd up a Parson,
Dame *Baucis* next they play'd their Farce on:
Instead of home-spun Coifs were seen
Good Pinners edg'd with *Colberteen*:   140
Her Petticoat, transform'd apace,
Became black *Sattin* flounc'd with Lace.
Plain *Goody* would no longer down;
'Twas *Madam*, in her Grogram Gown.
Philemon was in great Surprize,
And hardly could believe his Eyes:
Amaz'd to see her look so prim:
And she admir'd as much at him.

Thus happy in their Change of Life,
Were several Years the Man and Wife: 150
When on a Day, which prov'd their last,
Discoursing o'er old Stories past;
They went by chance, amidst their Talk,
To the Church-yard, to fetch a Walk:
When *Baucis* hastily cry'd out,
My Dear, I see your Forehead sprout!

Sprout, quoth the Man, what's this you tell us?
I hope you don't believe me jealous:
But yet, methinks, I feel it true;
And really yours is budding too—   160
Nay,—now I cannot stir my Foot;
It feels as if 'twere taking Root.

    Description would but tire my Muse:
In short, they both were turn'd to *Yews*.

    Old Goodman *Dobson*, of the Green,
Remembers he the Trees hath seen;
He'll talk of them from Noon to Night,
And goes with Folks to shew the Sight;
On *Sundays*, after Evening Prayer,
He gathers all the Parish there;   170
Points out the Place of either *Yew*:
Here *Baucis*, there *Philemon* grew:
'Till once, a Parson of our Town,
To mend his Barn, cut *Baucis* down;
At which, 'tis hard to be believ'd,
How much the other Tree was griev'd:
Grew scrubby, dy'd a-top, was stunted:
So, the next Parson stubb'd and burnt it.
          1709/1711

On Mrs. Biddy Floyd

WHEN *Cupid* did his Grandsire *Jove* intreat,
To form some Beauty by a new Receipt;
Jove sent and found far in a Country Scene,
Truth, Innocence, Good-Nature, Look serene;
From which Ingredients, first the dext'rous Boy
Pick'd the Demure, the Aukward, and the Coy:
The *Graces* from the Court did next provide

Breeding, and Wit, and Air, and decent Pride.
These *Venus* cleans'd from ev'ry spurious Grain
Of Nice, Coquet, Affected, Pert, and Vain.   10
Jove mix'd up all, and his best Clay employ'd;
Then call'd the happy Composition FLOYD.
                                        1709/1711

Apollo Outwitted

To the Hon. Mrs. Finch, (since Countess of
Winchelsea,) under the Name of Ardelia

PHŒBUS now short'ning every Shade,
    Up to the *Northern Tropick* came,
And thence beheld a lovely Maid
    Attending on a Royal Dame.

The God laid down his feeble Rays;
    Then lighted from his glitt'ring Coach;
But fenc'd his Head with his own Bays,
    Before he durst the Nymph approach.

Under those sacred Leaves, secure
    From common Lightning of the Skies,   10
He fondly thought he might endure
    The Flashes of *Ardelia*'s Eyes.

The Nymph, who oft had read in Books
    Of that bright God, whom Bards invoke,
Soon knew *Apollo* by his Looks,
    And guess'd his Business, e'er he spoke.

He in the old Celestial Cant,
    Confess'd his Flame, and swore by *Styx*,
Whate'er she would desire, to grant;
    But wise *Ardelia* knew his Tricks.   20

Ovid had warn'd her to beware
   Of stroling Gods, whose usual Trade is,
Under Pretence of taking Air,
   To pick up Sublunary Ladies.

Howe'er, she gave no flat Denial,
   As having Malice in her Heart;
And was resolv'd upon a Tryal,
   To cheat the God in his own Art.

Hear my Request, the Virgin said;
   Let which I please of all the Nine   30
Attend whene'er I want their Aid,
   Obey my Call, and only mine.

By Vow oblig'd, by Passion led,
   The God could not refuse her Prayer:
He wav'd his Wreath thrice o'er her Head,
   Thrice mutter'd something to the Air.

And now he thought to seize his Due,
   But she the Charm already try'd,
Thalia heard the Call, and flew
   To wait at bright *Ardelia*'s Side.   40

On Sight of this celestial Prude,
   Apollo thought it vain to stay,
Nor in her Presence durst be rude;
   But made his Leg, and went away.

He hop'd to find some lucky Hour,
   When on their Queen the Muses wait;
But *Pallas* owns *Ardelia*'s Power:
   For Vows divine are kept by Fate.

Then full of Rage *Apollo* spoke,
   Deceitful Nymph! I see thy Art;   50

And though I can't my Gift revoke,
    I'll disappoint its nobler Part.

Let stubborn Pride possess thee long,
    And be thou negligent of Fame;
With ev'ry Muse to grace thy Song,
    May'st thou despise a Poet's Name.

Of modest Poets thou be first,
    To silent Shades repeat thy Verse,
Till *Fame* and *Eccho* almost burst,
    Yet hardly dare one Line rehearse.   60

And last, my Vengeance to compleat;
    May you descend to take Renown,
Prevail'd on by the Thing you hate,
    A Whig, and one that wears a Gown.
                    1709/1711

A Description of the Morning

Now hardly here and there a Hackney-Coach
Appearing, shew'd the ruddy Morn's Approach.
Now *Betty* from her Master's Bed had flown,
And softly stole to discompose her own.
The Slip-shod 'Prentice from his Master's Door
Had par'd the Dirt, and sprinkled round the Floor.
Now *Moll* had whirl'd her Mop with dext'rous Airs,
Prepar'd to scrub the Entry and the Stairs.
The Youth [1]with broomy Stumps began to trace   9
The Kennel-Edge, where Wheels had worn the Place.
The Small-Coal Man was heard with Cadence deep;
Till drown'd in shriller Notes of *Chimney-sweep*.
Duns at his Lordship's Gate began to meet;

[1] *To find old Nails.*

And Brick-dust *Moll* had scream'd thro' half a Street.
The Turnkey now his Flock returning sees,
Duly let out a-Nights to steal for Fees.
The watchful Bailiffs take their silent Stands;
And School-boys lag with Satchels in their Hands.

1709/1711

The Virtues of Sid Hamet, the Magician's Rod

THE *Rod* was but a harmless Wand,
While *Moses* held it in his Hand;
But soon as e'er he *laid it down*
'Twas a devouring Serpent grown.

Our great Magician, *Hamet Sid*,
Reverses what the Prophet did:
His *Rod* was honest *English* Wood,
That senseless in a Corner stood,
Till metamorphos'd by his Grasp,
It grew an all-devouring Asp;   10
Would hiss, and sting, and roll and twist,
By the mere Virtue of his Fist:
But when he *laid it down*, as quick
Resum'd the Figure of a Stick.

So, to her Midnight Feasts the Hag
Rides on a Broomstick for a Nag,
That, rais'd by Magick of her Breech,
O'er Sea and Land conveys the Witch:
But with the Morning Dawn resumes
The peaceful State of common Brooms.   20

They tell us something strange and odd,
About a certain Magick *Rod*,

That bending down its Top divines
Whene'er the Soil has golden Mines:
Where there are none, it stands erect,
Scorning to shew the least Respect.
As ready was the Wand of *Sid*
To bend, where golden Mines were hid;
In *Scottish* Hills found precious Ore,
Where none e'er look'd for it before: 30
And by a *gentle Bow* divin'd
How well a *Cully*'s Purse was lin'd:
To a forlorn and broken *Rake*
Stood without Motion, like a Stake.

The *Rod* of *Hermes* was renown'd
For Charms above and under Ground;
To sleep could mortal Eye-lids fix,
And drive departed Souls to *Styx*.
That *Rod* was just a Type of *Sid*'s,
Which o'er a *British* Senate's Lids   40
Could scatter *Opium* full as well;
And drive as many *Souls to Hell*.

Sid's Rod was slender, white and tall,
Which oft he us'd to fish withal:
A Place was fasten'd to the Hook,
And many a Score of *Gudgeons* took;
Yet still so happy was his Fate,
He caught his *Fish*, and sav'd his *Bait*.

Sid's Brethren of the conj'ring Tribe
A Circle with their *Rod* describe;   50
Which proves a magical Redoubt,
To keep *mischievous Spirits out*:
Sid's Rod was of a larger Stride,
And made a Circle thrice as wide;
Where *Spirits* throng'd with hideous Din;
And he stood there to *take them in*.

But when th' enchanted *Rod* was broke,
They vanish'd in a stinking Smoke.

Achilles' Sceptre was of Wood,
Like *Sid*'s, but nothing near so good: 60
Though down from Ancestors divine,
Transmitted to the Heroes Line,
Thence thro' a long Descent of Kings,
Came an *Heir-loom* as *Homer* sings:
Tho' this Description looks so big,
That *Sceptre* was a sapless Twig;
Which, from the fatal Day, when first
It left the Forest, where 'twas nurs'd,
As *Homer* tells us o'er and o'er,
Nor Leaf, nor Fruit, nor Blossom bore.   70
Sid's Sceptre, full of Juice, did shoot
In golden Boughs, and golden Fruit;
And he, the *Dragon* never sleeping,
Guarded each fair *Hesperian* Pippin.
No *Hobby Horse*, with gorgeous Top,
The dearest in *Charles Mather*'s Shop,
Or glitt'ring Tinsel of *May-Fair*,
Could with this Rod of *Sid* compare.

Dear *Sid*, then why wer't thou so mad,
To break thy *Rod* like naughty Lad?   80
You should have kiss'd it in your Distress,
And then return'd it to *your Mistress*;
Or made it a *Newmarket* Switch,
And not a *Rod* for thy own Breech.
But since old *Sid* has broken this,
His next may be a *Rod in P—s.*

1710/1711

A Description of a City Shower

CAREFUL Observers may foretel the Hour
(By sure Prognosticks) when to dread a Show'r.
While Rain depends, the pensive Cat gives o'er
Her Frolicks, and pursues her Tail no more.
Returning home at Night you find the Sink
Strike your offended Sense with double Stink.
If you be wise, then go not far to dine,
You spend in Coach-hire more than save in Wine.
A coming Show'r your shooting Corns presage;
Old Aches throb, your hollow Tooth will rage: 10
Saunt'ring in Coffee-house is *Dulman* seen;
He damns the Climate, and complains of *Spleen*.

Mean while the South, rising with dabbled Wings,
A sable Cloud athwart the Welkin flings;
That swill'd more Liquor than it could contain,
And like a Drunkard gives it up again.
Brisk *Susan* whips her Linnen from the Rope,
While the first drizzling Show'r is born aslope:
Such is that Sprinkling, which some careless Quean
Flirts on you from her Mop; but not so clean: 20
You fly, invoke the Gods; then turning, stop
To rail; she singing, still whirls on her Mop.
Nor yet the Dust had shun'd the unequal Strife,
But aided by the Wind, fought still for Life;
And wafted with its Foe by vi'lent Gust,
[1]'Twas doubtful which was Rain, and which was Dust.
Ah! where must needy Poet seek for Aid,
When Dust and Rain at once his Coat invade?
Sole Coat, where Dust, cemented by the Rain,
Erects the Nap, and leaves a cloudy Stain.   30

---

[1] *'Twas doubtful which was Sea, and which was Sky.*
Garth Disp.

Now, in contiguous Drops the Flood comes down,
Threat'ning with Deluge this *devoted* Town.
To Shops in Crowds the daggled Females fly,
Pretend to cheapen Goods; but nothing buy.
The Templar spruce, while ev'ry Spout's abroach,
Stays till 'tis fair, yet *seems* to call a Coach.
The tuck'd-up Sempstress walks with hasty Strides,
While Streams run down her oil'd Umbrella's Sides.
Here various Kinds by various Fortunes led,
Commence Acquaintance underneath a Shed.   40
[1]Triumphant Tories, and desponding Whigs,
Forget their Feuds, and join to save their Wigs.
Box'd in a Chair the Beau impatient sits,
While Spouts run clatt'ring o'er the Roof by Fits;
And ever and anon with frightful Din
The Leather sounds; he trembles from within.
So, when *Troy* Chair-Men bore the Wooden-Steed,
Pregnant with *Greeks*, impatient to be freed;
(Those Bully *Greeks*, who, as the Moderns do,
Instead of paying Chair-Men, run them thro')   50
Laocoon struck the Out-side with his Spear,
And each imprison'd Hero quak'd for Fear.

Now from all Parts the swelling Kennels flow,
And bear their Trophies with them, as they go:
Filths of all Hues and Odours seem to tell
What Streets they sail'd from, by the Sight and Smell.
They, as each Torrent drives with rapid Force,
From *Smithfield*, or St. *Pulchre*'s shape their Course;
And in huge Confluent join at *Snow-Hill* Ridge,
Fall from the *Conduit* prone to *Holbourn Bridge*.   60

[1] N.B. *This was the first Year of the Earl of* OXFORD's *Ministry.*

¹Sweepings from Butcher's Stall, Dung, Guts, and
    Blood,
Drown'd Puppies, stinking Sprats, all drench'd in
    Mud,
Dead Cats, and Turnip-Tops come tumbling
    down the Flood.

1710/1711

---

¹ *These three last lines were intended against that licentious Manner of modern Poets, in making three Rhimes together, which they call* Triplets; *and the last of the three, was two or some Times more Syllables longer, called an* Alexandrian. *These* Triplets *and* Alexandrians *were brought in by* DRYDEN, *and other Poets in the Reign of* CHARLES II. *They were the mere Effect of Haste, Idleness, and Want of Money; and have been wholely avoided by the best Poets, since these Verses were written.*

PERSONAL POEMS

The Author upon Himself

*A few of the first Lines were wanting in the
Copy sent us by a Friend of the Author's
from* London

* * * * * * * *
  * * * * * * *
  * * * * * * *
* * * * * * * *

BY an old [redhair'd, murd'ring Hag] pursu'd,
A [1]crazy Prelate, and a [2]Royal Prude.
By dull Divines, who look with envious Eyes,
On ev'ry Genius, that attempts to rise;
And pausing o'er a Pipe, with doubtful Nod,
Give Hints, that Poets ne'er believe in God.
So, Clowns on Scholars as on Wizards look,
And take a Folio for a conj'ring Book.

S[*wift*] had the Sin of Wit, no venial Crime;
Nay, 'twas affirm'd, he sometimes dealt in Rhime:
Humour, and Mirth, had Place in all he writ: 11
He reconcil'd Divinity and Wit.
He mov'd, and bow'd, and talk'd with too much
    Grace;
Nor shew'd the Parson in his Gait or Face;
Despis'd luxurious Wines, and costly Meat;
Yet, still was at the Tables of the Great.
Frequented Lords; *saw those that saw the Queen*;
At [3]*Child's* or *Truby's* never once had been;

[1] *Dr.* SHARPE, *Archbishop of* York.
[2] *Her late M[ajesty].*
[3] *A Coffee-House and Tavern near St.* Paul's, *much frequented by
the Clergy.*

87

Where Town and Country Vicars flock in Tribes,
Secur'd by Numbers from the Laymen's Gibes;   20
And deal in Vices of the graver Sort,
Tobacco, Censure, Coffee, Pride, and Port.

But, after sage Monitions from his Friends,
His Talents to employ for nobler Ends;
To better Judgments willing to submit,
He turns to Politicks his dang'rous Wit.

And now, the publick Int'rest to support,
By *Harley S[wift]* invited comes to Court.
In Favour grows with Ministers of State;
Admitted private, when Superiors wait: 30
And, *Harley*, not asham'd his Choice to own,
Takes him to *Windsor* in his Coach, alone.
At *Windsor*, *S[wift]* no sooner can appear,
But, ¹*St. John* comes and whispers in his Ear;
The Waiters stand in Ranks; the Yeomen cry,
Make Room; as if a Duke were passing by.

Now ²*Finch* alarms the Lords; he hears for certain,
This dang'rous Priest is got behind the Curtain:
Finch, fam'd for tedious Elocution, proves
That *S[wift]* oils many a Spring, which *Harley* moves.
³*W[alpol]e* and *Ayslaby*, to clear the Doubt,   41
Inform the Commons, that the Secret's out:
'A *certain* Doctor is observ'd of late,
'To haunt a *certain* Minister of State:
'From whence, with half an Eye we may discover,
'The Peace is made, and *Perkin* must come over.'
York is from *Lambeth* sent, to shew the QUEEN

---

¹ *Then Secretary of State, now Lord* BOLINGBROKE, *the most universal Genius in Europe.*
² *Late Earl of* Nottingham, *who made a Speech in the House of Lords against the Author.*
³ *Those two made Speeches in the House of* Commons *against the* Author, *although the latter professed much Friendship for him.*

A dang'rous Treatise writ against the Spleen;
Which by the Style, the Matter, and the Drift,
'Tis thought could be the Work of none but S[wift].
Poor *York !* the harmless Tool of others Hate,   51
[1]He sues for Pardon, and repents too late.

Now, [Madam Coningsmark] her Vengeance vows
On S[wift]'s Reproaches for her [murdered Spouse];
From her red Locks her Mouth with Venom fills;
And thence into the Royal Ear instills.
The Q[ueen] incens'd, his Services forgot,
Leaves him a Victim to the vengeful *Scot*:
Now, through the Realm a [2]Proclamation spread,
To fix a Price on his devoted Head.   60
While innocent, he scorns ignoble Flight;
His watchful Friends preserve him by a Sleight.

By *Harley*'s Favour once again he shines;
Is now caress'd by Candidate Divines;
Who change Opinions with the changing Scene:
Lord! how were they mistaken in the Dean!
Now, [3]*Delawere* again familiar grows;
And, in S[wif]t's Ear thrusts half his powder'd Nose.
[4]The *Scottish* Nation, whom he durst offend,
Again apply, that S[wift] would be their Friend.   70
By Faction tir'd, with Grief he waits a while,

[1] *It is known that his Grace sent a Message to the Author, to desire his Pardon, and that he was very sorry for what he had said and done.*

[2] *The Proclamation was against the Author of a Pamphlet, called,* The Publick Spirit of the Whigs, *against which the* Scotch Lords *complained.*

[3] *Lord* DELAWERE, *then Treasurer of the Houshold, always caressing the Author at Court: But during the Tryal of the Printers before the House of Lords, and while the Proclamation hung over the Author, his Lordship would not seem to know him, till the Danger was past.*

[4] *The* Scotch Lords *treated and visited the Author more after the Proclamation than before, except the D. of* AR[GYL]E, *who would never be reconciled.*

His great contending Friends to reconcile.
Performs what Friendship, Justice, Truth require:
[1]What could he more, but decently retire?

1714/1735

In Sickness

Written soon after the Author's coming to live in
IRELAND, *upon the Queen's Death*, Oct. 1714.

'TIS true,—then why should I repine,
To see my Life so fast decline?
But, why obscurely here alone?
Where I am neither lov'd nor known.
My State of Health none care to learn;
My Life is here no Soul's Concern.
And, those with whom I now converse,
Without a Tear will tend my Herse.
Remov'd from kind *Arbuthnot*'s Aid,
Who knows his Art, but not his Trade;   10
Preferring his Regard for me
Before his Credit or his Fee.
Some formal Visits, Looks, and Words,
What meer Humanity affords,
I meet perhaps from three or four,
From whom I once expected more;
Which those who tend the Sick for Pay,
Can act as decently as they.
But, no obliging, tender Friend
To help at my approaching End;   20
My Life is now a Burthen grown
To other's e're it be my own.

[1] *The Author retired to a Friend in* Berkshire, *ten Weeks before
the Qu*[een] *died; and never saw the Ministry after.*

90

Ye formal Weepers for the Sick,
In your last Offices be quick:
And spare my absent Friends the Grief
To hear, yet give me no Relief;
Expir'd To-day, entomb'd To-morrow,
When known, will save a double Sorrow.

1714/1735

The Author's Manner of Living

On rainy Days alone I dine,
Upon a Chick, and Pint of Wine.
On rainy Days, I dine alone,
And pick my Chicken to the Bone:
But this my Servants much enrages,
No Scraps remain to save Board-wages.
In Weather fine I nothing spend,
But often spunge upon a Friend:
Yet where He's not so rich as I;
I pay my Club, and so God b'y'——.   10

1715?/1746

On Censure

Ye Wise, instruct me to endure
An Evil, which admits no Cure:
Or, how this Evil can be born,
Which breeds at once both Hate and Scorn,
Bare Innocence is no Support,
When you are try'd in Scandal's Court.
Stand high in Honour, Wealth, or Wit;
All others who inferior sit,
Conceive themselves in Conscience bound

To join, and drag you to the Ground.   10
Your Altitude offends the Eyes,
Of those who want the Pow'r to rise.
The World, a willing Stander-by,
Inclines to aid a specious Lye:
Alas! they would not do you wrong;
But, all Appearances are strong.

    Yet, whence proceeds this Weight we lay
On what detracting People say?
For, let Mankind discharge their Tongues
In Venom till they burst their Lungs,   20
Their utmost Malice cannot make
Your Head, or Tooth, or Finger ake:
Nor spoil your Shape, distort your Face,
Or put one Feature out of Place;
Nor, will you find your Fortune sink,
By what they speak, or what they think.
Nor can ten Hundred Thousand Lyes,
Make you less virtuous, learn'd, or wise.

    The most effectual Way to baulk
Their Malice, is—to let them talk.   30

                      1727/1735

Poems from the 'Holyhead Journal'

Mrs. Welsh's Chimney

WHEN Mrs. Welsh's Chimney smokes,
Tis a sign she'll keep her folks.
But, when of smoke the room is clear,
It is a sign we sha'nt stay here.

Holyhead

Sept. 25. 1727

Lo here I sit at holy head,
With muddy ale and mouldy bread:
I'm fastened both by wind and tide,
I see the ships at anchor ride.
All Christian vittals stink of fish,
I'm where my enemyes would wish.
Convict of lies is every Sign,
The Inn has not one drop of wine.
The Captain swears the sea's too rough,
He has not passengers enough.   10
And thus the Dean is forc'd to stay
Till others come to help the pay.
In Dublin they'd be glad to see
A packet though it brings in me.
They cannot say the winds are cross:
Your Politicians at a loss
For want of matter swears and fretts—
Are forced to read the old Gazettes.
I never was in haste before,
To reach that slavish hateful shore.   20
Before, I always found the wind
To me was most malicious kind,
But now the danger of a friend,
On whom my fears and hopes depend,
Absent from whom all Climes are curst,
With whom I'm happy in the worst,
With rage impatient makes me wait
A passage to the Land I hate.
Else, rather on this bleaky shore,
Where loudest winds incessant roar,   30
Where neither herb nor tree will thrive,
Where Nature hardly seems alive,
I'd go in freedom to my grave
Than Rule yon Isle, and be a slave.

Ireland

REMOVE me from this land of slaves,
Where all are fools, and all are knaves;
Where every knave and fool is bought,
Yet kindly sells himself for nought;
Where Whig and Tory fiercely fight
Who's in the wrong, who in the right;
And, when their country lies at stake,
They only fight for fighting sake,
While English sharpers take the pay,
And then stand by to see fair play.   10
Meantime the Whig is always winner,
And for his courage gets—a dinner.
His Excellency, too, perhaps
Spits in his mouth and stroaks his Chaps.
The humble whelp gives ev'ry vote—
To put the question strains his throat.
His Excellency's condescension
Will serve instead of place or pension.
When to the window he's trepan'd—
When my Lord shakes him by the hand,   20
Or, in the presence of beholders,
His arms upon the booby's shoulders—
You quickly see the gudgeon bite.
He tells his brother fools at night
How well the Governor's inclined—
So just, so gentle, and so kind.
He heard I kept a pack of hounds,
And longs to hunt upon my grounds,
He said our Ladyes were so fair,
The land had nothing to compare;   30
But that indeed which pleased me most,
He call'd my Dol a perfect toast.
He whispered public things at last,
Asked me how our elections past.
Some augmentation, Sir, you know,

94

Would make at least a handsome show.
New kings a compliment expect;
I shall not offer to direct.
There are some prating folks in town,
But, Sir, we must support the Crown.   40
Our letters say a Jesuit boasts
Of some invasion on your coasts.
The king is ready, when you will,
To pass another Popery bill;
And for dissenters, he intends
To use them as his truest friends.
I think they justly ought to share
In all employments we can spare.
Next, for encouragement of spinning,
A duty might be laid on linen.   50
An act for laying down the plough—
England will send you corn enough;
Another act that absentees
For licences shall pay no fees.
If England's friendship you would keep,
Feed nothing on your lands but sheep;
But make an act, severe and full,
To bring up all who smuggle wool.
And then he kindly gave me hints
That all our wives should go in chintz.   60
To-morrow I shall tell you more,
For I'm to dine with him at four.
   This was the speech, and here's the jest—
His arguments convinced the rest.
Away he runs, with zealous hotness,
Exceeding all the fools of Totness,
To move that all the nation round
Should pay a guinea in the pound;
Yet should this blockhead beg a place,
Either from Excellence or Grace,   70
'Tis pre-engaged, and in his room
Townshend's cast page or Walpole's groom.

On Lord Carteret's Arms

Given, as the custom is, at every Inn where
the Lord Lieutenant dines or lies,
with all the bills in a long parchment

'Tis twenty to one
When Carteret is gone,
These praises we blot out;
The truth will be got out,
And then we'll be smart on
His lordship as Wharton;
Or Shrewsbury's duke,
With many rebuke;
Or Bolton the wise,
With his Spanish flyes;   10
Or Grafton the deep,
Either drunk or asleep.
These titles and arms
Will then lose their charms,
If somebody's grace
Should come in his place.
And thus it goes round—
We praise and confound.
They can do no good,
Nor would if they could.   20
To injure the nation
Is recommendation;
And why should they save her
By losing their favour?
Poor kingdom, thou woulds't be that governor's
    debtor,
Who kindly would leave thee no worse nor no better.

1727/1882

The Power of Time[1]

IF neither Brass, nor Marble, can withstand
The mortal Force of *Time*'s destructive Hand:
If Mountains sink to Vales, if Cities die,
And less'ning Rivers mourn their Fountains dry:
When my old Cassock, said a *Welch* Divine,
Is out at Elbows; why should I repine?

1727/1735

The Dean to Himself on Saint Cecilia's Day

GRAVE Dean of St. Patrick's, how comes it to pass,
That you, who know music no more than an ass,
That you, who so lately were writing of Drapiers,
Should lend your Cathedral to players and scrapers?
To act such an opera once in a year,
So offensive to ev'ry true Protestant ear,
With trumpets, and fiddles, and organs, and singing,
Will sure the Pretender and Popery bring in.
No Protestant prelate, his Lordship, or Grace,
Durst there shew his Right or Most Reverend face: 10
How would it pollute their crosiers and rochets,
To listen to minims, and quavers, and crotchets?

1730/1765

The Day of Judgement

WITH a Whirl of Thought oppress'd,
I sink from Reverie to Rest.
An horrid Vision seiz'd my Head,
I saw the Graves give up their Dead.

[1] Scarron *hath a large Poem on the same Subject.*

97

Jove, arm'd with Terrors, burst the Skies,
And Thunder roars, and Light'ning flies!
Amaz'd, confus'd, its Fate unknown,
The World stands trembling at his Throne.
While each pale Sinner hangs his Head,
Jove, nodding, shook the Heav'ns, and said,   10
'Offending Race of Human King,
By Nature, Reason, Learning, blind;
You who thro' Frailty step'd aside,
And you who never fell—*thro' Pride*;
You who in different Sects have shamm'd,
And come to see each other damn'd;
(So some Folks told you, but they knew
No more of Jove's Designs than you)
The World's mad Business now is o'er,
And I resent these Pranks no more.   20
I to such Blockheads set my Wit!
I damn such Fools!—Go, go, you're bit.'
                    1731?/1744

Midnight Memorandum

                                    Dec. 27, 1733.
    I waked at two this morning with the two above
lines in my head, which I had made in my sleep, and I
wrote them down in the dark, lest I should forget
them. But as the original words being writ in the dark,
may possibly be mistaken by a careless or unskilful
transcriber, I shall give a fairer copy, that two such
precious lines may not be lost to posterity:

        I walk before no man, a hawk in his fist,
        Nor am I a brilliant, whenever I list.
                                    1733/1913

98

On his own Deafness

Vertiginosus, inops, surdus, male gratus amicis;
Non campana sonans, tonitru non ab Jove missum,
Quod mage mirandum, saltem si credere fas est,
Non clamosa meas mulier jam percutit aures.

DEAF, giddy, helpless, left alone,
To all my Friends a Burthen grown,
No more I hear my Church's Bell,
Than if it rang out for my Knell:
At Thunder now no more I start,
Than at the Rumbling of a Cart:
Nay, what's incredible, alack!
I hardly hear a Woman's Clack.
                    1734/1734

POEMS TO VANESSA

Cadenus and Vanessa

THE *Shepherds* and the *Nymphs* were seen
Pleading before the *Cyprian* Queen,
The Council for the Fair began,
Accusing that false Creature *Man*:
The Brief with weighty Crimes was charg'd,
On which the Pleader much enlarg'd:
That, *Cupid* now has lost his Art,
Or blunts the Point of ev'ry Dart:
His Altar now no longer smokes,
His Mother's Aid no Youth invokes: 10
This tempts Free-thinkers to refine,
And bring in doubt their Pow'r divine.
Now Love is dwindled to Intrigue,
And Marriage grown a Money-League.
Which Crimes aforesaid, (*with her Leave*)
Were (*as he humbly did conceive*)
Against our Sov'reign Lady's Peace,
Against the Statute in that Case,
Against her Dignity and Crown:
Then pray'd an Answer, and sat down.   20

The *Nymphs* with Scorn beheld their Foes:
When the Defendant's Council rose;
And, what no Lawyer ever lack'd,
With Impudence own'd all the Fact:
But, what the gentlest Heart would vex,
Laid all the Fault on t'other Sex.
That modern Love is no such Thing,
As what those antient Poets sing;
A Fire celestial, chaste, refin'd,
Conceiv'd and kindled in the Mind;   30
Which, having found an equal Flame,

Unites, and both become the same;
In different Breasts together burn,
Together both to Ashes turn.
But Women now feel no such Fire;
And only know the gross Desire.
Their Passions move in lower Spheres,
Where-e'er Caprice or Folly steers:
A Dog, a Parrot, or an Ape,
Or, some worse Brute in human Shape,   40
Engross the Fancies of the Fair,
The few soft Moments they can spare,
From Visits to receive and pay;
From Scandal, Politicks, and Play;
From Fans, and Flounces, and Brocades,
From Equipage and Park-Parades;
From all the Thousand Female Toys;
From every Trifle that employs
The Out or Inside of their Heads,
Between their Toylets and their Beds.   50

In a dull Stream, which moving slow,
You hardly see the Current flow;
If a small Breeze obstructs the Course,
It whirls about for want of Force;
And in its narrow Circle gathers
Nothing but Chaff, and Straw, and Feathers:
The Current of a Female Mind
Stops thus, and turns with ev'ry Wind;
Thus whirling round, together draws
Fools, Fops, and Rakes, for Chaff and Straws.
Hence we conclude, no Women's Hearts   61
Are won by Virtue, Wit, and Parts:
Nor are the Men of Sense to blame,
For Breasts incapable of Flame;
The Fault must on the *Nymphs* be plac'd,
Grown so corrupted in their Taste.

104

The Pleader having spoke his best,
Had Witness ready to attest;
Who fairly could on Oath depose,
When Questions on the Fact arose,   70
That ev'ry Article was true;
Nor further those Deponents knew:
Therefore he humbly would insist,
The Bill might be with Costs dismist.

The Cause appear'd of so much Weight,
That *Venus*, from her Judgment-Seat,
Desir'd them not to talk so loud,
Else she must interpose a Cloud:
For, if the Heav'nly Folk should know
These Pleadings *in the Courts below*,   80
That Mortals here disdain to love;
She ne'er could shew her Face above:
For Gods, their Betters, are too wise
To value that which Men despise:
And then, said she, my Son and I,
Must strole in Air 'twixt Land and Sky;
Or else, shut out from Heaven and Earth,
Fly to the Sea, my Place of Birth;
There live with daggl'd *Mermaids* pent,
And keep on Fish perpetual *Lent*.   90

But, since the Case appear'd so nice,
She thought it best to take Advice.
The *Muses*, by their King's Permission,
Tho' Foes to Love, attend the Session;
And on the Right Hand took their Places
In Order; on the Left, the *Graces*:
To whom she might her Doubts propose
On all Emergencies that rose.
The *Muses* oft were seen to frown;
The *Graces* half asham'd look'd down;   100

And 'twas observ'd, there were but few,
Of either Sex, among the Crew,
Whom she or her Assessors knew.
The Goddess soon began to see
Things were not ripe for a Decree:
And said, she must consult her Books,
The Lovers *Fleta's*, *Bractons*, *Cokes*.
First, to a dapper Clerk she beckon'd,
To turn to *Ovid*, Book the Second:
She then referr'd them to a Place   110
In Virgil (*vide Dido's* Case:)
As for *Tibullus's* Reports,
They never pass'd for Law in Courts;
For *Cowley's* Briefs, and Pleas of *Waller*,
Still their Authority was smaller.

There was on both Sides much to say:
She'd hear the Cause another Day;
And so she did, and then a Third:
She heard it—there she kept her Word;
But with Rejoinders and Replies,   120
Long Bills, and Answers, stuff'd with Lies;
Demur, Imparlance, and Essoign,
The Parties ne'er could Issue join:
For Sixteen Years the Cause was spun,
And then stood where it first begun.

Now, gentle *Clio*, sing or say,
What *Venus* meant by this Delay.
The Goddess much perplex'd in Mind,
To see her Empire thus declin'd;
When first this grand Debate arose   130
Above her Wisdom to compose,
Conceiv'd a Project in her Head,
To work her Ends; which if it sped,
Wou'd shew the Merits of the Cause,
Far better than consulting Laws.

In a glad Hour, *Lucina*'s Aid
Produc'd on Earth a wond'rous Maid,
On whom the Queen of Love was bent
To try a new Experiment:
She threw her Law-books on the Shelf,   140
And thus debated with her self.

   Since Men alledge, they ne'er can find
Those Beauties in a Female Mind,
Which raise a Flame that will endure
For ever, uncorrupt and pure;
If 'tis with Reason they complain,
This Infant shall restore my Reign.
I'll search where ev'ry Virtue dwells,
From Courts inclusive, down to Cells,
What Preachers talk, or Sages write;   150
These I will gather and unite;
And represent them to Mankind
Collected in that Infant's Mind.

   This said, she plucks in Heav'ns high Bowers,
A Sprig of *Amaranthine* Flow'rs;
In Nectar thrice infuses Bays;
Three Times refin'd in *Titan*'s Rays:
Then calls the *Graces* to her Aid;
And sprinkles thrice the new-born Maid:
From whence the tender Skin assumes   160
A Sweetness above all Perfumes;
From whence a Cleanliness remains,
Incapable of outward Stains;
From whence that Decency of Mind,
So lovely in the Female Kind;
Where not one careless Thought intrudes,
Less modest than the Speech of Prudes:
Where never Blush was call'd in Aid;
That spurious Virtue in a Maid;

A Virtue but at second-hand;   170
They blush because they understand.

    The *Graces* next wou'd act their Part,
And shew'd but little of their Art;
Their Work was half already done,
The Child with native Beauty shone;
The outward Form no Help requir'd:
Each breathing on her thrice, inspir'd
That gentle, soft, engaging Air,
Which, in old Times, adorn'd the Fair:
And said, '*Vanessa* be the Name,   180
'By which thou shalt be known to Fame:
'*Vanessa*, by the Gods enroll'd:
'Her Name on Earth—shall not be told.'

    But still the Work was not compleat;
When *Venus* thought on a Deceit:
Drawn by her Doves, away she flies,
And finds out *Pallas* in the Skies:
Dear *Pallas*, I have been this Morn
To see a lovely infant born:
A Boy in yonder Isle below,   190
So like my own, without his Bow:
By Beauty could your Heart be won,
You'd swear it is *Apollo*'s Son;
But it shall ne'er be said, a Child
So hopeful has by me been spoil'd;
I have enough besides to spare,
And give him wholly to your Care.

    Wisdom's above suspecting Wiles:
The Queen of Learning gravely smiles;
Down from *Olympus* comes with Joy,   200
Mistakes *Vanessa* for a Boy;
Then sows within her tender Mind
Seeds, long unknown to Womankind,

For manly Bosoms chiefly fit,
The Seeds of Knowledge, Judgment, Wit.
Her Soul was suddenly endu'd
With Justice, Truth and Fortitude;
With Honour, which no Breath can stain,
Which Malice must attack in vain;
With open Heart and bounteous Hand: 210
But *Pallas* here was at a Stand;
She knew in our degen'rate Days
Bare Virtue could not live on Praise;
That Meat must be with Money bought;
She therefore, upon second Thought,
Infus'd, yet as it were by Stealth,
Some small Regard for State and Wealth:
Of which, as she grew up, there stay'd
A Tincture in the prudent Maid:
She manag'd her Estate with Care,   220
Yet lik'd three Footmen to her Chair.
But lest he should neglect his Studies,
Like a young Heir, the thrifty Goddess
(For fear young Master should be spoil'd,)
Wou'd use him like a younger Child;
And, after long computing, found
'Twou'd come to just Five thousand Pound.

The Queen of Love was pleas'd, and proud,
To see *Vanessa* thus endow'd;
She doubted not, but such a Dame   230
Thro' ev'ry Breast would dart a Flame;
That ev'ry rich and lordly Swain
With Pride would drag about her Chain;
That Scholars should forsake their Books,
To study bright *Vanessa*'s Looks:
As she advanc'd, that Womankind
Wou'd by her Model form their Mind;
And all their Conduct would be try'd
By her, as an unerring Guide,

Offending Daughters oft' would hear   240
Vanessa's Praise rung in their Ear:
Miss *Betty*, when she does a Fault,
Lets fall her Knife, or spills the Salt,
Will thus be by her Mother chid;
"Tis what *Vanessa* never did.'
Thus, by the Nymphs and Swains ador'd,
My Pow'r shall be again restor'd,
And happy Lovers bless my Reign—
So *Venus* hop'd, but hop'd in vain.

    For, when in Time, the *Martial Maid*   250
Found out the Trick, that *Venus* play'd,
She shakes her Helm, she knits her Brows,
And fir'd with Indignation vows,
To-morrow e'er the setting Sun,
She'd all undo, that she had done.

    But, in the Poets we may find,
A wholesome Law, Time out of Mind,
Had been confirmed by Fate's decree;
That God's, of whatsoe'er Degree,
Resume not what themselves have giv'n,   260
Or any Brother God in Heav'n:
Which keeps the Peace among the Gods,
Or, they must always be at Odds,
And *Pallas*, if she broke the Laws,
Must yield her Foe the stronger Cause;
A Shame to one, so much ador'd
For Wisdom at *Jove*'s Council-Board.
Besides, she fear'd, the Queen of Love
Wou'd meet with better Friends above:
And tho' she must with Grief reflect,   270
To see a mortal Virgin deck'd
With Graces hitherto unknown
To female Breasts, except her own;
Yet she wou'd act, as best became

110

A Goddess of unspotted Fame;
She knew by Augury divine,
Venus would fail in her Design:
She studied well the Point, and found,
Her Foes Conclusions were not sound;
From Premisses erroneous brought,   280
And therefore the Deductions nought;
And must have contrary Effects
To what her treach'rous Foe expects.

    In proper Season *Pallas* meets
The Queen of Love, whom thus she greets:
(For Gods we are by *Homer* told
Can in Celestial Language scold)
Perfidious Goddess! but in vain
You form'd this Project in your Brain;
A Project for thy Talents fit,   290
With much Deceit, and little Wit:
Thou hast, as thou shalt quickly see,
Deceiv'd thy self, instead of me;
For how can heav'nly Wisdom prove
An Instrument to earthly Love?
Know'st thou not yet, that Men commence
Thy Votaries for want of Sense?
Nor shall *Vanessa* be the Theme
To manage thy abortive Scheme:
She'll prove the greatest of thy Foes   300
And yet I scorn to interpose;
But using neither Skill, nor Force,
Leave all Things to their nat'ral Course.

    The Goddess thus pronounc'd her Doom:
When, lo! *Vanessa* in her Bloom,
Advanc'd like *Atalanta*'s Star,
But rarely seen, and seen from far:
In a new World with Caution stept,
Watch'd all the Company she kept,

Well knowing from the Books she read   310
What dang'rous Paths young Virgins tread:
Would seldom at the Park appear,
Nor saw the Play-house twice a Year;
Yet not incurious, was inclin'd
To know the Converse of Mankind.

   First issu'd from Perfumers Shops,
A Croud of fashionable Fops;
They ask'd her, how she lik'd the Play;
Then told the Tattle of the Day;
A Duel fought last Night at Two,   320
About a Lady—you know who:
Mention'd a new *Italian*, come
Either from *Muscovy* or *Rome*;
Gave Hints of who and who's together;
Then fell to talking of the Weather:
Last Night was so extremely fine,
The Ladies walk'd till after Nine.
Then in soft Voice and Speech absurd,
With Nonsense ev'ry second Word,
With Fustian from exploded Plays,   330
They celebrate her Beauty's Praise;
Run o'er their Cant of stupid Lyes,
And tell the Murders of her Eyes.

   With silent Scorn *Vanessa* sat,
Scarce list'ning to their idle Chat;
Further than sometimes by a Frown,
When they grew pert, to pull them down.
At last she spitefully was bent
To try their Wisdom's full Extent;
And said she valu'd nothing less   340
Than Titles, Figure, Shape, and Dress:
That Merit should be chiefly plac'd
In Judgment, Knowledge, Wit, and Taste:
And these, she offer'd to dispute,

Alone distinguish'd Man from Brute:
That, present Times have no Pretence
To Virtue, in the noblest Sense,
By *Greeks* and *Romans* understood,
To perish for our Country's Good.
She nam'd the antient Heroes round,   350
Explain'd for what they were renown'd:
Then spoke with Censure, or Applause,
Of foreign Customs, Rites, and Laws.
Thro' Nature, and thro' Art she rang'd,
And gracefully her Subject chang'd:
In vain: Her Hearers had no share
In all she spoke, except to stare.
Their Judgment was upon the Whole,
—That Lady is the dullest Soul—
Then tipt their Forehead in a Jeer,   360
As who should say—she wants it here;
She may be handsome, young, and rich,
But none will burn her for a Witch.

   A Party next of glitt'ring Dames,
From round the Purlieus of St. *James*',
Came early, out of pure good Will,
To see the Girl in Dishabille.
Their Clamour 'lighting from their Chairs,
Grew louder all the Way up Stairs;
At Entrance loudest; where they found   370
The Room with Volumes litter'd round.
Vanessa held *Montaigne*, and read,
Whilst Mrs. *Susan* comb'd her Head:
They call'd for Tea and Chocolate,
And fell into their usual Chat;
Discoursing with important Face,
On Ribbons, Fans, and Gloves, and Lace;
Shew'd Patterns just from *India* brought,
And gravely ask'd her what she thought;
Whether the Red or Green were best,   380

And what they cost? *Vanessa* guess'd,
As came into her Fancy first,
Nam'd half the Rates, and lik'd the worst.
To Scandal next—What aukward Thing
Was that, last *Sunday* in the Ring?
—I'm sorry *Mopsa* breaks so fast;
I said her Face would never last.
Corinna, with that youthful Air,
Is thirty, and a Bit to spare:
Her Fondness for a certain Earl   390
Began, when I was but a Girl.
Phillis, who but a Month ago
Was marry'd to the *Tunbridge* Beau,
I saw coquetting t'other Night,
In Publick with that odious Knight.

    They rally'd next *Vanessa*'s Dress;
That Gown was made for old Queen *Bess*.
Dear Madam, let me set your Head:
Don't you intend to put on Red?
A Petticoat without a Hoop!   400
Sure, you are not asham'd to stoop;
With handsome Garters at your Knees,
No Matter what a Fellow sees.

    Fill'd with Disdain, with Rage inflam'd,
Both of her self and Sex asham'd,
The Nymph stood silent out of Spight,
Nor would vouchsafe to set them right.
Away the fair Detractors went,
And gave, by Turns, their Censures Vent.
She's not so handsome in my Eyes: 410
For Wit, I wonder where it lies.
She's fair and clean, and that's the most;
But why proclaim her for a Toast?
A Baby Face, no Life, nor Airs,
But what she learnt at Country Fairs;

Scarce knows what Diff'rence is between
Rich *Flanders* Lace, and Colberteen.
I'll undertake my little *Nancy*
In Flounces hath a better Fancy.
With all her Wit, I would not ask   420
Her Judgment, how to buy a Mask;
We begg'd her but to patch her Face,
She never hit one proper Place;
Which ev'ry Girl at five Years old
Can do, as soon as she is told.
I own, that out-of-fashion Stuff
Becomes the *Creature* well enough.
The Girl might pass, if we could get her
To know the World a little better.
(*To know the World:* A modern Phrase   430
For Visits, Ombre, Balls, and Plays.)

      Thus, to the World's perpetual Shame,
The *Queen of Beauty* lost her Aim.
Too late with Grief she understood,
Pallas had done more Harm than Good:
For great Examples are but vain,
Where Ignorance begets Disdain.
Both Sexes arm'd with Guilt and Spite,
Against *Vanessa*'s Pow'r unite;
To copy her, few Nymphs aspir'd;   440
Her Virtues fewer Swains admir'd:
So, Stars beyond a certain Height
Give Mortals neither Heat nor Light.

      Yet some of either Sex, endow'd
With Gifts superior to the Crowd,
With Virtue, Knowledge, Taste, and Wit,
She condescended to admit:
With pleasing Arts she could reduce
Mens Talents to their proper Use;
And with Address each Genius held   450

To that wherein it most excell'd;
Thus making others Wisdom known,
Could please them, and improve her own.
A modest Youth said something new:
She plac'd it in the strongest View.
All humble Worth she strove to raise;
Would not be prais'd, yet lov'd to praise.
The Learned met with free Approach,
Altho' they came not in a Coach.
Some Clergy too she would allow,   460
Nor quarrell'd at their awkward Bow;
But this was for *Cadenus*' Sake;
A Gownman of a diff'rent Make;
Whom *Pallas*, once *Vanessa*'s Tutor,
Had fix'd on for her Coadjutor.

    But *Cupid*, full of Mischief, longs
To vindicate his Mother's Wrongs,
On *Pallas* all Attempts are vain;
One Way he knows to give her Pain;
Vows, on *Vanessa*'s Heart to take   470
Due Vengeance for her Patron's Sake.
Those early Seeds by *Venus* sown,
In Spight of *Pallas* now were grown;
And *Cupid* hop'd they would improve
By Time, and ripen into Love.
The Boy made use of all his Craft,
In vain discharging many a Shaft,
Pointed at Col'nels, Lords, and Beaux:
Cadenus warded off the Blows;
For placing still some Book betwixt,   480
The Darts were in the Cover fix't;
Or often blunted and recoil'd,
On *Plutarch*'s Morals struck, were spoil'd.

    The Queen of Wisdom could foresee,
But not prevent the Fates Decree:

And human Caution tries in vain
To break that Adamantine Chain.
Vanessa, tho' by *Pallas* taught,
By *Love* invulnerable thought,
Searching in Books for Wisdom's Aid,   490
Was, in the very Search, betray'd.

    Cupid, tho' all his Darts were lost,
Yet still resolv'd to spare no Cost;
He could not answer to his Fame
The Triumphs of that stubborn Dame;
A Nymph so hard to be subdu'd,
Who neither was Coquet nor Prude.
I find, said he, she wants a Doctor,
Both to adore her, and instruct her;
I'll give her what she most admires;   500
Among those venerable Sires.
Cadenus is a Subject fit,
Grown old in Politicks and Wit;
Caress'd by Ministers of State,
Of half Mankind the Dread and Hate;
Whate'er Vexations Love attend,
She need no Rivals apprehend:
Her Sex, with universal Voice,
Must laugh at her capricious Choice.

    Cadenus many Things had writ;   510
Vanessa much esteem'd his Wit,
And call'd for his Poetick Works;
Mean time the Boy in secret lurks,
And, while the Book was in her Hand,
The Urchin from his private Stand
Took Aim, and shot with all his Strength
A Dart of such prodigious Length;
It pierc'd the feeble Volume thro',
And deep transfix'd her Bosom too.
Some Lines more moving than the rest,   520

Stuck to the Point that pierc'd her Breast;
And born directly to her Heart,
With Pains unknown increas'd the Smart.

Vanessa, not in Years a Score,
Dreams of a Gown of Forty-four;
Imaginary Charms can find,
In Eyes with Reading almost blind:
Cadenus now no more appears
Declin'd in Health, advanc'd in Years:
She fancies Musick in his Tongue,   530
Nor further looks, but thinks him young.
What Mariner is not afraid
To venture in a Ship decay'd?
What Planter will attempt to yoke
A Sapling with a falling Oak?
As Years increase, she brighter shines,
Cadenus with each Day declines,
And he must fall a Prey to Time,
While she continues in her Prime.

Cadenus, common Forms apart,   540
In every Scene had kept his Heart;
Had sigh'd and languish'd, vow'd and writ,
For Pastime, or to shew his Wit:
But Books, and Time, and State Affairs,
Had spoil'd his fashionable Airs;
He now cou'd praise, esteem, approve,
But understood not what was Love:
His Conduct might have made him styl'd
A Father, and the Nymph his Child.
That innocent Delight he took   550
To see the Virgin mind her Book,
Was but the Master's secret Joy
In School to hear the finest Boy.
Her Knowledge with her Fancy grew;
She hourly press'd for something new:

Ideas came into her Mind
So fast, his Lessons lagg'd behind:
She reason'd, without plodding long;
Nor ever gave her Judgment wrong.
But now a sudden Change was wrought,   560
She minds no longer what he taught.
[She wish'd her Tutor were her Lover;
Resolv'd she would her Flame discover:
And when *Cadenus* would expound
Some Notion subtil or profound,
The Nymph would gently press his Hand,
As if she seem'd to understand;
Or dext'rously dissembling Chance,
Would sigh, and steal a secret Glance.]
Cadenus was amaz'd to find
Such Marks of a distracted Mind;
For tho' she seem'd to listen more
To all he spoke, than e'er before;
He found her Thoughts would absent range,
Yet guess'd not, whence could spring the Change.
And first, he modestly conjectures,
His Pupil might be tir'd with Lectures;
Which help'd to mortify his Pride,   570
Yet gave him not the Heart to chide:
But in a mild dejected Strain,
At last he ventur'd to complain:
Said, she should be no longer teiz'd;
Might have her Freedom when she pleas'd:
Was now convinc'd he acted wrong,
To hide her from the World so long;
And in dull Studies to engage,
One of her tender Sex and Age:
That ev'ry Nymph with Envy own'd,   580
How she might shine in the *Grand Monde*:
And ev'ry Shepherd was undone
To see her cloister'd like a Nun.
This was a visionary Scheme,

He wak'd and found it but a Dream;
A Project far above his Skill;
For Nature must be Nature still.
If he were bolder than became
A Scholar to a courtly Dame,
She might excuse a Man of Letters;   590
Thus Tutors often treat their Betters.
And since his Talk offensive grew,
He came to take his last Adieu.

Vanessa, fill'd with just Disdain,
Would still her Dignity maintain;
Instructed from her early Years
To scorn the Art of Female Tears.

Had he employ'd his Time so long
To teach her what was Right and Wrong,
Yet cou'd such Notions entertain,   600
That all his Lectures were in vain?
She own'd the Wand'ring of her Thoughts,
But he must answer for her Faults.
She well remember'd to her Cost,
That all his Lessons were not lost.
Two Maxims she could still produce,
And sad Experience taught their Use:
That Virtue, pleas'd by being shown,
Knows nothing which it dare not own;
Can make us, without Fear disclose   610
Our inmost Secrets to our Foes:
That common Forms were not design'd
Directors to a noble Mind.
Now, said the Nymph, to let you see,
My Actions with your Rules agree,
That I can vulgar Forms despise,
And have no Secrets to disguise:
[I'll fully prove your Maxims True,
By owning here my Love for you.]

I knew by what you said and writ,
How dang'rous Things were Men of Wit;
You caution'd me against their Charms,   620
But never gave me equal Arms:
Your Lessons found the weakest Part,
Aim'd at the Head, and reach'd the Heart.

   Cadenus felt within him rise
Shame, Disappointment, Guilt, Surprize.
He knew not how to reconcile
Such Language, with her usual Style:
And yet her Words were so exprest,
He could not hope she spoke in Jest.
His Thoughts had wholly been confin'd   630
To form and cultivate her Mind.
He hardly knew, till he was told,
Whether the Nymph were young or old:
Had met her in a publick Place,
Without distinguishing her Face.
Much less could his declining Age,
Vanessa's earliest Thoughts engage:
And, if her Youth Indifference met,
His Person must Contempt beget.
Or, grant her Passion be sincere,   640
How shall his Innocence be clear?
Appearances were all so strong,
The World must think him in the wrong;
Wou'd say, he made a treach'rous Use
Of Wit, to flatter and seduce:
The Town wou'd swear he had betray'd,
By Magick Spells, the harmless Maid;
And ev'ry Beau wou'd have his Jokes,
That Scholars were like other Folks:
That when Platonick Flights are over,   650
The Tutor turns a mortal Lover:
So tender of the Young and Fair;
It shew'd a true paternal Care:

Five thousand Guineas in her Purse,
The Doctor might have fancy'd worse.

Hardly at length he Silence broke,
And faulter'd ev'ry Word he spoke:
Interpreting her Complaisance,
Just as a Man *sans Consequence*.
She rally'd well, he always knew;   660
Her Manner now was something new:
And what she spoke was in an Air,
As serious as a Tragick Play'r.
But those, who aim at Ridicule,
Shou'd fix upon some certain Rule;
Which fairly hints they are in Jest,
Else he must enter his Protest:
For, let a Man be ne'er so wise,
He may be caught with sober Lies;
A Science, which he never taught,   670
And, to be free, was dearly bought:
For, take it in its proper Light,
'Tis just what Coxcombs call, *A Bite*.

But, not to dwell on Things minute;
Vanessa finish'd the Dispute;
Brought weighty Arguments to prove,
That Reason was her Guide in Love.
She thought he had himself describ'd,
His Doctrines, when she first imbib'd;
[From him transfus'd into her Breast
With Pleasure not to be exprest.]
What he had planted, now was grown;   680
His Virtues she might call her own;
As he approves, as he dislikes,
Love or Contempt her Fancy strikes.
Self-love, in Nature rooted fast,
Attends us first, and leaves us last:
Why she likes him, admire not at her,

She loves her self, and that's the Matter.
How was her Tutor wont to praise
The Genius's of ancient Days!
(Those Authors he so oft' had nam'd   690
For Learning, Wit, and Wisdom fam'd;)
Was struck with Love, Esteem, and Awe,
For Persons whom he never saw.
Suppose *Cadenus* flourish'd then,
He must adore such God-like Men.
If one short Volume could comprise
All that was witty, learn'd, and wise,
How wou'd it be esteem'd, and read,
Altho' the Writer long were dead?
If such an Author were alive,   700
How all would for his Friendship strive;
And come in Crowds to see his Face:
And this she takes to be her Case:
Cadenus answer'd ev'ry End,
The Book, the Author, and the Friend.
The utmost her Desires will reach,
Is but to learn what he can teach;
His Converse is a System, fit
Alone to fill up all her Wit;
While ev'ry Passion of her Mind   710
In him is center'd and confin'd.

   Love can with Speech inspire a Mute;
And taught *Vanessa* to dispute.
This Topick, never touch'd before,
Display'd her Eloquence the more:
Her Knowledge, with such Pains acquir'd,
By this new Passion grew inspir'd:
Thro' this she made all Objects pass,
Which gave a Tincture o'er the Mass:
As Rivers, tho' they bend and twine,   720
Still to the Sea their Course incline:
Or, as Philosophers, who find

Some fav'rite System to their Mind;
In ev'ry Point to make it fit,
Will force all Nature to submit.

Cadenus, who could ne'er suspect
His Lessons would have such Effect,
Or be so artfully apply'd;
Insensibly came on her Side:
It was an unforeseen Event,   730
Things took a Turn he never meant.
Whoe'er excels, in what we prize,
Appears a Hero to our Eyes;
Each Girl, when pleas'd with what is taught,
Will have the Teacher in her Thought:
When Miss delights in her Spinnet,
A Fidler may a Fortune get:
A Blockhead with melodious Voice,
In Boarding-Schools can have his Choice:
And oft' the Dancing-Master's Art   740
Climbs from the Toe to touch the Heart.
In Learning let a Nymph delight,
The Pedant gets a Mistress by't.
Cadenus, to his Grief and Shame,
Cou'd scarce oppose *Vanessa*'s Flame;
And tho' her Arguments were strong,
At least could hardly wish them wrong.
Howe'er it came, he could not tell,
But sure she never talk'd so well.
His Pride began to interpose;   750
Preferr'd before a Crowd of Beaux:
So bright a Nymph to come unsought,
Such Wonder by his Merit wrought;
'Tis Merit must with her prevail,
He never knew her Judgment fail;
She noted all she ever read,
And had a most discerning Head.

'Tis an old Maxim in the Schools,
That Flattery's the Food of Fools;
Yet now and then your Men of Wit   760
Will condescend to take a Bit.
So when *Cadenus* could not hide,
He chose to justify his Pride;
Const'ring the Passion she had shown,
Much to her Praise, more to his own.
Nature in him had Merit plac'd;
In her, a most judicious Taste.
Love, hitherto a transient Guest,
Ne'er held Possession of his Breast;
So, long attending at the Gate,   770
Disdain'd to enter in so late.
Love, why do we one Passion call?
When 'tis a Compound of them all;
Where hot and cold, where sharp and sweet,
In all their Equipages meet:
Where Pleasures mix'd with Pains appear,
Sorrow with Joy, and Hope with Fear;
Wherein his Dignity and Age
Forbid *Cadenus* to engage:
But Friendship in its greatest Height,   780
A constant, rational Delight,
On Virtue's Basis fix'd to last,
When Love's Allurements long are past;
Which gently warms, but cannot burn;
He gladly offers in return:
His want of Passion will redeem,
With Gratitude, Respect, Esteem:
With that Devotion we bestow,
When Goddesses appear below.

While thus *Cadenus* entertains   790
Vanessa in exalted Strains,
The Nymph, in sober Words, intreats
A Truce with all sublime Conceits:

For why such Raptures, Flights, and Fancies,
To her, who durst not read Romances;
In lofty Style to make Replies,
Which he had taught her to despise.
But when her Tutor will affect
Devotion, Duty, and Respect,
He fairly abdicates his Throne;   800
The Government is now her own:
He has a Forfeiture incurr'd:
She vows to take him at his Word;
And hopes he will not think it strange,
If both shou'd now their Stations change.
The Nymph will have her Turn, to be
The Tutor; and the Pupil, he:
Tho' she already can discern,
Her Scholar is not apt to learn;
Or wants Capacity to reach   810
The Science she designs to teach:
Wherein his Genius was below
The Skill of ev'ry common Beau;
Who, tho' he cannot spell, is wise
Enough to read a Lady's Eyes;
And will each accidental Glance
Interpret for a kind Advance.

But what Success *Vanessa* met,
Is to the World a Secret yet:
Whether the Nymph, to please her Swain,   820
Talks in a high romantick Strain;
Or whether he at last descends,
To act with less Seraphick Ends;
Or, to compound the Business, whether
They temper Love and Books together;
Must never to Mankind be told,
Nor shall the conscious Muse unfold.

Mean while, the mournful *Queen of Love*
Led but a weary Life above.
She ventures now to leave the Skies,   830
Grown by *Vanessa*'s Conduct wise:
For, tho' by one perverse Event
Pallas had cross'd her first Intent,
Tho' her Design was not obtain'd,
Yet had she much Experience gain'd;
And by the Project vainly try'd,
Cou'd better now the *Cause* decide.

She gave due Notice, that both Parties,
[1]*Coram Regina prox' die Martis*,
Should at their Peril, without fail,   840
Come and appear, and save their Bail.
All met, and Silence thrice proclaim'd,
One Lawyer to each Side was nam'd.
The Judge discover'd in her Face,
Resentments for her late Disgrace;
And, full of Anger, Shame, and Grief,
Directed them to mind their Brief;
Nor spend their Time to shew their Reading;
She'd have a summary Proceeding.
She gather'd, under ev'ry Head,   850
The Sum of what each Lawyer said;
Gave her own Reasons last; and then
Decreed the Cause against the *Men*.

But, in a weighty Case like this,
To shew she did not judge amiss,
Which evil Tongues might else report:
She made a Speech in open Court;
Wherein she grievously complains,
'How she was cheated by the Swains:
On whose Petition, (humbly shewing,   860
That Women were not worth the wooing;

---

[1] *Before the Queen on* Tuesday *next.*

And, that unless the Sex would mend,
The Race of Lovers soon must end:)
'She was at Lord knows what Expence
'To form a Nymph of Wit and Sense;
'A Model for her Sex design'd,
'Who never could one Lover find.
'She saw her Favour was misplac'd;
'The Fellows had a wretched Taste;
'She needs must tell them to their Face,   870
'They were a stupid, senseless Race:
'And were she to begin agen,
'She'd study to reform the *Men*;
'Or add some Grains of Folly more
'To *Women* than they had before,
'To put them on an equal Foot;
'And this, or nothing else, wou'd do't.
'This might their mutual Fancy strike,
'Since every Being loves its *Like*.

    'But now, repenting what was done,   880
'She left all Business to her Son,
'She puts the World in his Possession,
'And let him use it at Discretion.'

    The Cry'r was order'd to dismiss
The Court; who made his last *O yes!*
The Goddess would no longer wait;
But rising from her Chair of State,
Left all below at Six and Sev'n;
Harness'd her Doves and flew to Heav'n.
                              1719?/1726

A Rebus written by a Lady[1]
On the Rev. Dean Swift

With his Answer

CUT the Name of the MAN who his
    Mistress deny'd,   *Jo—seph.*
And let the *first* of it, be only
    apply'd
To join with the *Prophet* who   *Nathan.*
    DAVID did chide.
Then say what a *Horse* is that runs very *fast*,
And that which deserves to be *first* put the *last*;
Spell all then, and put them together, to find
The NAME and the VIRTUES of *Him* I designed.
Like the *Patriarch* in *Egypt*, he's vers'd in the *State*,
Like the *Prophet* in *Jeury*, he's free with the *Great*.
Like a *Racer* he flies to succour with Speed,   10
When his *Friends* want his Aid, or Desert is in Need.

THE ANSWER

The NYMPH who wrote this in an amorous Fit,
I cannot but Envy the Pride of her *Wit*.
Which thus she will venture profusely to throw,
On so mean a *Design*, and a *Subject* so low.
For mean's her *Design*, and her *Subject* as mean,
The *First* but a REBUS, the *Last* but a DEAN.
A *Dean*'s but a *Parson*, and what is a *Rebus*?
A Thing never known to the *Muses* or *Phœbus*:
The Corruption of Verse, for when all is done,   20
It is but a *Paraphrase* made on a *Punn*;
But a Genius like her's no Subject can stifle,
It shews and discovers itself through a *Trifle*.
By reading this *Trifle*, I quickly began
To find her a great *Wit*, but the *Dean* a small Man.

[1] Mrs. *Vanhomrigh.*—Faulkner.

Rich Ladies will furnish their Garrets with Stuff,
Which others for Mantuas wou'd think fine enuff;
So the *Wit* that is lavishly thrown away here,
Might furnish a Second Rate *Poet* a Year:
Thus much for the *Verse*, we proceed to the next,   30
Where the NYMPH has entirely forsaken her *Text*:
Her fine Panegyricks are quite out of Season,
And what *She* describes to be *Merit* is *Treason*:
The Changes which Faction has made in the State,
Have put the *Dean*'s Politicks quite out of Date:
Now no one regards what he utters with Freedom,
And should he write *Pamphlets*, no Great Man wou'd
      read 'em;
And shou'd *Want* or *Desert* stand in need of his *Aid*,
This *Racer* wou'd prove but a dull founder'd *Jade*.

                                                    1719?/?

Verses to Vanessa

NYMPH, would you learn the only art,
To keep a worthy lover's heart;
First, to adorn your person well,
In utmost cleanliness excel:
And though you must the fashions take,
Observe them, but for fashion's sake:
The strongest reason will submit
To virtue, honour, sense, and wit:
To such a nymph, the wise and good,
Cannot be faithless, if they would,   10
For vices all have different ends,
But virtue still to virtue tends;
And when your lover is not true,
'Tis virtue fails in him, or you;
And either he deserves disdain,
Or you without a cause complain;

But here Vanessa cannot err,
Nor are these rules applied to her:
For who could such a nymph forsake,
Except a blockhead, or a rake;   20
Or how could she her heart bestow,
Except where wit and virtue grow.

                                    1720/1814

'Dorinda dreams of dress a-bed'

DORINDA dreams of dress a-bed,
   'Tis all her thought and art;
Her lace hath got within her head,
   Her stays stick to her heart.

                                    1720/1814

'A fig for partridges and quails'

A FIG for partridges and quails;—
Ye dainties, I know nothing of ye;
   But on the highest mount in Wales
Would choose in peace to drink my coffee.

                                    1720/1814

POEMS TO STELLA

Stella's Birth-Day

1718-19

STELLA this Day is Thirty-four,
(We shan't dispute a Year or more:)
However *Stella*, be not troubled,
Although thy Size and Years are doubled,
Since first I saw thee at Sixteen,
The brightest Virgin on the Green.
So little is thy Form declin'd;
Made up so largely in thy Mind.

Oh! would it please the Gods, to *split*
Thy Beauty, Size, and Years, and Wit;   10
No Age could furnish out a Pair
Of Nymphs so graceful, wise, and fair:
With half the Lustre of your Eyes,
With half your Wit, your Years, and Size.
And then, before it grew too late,
How should I beg of gentle Fate,
(That either Nymph might have her Swain,)
To split my Worship too in twain.

                                      1719/1735

To Stella Visiting Me
in my Sickness

PALLAS, observing *Stella*'s Wit
Shine more than for her Sex was fit;
And that her Beauty, soon or late,
Might breed Confusion in the State;

In high Concern for human Kind,
Fixt *Honour* in her Infant Mind.

But, (not in Wranglings to engage
With such a stupid vicious Age,)
If *Honour* I would here define,
It answers *Faith* in Things divine;   10
As nat'ral Life the Body warms,
And Scholars teach, the Soul informs;
So Honour animates the Whole,
And is the Spirit of the Soul.

Those num'rous Virtues which the Tribe
Of tedious Moralists describe,
And by such various Titles call;
True Honour comprehends them all.
Let Melancholy rule supreme,
Cholar preside, or Blood, or Phlegm;   20
It makes no Diff'rence in the Case,
Nor is Complexion Honour's Place.

But, lest we should, for Honour take
The drunken Quarrels of a Rake;
Or think it seated in a Scar;
Or on a proud triumphal Car;
Or in the Payment of a Debt
We lose with Sharpers at Piquet;
Or, when a Whore, in her Vocation,
Keeps punctual to an Assignation;   30
Or that on which his Lordship swears,
When vulgar Knaves would lose their Ears:
Let *Stella*'s fair Example preach,
A Lesson she alone can teach.

In Points of Honour to be try'd,
All Passions must be laid aside;

Ask no Advice, but think alone:
Suppose the Question not your own:
How shall I act? is not the Case;
But how would *Brutus* in my Place?   40
In such a Cause would *Cato* bleed?
And how would *Socrates* proceed?

Drive all Objections from your Mind,
Else you relapse to human Kind:
Ambition, Avarice, and Lust,
And factious Rage, and Breach of Trust;
And Flatt'ry tipt with nauseous Fleer,
And guilty Shame, and servile Fear,
Envy, and Cruelty, and Pride,
Will in your tainted Heart preside.   50

Heroes and Heroins of old,
By *Honour* only were inroll'd
Among their Brethren of the Skies;
To which (though late) shall *Stella* rise.
Ten thousand Oaths upon Record,
Are not so sacred as her Word;
The World shall in its Atoms end,
E'er *Stella* can deceive a Friend.
By *Honour* seated in her Breast,
She still determines what is best: 60
What Indignation in her Mind
Against Enslavers of Mankind!
Base Kings and Ministers of State,
Eternal Objects of her Hate.

She thinks, that Nature ne'er design'd
Courage to Man alone confin'd:
Can Cowardice her Sex adorn,
Which most exposes ours to Scorn;
She wonders where the Charm appears
In *Florimel*'s affected Fears: 70

For *Stella* never learn'd the Art,
At proper times to scream and start;
Nor calls up all the House at Night,
And swears she saw a thing in White:
Doll never flies to cut her Lace,
Or throw cold Water in her Face,
Because she heard a sudden Drum,
Or found an Earwig in a Plum.

Her Hearers are amaz'd from whence
Proceeds that Fund of Wit and Sense;   80
Which though her Modesty would shroud,
Breaks like the Sun behind a Cloud;
While Gracefulness its Art conceals,
And yet through ev'ry Motion steals.

Say, *Stella*, was *Prometheus* blind,
And forming you, mistook your Kind;
No: 'Twas for you alone he stole
The Fire that forms a manly Soul;
Then to compleat it ev'ry way,
He moulded it with Female Clay: 90
To that you owe the nobler Flame,
To this, the Beauty of your Frame.

How would Ingratitude delight?
And, how would Censure glut her Spight?
If I should *Stella*'s Kindness hide
In Silence, or forget with Pride,
When on my sickly Couch I lay,
Impatient both of Night and Day,
Lamenting in unmanly Strains,
Call'd ev'ry Pow'r to ease my Pains: 100
Then *Stella* ran to my Relief,
With chearful Face, and inward Grief:
And, though by Heav'ns severe Decree
She suffers hourly more than me:

No cruel Master could require
From Slaves employ'd for daily Hire,
What *Stella*, by her Friendship warm'd,
With Vigour and Delight perform'd:
My sinking Spirits, now supplies,
With Cordials in her Hands and Eyes;   110
Now, with soft and silent Tread,
Unheard she moves about my Bed.
I see her taste each nauseous Draught,
And so obligingly am caught;
I bless the Hand from whence they came,
Nor dare distort my Face for shame.

Best Pattern of true Friends, beware;
You pay too dearly for your Care:
If, while your Tenderness secures
My Life, it must endanger yours.   120
For such a Fool was never found,
Who pull'd a Palace to the Ground,
Only to have the Ruins made
Materials for an House decay'd.

1720/1727

To Stella, who Collected and Transcribed his Poems

As when a lofty Pile is rais'd,
We never hear the Workmen prais'd,
Who bring the Lime, or place the Stones,
But all admire *Inigo Jones*:
So, if this Pile of scatter'd Rhymes
Should be approv'd in After-times;
If it both pleases and endures,
The Merit and the Praise are yours.

139

Thou, *Stella*, wert no longer young,
When first for thee my Harp I strung;   10
Without one Word of *Cupid*'s Darts,
Of killing Eyes, or bleeding Hearts:
With Friendship and Esteem possest,
I ne'er admitted Love a Guest.

In all the Habitudes of Life,
The Friend, the Mistress, and the Wife,
Variety we still pursue,
In Pleasure seek for something new:
Or else, comparing with the rest,
Take Comfort, that our own is best: 20
(The best we value by the worst,
As Tradesmen shew their Trash at first:)
But his Pursuits are at an End,
Whom *Stella* chuses for a *Friend*.

A Poet, starving in a Garret,
Conning old Topicks like a Parrot,
Invokes his Mistress and his Muse,
And stays at home for Want of Shoes:
Should but his Muse descending drop
A Slice of Bread, and Mutton-Chop;   30
Or kindly when his Credit's out,
Surprize him with a Pint of ¹*Stout*;
Or patch his broken Stocking Soals;
Or send him in a Peck of Coals;
Exalted in his mighty Mind
He flies, and leaves the Stars behind;
Counts all his Labours amply paid,
Adores her for the timely Aid.

Or, should a Porter make Enquiries
For *Chloe, Sylvia, Phillis, Iris*;   40
Be told the Lodging, Lane, and Sign,

¹ *A Cant Word for Strong-Beer.*

The Bow'rs that hold those Nymphs divine;
Fair *Chloe* would perhaps be found
With Footmen tippling under Ground;
The charming *Sylvia* beating Flax,
Her shoulders mark'd with bloody Tracks;
Bright *Phillis* mending ragged Smocks;
And radiant *Iris* in the Pox.

These are the Goddesses enroll'd
In *Curl*'s Collections, new and old,   50
Whose scoundrel Fathers would not know
        'em,
If they should meet 'em in a Poem.

True Poets can depress and raise;
Are Lords of Infamy and Praise:
They are not scurrilous in Satire,
Nor will in Panegyrick flatter.
Unjustly Poets we asperse;
Truth shines the brighter, clad in Verse:
And all the Fictions they pursue,
Do but insinuate what is true.   60

Now, should my Praises owe their Truth
To Beauty, Dress, or Paint, or Youth,
What Stoicks call *without our Power*;
They could not be insur'd an Hour:
'Twere grafting on an annual Stock,
That must our Expectation mock,
And making one luxuriant Shoot,
Die the next Year for want of Root:
Before I could my Verses bring,
Perhaps you're quite another Thing.   70

So *Mævius*, when he drain'd his Skull
To celebrate some Suburb Trull;
His Similies in Order set,

141

And ev'ry Crambo he could get;
Had gone through all the common Places,
Worn out by Wits who rhyme on Faces;
Before he could his Poem close,
The lovely Nymph had lost her Nose.

Your Virtues safely I commend;
They on no Accidents depend: 80
Let Malice look with all her Eyes,
She dares not say, the Poet lyes.

Stella, when you these Lines transcribe,
Lest you should take them for a Bribe;
Resolv'd to mortify your Pride,
I'll here expose your weaker Side.

Your Spirits kindle to a Flame,
Mov'd with the lightest touch of Blame;
And when a Friend in Kindness tries
To shew you where your Error lies,   90
Conviction does but more incense;
Perverseness is your whole Defence:
Truth, Judgment, Wit, give Place to Spight,
Regardless both of Wrong and Right.
Your Virtues, all suspended, wait
Till Time hath open'd Reason's Gate:
And what is worse, your Passion bends
Its Force against your nearest Friends;
Which Manners, Decency, and Pride,
Have taught you from the World to hide. 100
In vain; for see, your Friend hath brought
To publick Light your *only* Fau't;
And yet a Fault we often find
Mix'd in a noble generous Mind;
And may compare to *Ætna's* Fire,
Which, tho' with trembling, all admire;
The Heat, that makes the Summit glow,

Enriching all the Vales below.
Those, who in warmer Climes complain,
From *Phœbus*' Rays they suffer Pain;   110
Must own, that Pain is largely paid
By gen'rous Wines beneath a Shade.

Yet, when I find your Passions rise,
And Anger sparkling in your Eyes,
I grieve those Spirits should be spent,
For nobler Ends by Nature meant.
One Passion with a diff'rent Turn,
Makes Wit inflame, or Anger burn;
So the Sun's Heat, by diff'rent Pow'rs,
Ripens the Grape, the Liquor sours.   120
Thus *Ajax*, when with Rage possest,
By *Pallas* breath'd into his Breast,
His Valour would no more employ,
Which might alone have conquer'd *Troy*;
But, blinded by Resentment, seeks
For Vengeance on his Friends, the *Greeks*.

You think this Turbulence of Blood
From stagnating preserves the Flood;
Which, thus fermenting, by Degrees
Exalts the Spirits, sinks the Lees.   130

Stella, for once you reason wrong;
For should this Ferment last too long,
By Time subsiding, you may find
Nothing but Acid left behind.
From Passion you may then be freed,
When Peevishness and Spleen succeed.

Say *Stella*, when you copy next,
Will you keep strictly to the Text?
Dare you let these Reproaches stand,
And to your Failing set your Hand?   140

Or if these Lines your Anger fire,
Shall they in baser Flames expire?
Whene'er they burn, if burn they must,
They'll prove my Accusation just.

                                        1720/1727

Stella's Birth-Day

1720-1

ALL Travellers at first incline
Where'er they see the fairest Sign;
And if they find the Chambers neat,
And like the Liquor, and the Meat,
Will call again, and recommend
The *Angel*-Inn to ev'ry Friend:
What though the Painting grows decay'd,
The House will never lose its Trade:
Nay, tho' the treach'rous Tapster *Thomas*
Hangs a new *Angel* two doors from us,   10
As fine as Dawbers Hand can make it,
In hopes that Strangers may mistake it;
We think it both a Shame and Sin
To quit the true old *Angel*-Inn.

Now, this is *Stella*'s Case in fact,
An *Angel*'s Face, a little crack'd:
(Could Poets, or could Painters fix
How *Angels* look at Thirty-six:)
This drew us in at first, to find
In such a Form an *Angel*'s Mind;   20
And ev'ry Virtue now supplies
The fainting Rays of *Stella*'s Eyes.
See, at her Levee crowding Swains;
Whom *Stella* freely entertains
With Breeding, Humour, Wit and Sense:

144

And puts them to so small Expence:
Their Mind so plentifully fills,
And makes such reasonable Bills;
So little gets for what she gives,
We really wonder how she lives!   30
And had her Stock been less, no doubt,
She must have long ago run out.

   Then who can think we'll quit the Place,
When *Doll* hangs out a newer Face;
Or stop and light at *Cloe*'s Head,
With Scraps and Leavings to be fed.

   Then *Cloe*, still go on to prate
Of Thirty-six and Thirty-eight:
Pursue your Trade of Scandal-picking,
Your Hints, that *Stella* is no *Chicken*:   40
Your Innuendo's, when you tell us,
That *Stella* loves to talk with Fellows:
And let me warn you to believe
A Truth, for which your Soul should grieve:
That should you live to see the Day
When *Stella*'s Locks must all be grey:
When Age must print a furrow'd Trace
On ev'ry Feature of her Face:
Though you, and all your senseless Tribe,
Could Art, or Time, or Nature Bribe,   50
To make you look like Beauty's Queen,
And hold for ever at Fifteen:
No Bloom of Youth can ever blind
The Cracks and Wrinkles of your Mind:
All Men of Sense will pass your Door,
And crowd to *Stella*'s at Fourscore.
                                1720/1727

145

To Stella,
on her Birthday

1721–2

WHILE, Stella, to your lasting praise
The Muse her annual tribute pays,
While I assign myself a task
Which you expect, but scorn to ask;
If I perform this task with pain,
Let me of partial fate complain;
You every year the debt enlarge,
I grow less equal to the charge:
In you each virtue brighter shines,
But my poetick vein declines;   10
My harp will soon in vain be strung,
And all your virtues left unsung.
For none among the upstart race
Of poets dare assume my place;
Your worth will be to them unknown,
They must have Stellas of their own;
And thus, my stock of wit decay'd,
I dying leave the debt unpaid,
Unless Delany, as my heir,
Will answer for the whole arrear.   20

1722/1766

Stella's Birth-Day
A great Bottle of Wine, long buried,
being that Day dug up

1722–3

RESOLV'D my annual Verse to pay,
By Duty bound, on *Stella's* Day;
Furnish'd with Paper, Pens, and Ink,

I gravely sat me down to think:
I bit my Nails, and scratch'd my Head,
But found my Wit and Fancy fled:
Or, if with more than usual Pain,
A Thought came slowly from my Brain,
It cost me, Lord knows, how much Time
To shape it into Sense and Rhyme: 10
And, what was yet a greater Curse,
Long-thinking made my Fancy worse.

Forsaken by th' inspiring Nine,
I waited at *Apollo*'s Shrine;
I told him what the World would say
If *Stella* were unsung To-day;
How I should hide my head for Shame,
When both the *Jacks* and *Robin* came;
How *Ford* would frown, how *Jim* would leer;
How *Sheridan* the Rogue would sneer: 20
And swear it does not always follow,
That *Semel'n anno ridet Apollo.*
I have assur'd them twenty Times,
That *Phœbus* help'd me in my Rhymes;
Phœbus inspir'd me from above,
And He and I were Hand and Glove,
But finding me so dull and dry since,
They'll call it all poetick Licence:
And when I brag of Aid Divine,
Think *Eusden*'s Right as good as mine.   30

Nor do I ask for *Stella*'s Sake;
'Tis my own Credit lies at Stake.
And *Stella* will be sung, while I
Can only be a Stander-by.

Apollo, having thought a little,
Return'd this Answer to a Tittle.

147

Though you should live like old
    Methusalem,
I furnish Hints, and you should use all 'em;
You yearly sing as she grows old,
You'd leave her Virtues half untold;   40
But to say Truth, such Dullness reigns
Through the whole set of *Irish* Deans;
I'm daily stunn'd with such a Medley,
Dean *W[oo]d*, Dean *D[anie]l*, and Dean
    Smedley,
That, let what Dean soever come,
My Orders are, I'm not at Home;
And if your Voice had not been loud,
You must have pass'd among the Crowd.

But now, your Danger to prevent,
You must apply to [1]Mrs. *Brent*.   50
For she, as Priestess, knows the Rites,
Wherein the God of *Earth* delights.
First, nine Ways looking, let her stand
With an old Poker in her Hand;
Let her describe a Circle round
In [2]*Saunder*'s Cellar on the Ground:
A Spade let prudent [3]*Archy* hold,
And with Discretion dig the Mould:
Let *Stella* look with watchful Eye,
[4]*Rebecca*, [5]*Ford*, and *Grattans* by.   60

Behold the Bottle, where it lies
With Neck elated tow'rds the Skies!
The God of Winds and God of Fire,
Did to its wond'rous Birth conspire;
And *Bacchus*, for the Poet's Use,
Pour'd in a strong inspiring Juice:

[1] *The House-keeper.*   [2] *The Butler.*   [3] *The Footman.*
[4] *A Lady, Friend to* Stella.
[5] *Gentlemen, Friends to the Author.*

See! as you raise it from its Tomb,
It drags behind a spacious Womb,
And in the spacious Womb contains
A sov'reign Med'cine for the Brains.   70

You'll find it soon, if Fate consents;
If not, a Thousand Mrs. *Brents*,
Ten Thousand *Archys* arm'd with Spades,
May dig in vain to *Pluto*'s Shades.

From thence a plenteous Draught infuse,
And boldly then invoke the Muse:
(But first let [1]*Robert* on his Knees,
With Caution drain it from the Lees)
The Muse will at your Call appear,
With *Stella*'s Praise to crown the Year.   80
                                    1723/1727

Stella at Wood-Park

A House of Charles Ford, Esq; eight
Miles from Dublin

—*Cuicunque nocere volebat
Vestimenta dabat pretiosa.*

DON *Carlos* in a merry Spight,
Did *Stella* to his House invite:
He entertain'd her half a Year
With gen'rous Wines and costly Chear.
Don *Carlos* made her chief Director,
That she might o'er the Servants hector.
In half a Week the Dame grew nice,
Got all things at the highest Price.
Now at the Table-Head she sits,
Presented with the nicest Bits: 10

[1] *The Valet.*

149

She look'd on Partridges with Scorn,
Except they tasted of the Corn:
A Haunch of Ven'son made her sweat,
Unless it had the right *Fumette*.
Don *Carlos* earnestly would beg,
Dear Madam, try this Pigeon's Leg;
Was happy when he could prevail
To make her only touch a Quail.
Through Candle-Light she view'd the Wine,
To see that ev'ry Glass was fine.   20
At last grown prouder than the D—l,
With feeding high, and Treatment civil,
Don *Carlos* now began to find
His Malice work as he design'd;
The Winter-Sky began to frown,
Poor *Stella* must pack off to Town.
From purling Streams and Fountains bub-
     bling,
To ¹*Liffy*'s stinking Tide in *Dublin*:
From wholsome Exercise and Air
To sossing in an easy Chair;   30
From Stomach sharp and hearty feeding,
To piddle like a Lady breeding:
From ruling there the Houshold singly,
To be directed here by ²*Dingly*:
From ev'ry Day a lordly Banquet,
To half a joint, and God be thanked:
From ev'ry Meal *Pontack* in Plenty,
To half a Pint one Day in Twenty.
From Ford attending at her Call,
To Visits of [*Archdeacon Wall*].   40
From *Ford*, who thinks of nothing mean,
To the poor Doings of the D[ea]n.
From growing Richer with good Chear,
To running out by starving here.

¹ *The River that runs through* Dublin.
² *A Lady. The two Ladies lodged together.*

But now arrives the dismal Day:
She must return to ¹*Ormond-Key*:
The Coachman stopt, she lookt, and swore
The Rascal had mistook the Door:
At coming in you saw her stoop;
The Entry brushed against her Hoop: 50
Each Moment rising in her Airs,
She curst the narrow winding Stairs:
Began a Thousand Faults to spy;
The Cieling hardly six Foot high;
The smutty Wainscot full of Cracks,
And half the Chairs with broken Backs:
Her Quarter's out at *Lady-Day*,
She vows she will no longer stay,
In Lodgings, like a poor *Grizette*,
While there are Lodgings to be lett.   60

Howe'er, to keep her Spirits up,
She sent for Company to sup;
When all the while you might remark,
She strove in vain to ape *Wood-Park*.
Two Bottles call'd for, (half her Store;
The Cupboard could contain but four;)
A Supper worthy of her self,
Five *Nothings* in five Plates of *Delph*.

Thus, for a Week the Farce went on;
When all her Country-Savings gone: 70
She fell into her former Scene,
Small Beer, a Herring, and the D[ea]n.

Thus far in jest. Though, now I fear,
You think my Jesting too severe:
But Poets when a Hint is new
Regard not whether false or true:
Yet Raillery gives no Offence,

¹ *Where both the Ladies lodged.*

151

Where Truth has not the least Pretence;
Nor can be more securly plac't
Than on a Nymph of *Stella*'s Taste.　　　80
I must confess, your Wine and Vittle
I was too hard upon *a little*;
Your Table neat, your Linnen fine;
And, though in Miniature, you shine.
Yet, when you sigh to leave *Wood-Park*,
The Scene, the Welcome, and the Spark,
To languish in this odious Town,
And pull your haughty Stomach down;
We think you quite mistake the Case;
The Virtue lies not in the Place:　　　90
For though my Raillery were true,
A Cottage is *Wood-Park* with you.
1723/1735

To Stella

Written on the Day of her Birth, but not
on the Subject, when I was sick in bed

1723–4

TORMENTED with incessant pains,
Can I devise poetic strains?
Time was, when I could yearly pay
My verse on Stella's native day:
But now, unable grown to write,
I grieve she ever saw the light.
Ungrateful; since to her I owe
That I these pains can undergo.
She tends me, like an humble slave;
And, when indecently I rave,　　　10
When out my brutish passions break,
With gall in ev'ry word I speak,
She, with soft speech, my anguish chears,

152

Or melts my passions down with tears:
Although 'tis easy to descry
She wants assistance more than I;
Yet seems to feel my pains alone,
And is a Stoic in her own.
When, among scholars, can we find
So soft, and yet so firm a mind?   20
All accidents of life conspire
To raise up Stella's virtue higher;
Or else, to introduce the rest
Which had been latent in her breast.
Her firmness who could e'er have known,
Had she not evils of her own?
Her kindness who could ever guess,
Had not her friends been in distress?
Whatever base returns you find
From me, dear Stella, still be kind;   30
In your own heart you'll reap the fruit,
Tho' I continue still a brute.
But when I once am out of pain,
I promise to be good again:
Meantime your other juster friends
Shall for my follies make amends:
So may we long continue thus,
Admiring you, you pitying us.

                                          1724/1765

Stella's Birth-Day

1724–5

As, when a beauteous Nymph decays,
We say, she's past her Dancing Days;
So, Poets lose their Feet by Time,
And can no longer dance in Rhyme.
Your annual Bard had rather chose

To celebrate your Birth in Prose.
Yet, merry Folks, who want by chance,
A Pair to make a Country-Dance,
Call the old House-keeper, and get her
To fill a Place, for want of better.   10
While *Sheridan* is off the Hooks,
And Friend *Delany* at his Books,
That *Stella* may avoid Disgrace,
Once more the *D[ea]n* supplies their Place.

   Beauty and Wit, too sad a Truth,
Have always been confin'd to Youth;
The God of Wit, and Beauty's Queen,
He Twenty-one, and she Fifteen:
No Poet ever sweetly sung,
Unless he were like *Phœbus*, young;   20
Nor ever Nymph inspir'd to rhyme,
Unless like *Venus*, in her Prime.
At fifty-six, if this be true,
Am I a Poet fit for you?
Or at the Age of Forty-three
Are you a Subject fit for me?
Adieu bright Wit, and radiant Eyes;
You must be grave, and I be wise.
Our Fate in vain we would oppose,
But I'll be still your Friend in Prose;   30
Esteem and Friendship to express,
Will not require poetick Dress;
And if the Muse deny her Aid
To have them *sung*, they must be *said*.

   But, *Stella* say, what evil Tongue
Reports you are no longer young?
That *Time* sits with his Scythe to mow,
Where erst sate *Cupid* with his Bow;
That half your Locks are turn'd to grey:
I'll ne'er believe a Word they say.   40

'Tis true, but let it not be known,
My Eyes are somewhat dimmish grown:
For Nature, always in the Right,
To your Decays adapts my Sight;
And Wrinkles undistinguish'd pass,
For I'm asham'd to use a Glass;
And, 'till I see them with these Eyes,
Whoever says you have them, lyes.

    No Length of Time can make you quit
Honour and Virtue, Sense and Wit: 50
Thus you may still be young to me,
While I can better *hear* than *see*:
Oh, ne'er may Fortune shew her Spight,
To make me *deaf*, and mend my *Sight*.
1725/1727

A Receipt to restore Stella's Youth

    THE Scottish Hinds too poor to house
In frosty Nights their starving Cows,
While not a Blade of Grass, or Hay,
Appears from *Michaelmas* to *May*;
Must let their Cattle range in vain
For Food, along the barren Plain;
Meager and lank with fasting grown,
And nothing left but Skin and Bone;
Expos'd to Want, and Wind, and Weather,
They just keep Life and Soul together,   10
'Till Summer Show'rs and Ev'ning Dew,
Again the verdant Glebe renew;
And as the Vegetables rise,
The famish't Cow her Want supplies;

155

Without an Ounce of last Year's Flesh,
Whate'er she gains is young and fresh;
Grows plump and round, and full of Mettle,
As rising from *Medea*'s Kettle;
With Youth and Beauty to enchant
Europa's counterfeit Gallant.   20

Why, *Stella*, should you knit your Brow,
If I compare you to the Cow?
'Tis just the Case: For you have fasted
So long till all your Flesh is wasted,
And must against the warmer Days,
Be sent to ¹*Quilca* down to graze;
Where Mirth, and Exercise, and Air,
Will soon your Appetite repair,
The Nutriment will from within,
Round all your Body, plump your Skin;   30
Will agitate the lazy Flood,
And fill your Veins with sprightly Blood:
Nor Flesh nor Blood will be the same,
Nor ought of *Stella*, but the Name;
For, what was ever understood
By human Kind, but Flesh and Blood?
And if your Flesh and Blood be new,
You'll be no more your former *You*,
But for a blooming Nymph will pass,
Just Fifteen, coming Summer's Grass: 40
Your jetty Locks with Garlands crown'd,
While all the 'Squires from nine Miles
    round,
Attended by a Brace of Curs,
With Jockey Boots, and Silver Spurs;
No less than Justices o' *Quorum*,
Their Cow-boys bearing Cloaks before 'um,
Shall leave deciding broken Pates,
To kiss your Steps at *Quilca* Gates;

¹ *A Friend's House seven or eight Miles from Dublin.*

But, lest you should my Skill disgrace,
Come back before you're out of Case: 50
For, if to *Michaelmas* you stay,
The new-born Flesh will melt away;
The 'Squires in Scorn will fly the House
For better Game, and look for Grouse:
But here, before the Frost can marr it,
We'll make it firm with Beef and Claret.

                                        1725/1735

Stella's Birth-Day

1726-7

THIS Day, whate'er the Fates decree,
Shall still be kept with Joy by me:
This Day then, let us not be told,
That you are sick, and I grown old,
Nor think on our approaching Ills,
And talk of Spectacles and Pills.
To-morrow will be time enough
To hear such mortifying Stuff.
Yet, since from Reason may be brought
A better and more pleasing Thought,   10
Which can, in spight of all Decays,
Support a few remaining Days:
From not the gravest of Divines,
Accept, for once, some serious Lines.

   Although we now can form no more
Long Schemes of Life, as heretofore;
Yet you, while Time is running fast,
Can look with Joy on what is past.

   Were future Happiness and Pain,
A mere Contrivance of the Brain,   20

As *Atheists* argue, to entice,
And fit their Proselytes for Vice;
(The only Comfort they propose,
To have Companions in their Woes.)
Grant this the Case; yet sure 'tis hard,
That Virtue, stil'd its own Reward,
And by all Sages understood
To be the chief of human Good,
Should acting, die, nor leave behind
Some lasting Pleasure in the Mind;　　　30
Which by Remembrance will asswage
Grief, Sickness, Poverty, and Age;
And strongly shoot a radiant Dart
To shine through Life's declining Part.

Say, *Stella*, feel you no Content,
Reflecting on a Life well spent?
Your skilful Hand employ'd to save
Despairing Wretches from the Grave;
And then supporting with your Store,
Those whom you dragg'd from Death
　　　before:　　　40
(So Providence on Mortals waits,
Preserving what it first creates)
Your generous Boldness to defend
An innocent and absent Friend:
That Courage which can make you just,
To Merit humbled in the Dust:
The Detestation you express
For Vice in all its glitt'ring Dress:
That Patience under tort'ring Pain,
Where stubborn Stoicks would complain. 50

Shall these, like empty shadows, pass,
Or Forms reflected from a Glass?
Or mere Chimæra's in the Mind,
That fly and leave no Marks behind?

Does not the Body thrive and grow
By Food of twenty Years ago?
And, had it not been still supply'd,
It must a thousand times have dy'd.
Then, who with Reason can maintain,
That no Effects of Food remain?   60
And is not Virtue in Mankind
The Nutriment that feeds the Mind?
Upheld by each good Action past,
And still continu'd by the last:
Then, who with Reason can pretend,
That all Effects of Virtue end?

    Believe me, *Stella*, when you show
That true Contempt for Things below,
Nor prize your Life for other Ends,
Than merely to oblige your Friends;   70
Your former Actions claim their Part,
And join to fortify your Heart.
For Virtue, in her daily Race,
Like *Janus*, bears a double Face;
Looks back with Joy where she has gone,
And therefore goes with Courage on.
She at your sickly Couch will wait,
And guide you to a better State.

    O then, whatever Heav'n intends,
Take Pity on your pitying Friends;   80
Nor let your Ills affect your Mind,
To fancy they can be unkind.
Me, surely Me, you ought to spare,
Who gladly would your Suff'rings share;
Or give my Scrap of Life to you,
And think it far beneath your Due:
You, to whose Care so oft I owe,
That I'm alive to tell you so.

1727/1727

POEMS
AT MARKET HILL

Lady Acheson Weary of the Dean

THE Dean would visit *Market-hill*,
    Our Invitation was but slight;
I said,—Why let him, if he will,
    And so I bid Sir *A[rthu]r* write.

His Manners would not let him wait,
    Lest we should think ourselves neglected;
And, so we saw him at our Gate
    Three Days before he was expected.

After a Week, a Month, a Quarter,
    And Day succeeding after Day,   10
Says not a word of his Departure,
    'Though not a Soul would have him stay.

I've said enough to make him blush,
    Methinks, or else the Devil's in't;
But he cares not for it a Rush,
    Nor, for my Life, will take the Hint.

But you, my Dear, may let him know,
    In civil Language, if he stays,
How deep and foul the Roads may grow,
    And that he may command the Chaise.   20

Or you may say—my Wife intends,
    (Though I should be exceeding proud)
This Winter to invite some Friends,
    And, Sir, I know, you hate a Crowd.

Or, Mr. Dean—I should with Joy
   Beg you would here continue still,
But we must go to [1]*Aghnacloy*,
   Or, Mr. *Moore* will take it ill.

The House Accounts are daily rising,
   So much his Stay doth swell the Bills: 30
My dearest Life, it is surprizing,
   How much he eats, how much he swills.

His Brace of Puppies how they stuff,
   And they must have three Meals a Day,
Yet never think they get enough;
   His Horses too eat all our Hay.

Oh! if I could, how I would maul
   His Tallow Face, and Wainscot Paws,
His Beetle-brows and Eyes of Wall,
   And make him soon give up the Cause.   40

Must I be ev'ry Moment chid
   With [2]Skinny, Bonia, Snip and Lean;
Oh! that I could but once be rid
   Of this insulting Tyrant Dean!

                   1728?/1730

My Lady's Lamentation
and Complaint against the Dean

    SURE never did man see
    A wretch like poor Nancy,
    So teaz'd day and night
    By a Dean and a Knight;

[1] The Seat of *Acheson Moore*, Esq.
[2] The Dean used to call Lady *Acheson* by those Names.

164

To punish my sins,
Sir Arthur begins,
And gives me a wipe
With Skinny and Snipe:
His malice is plain,
Hallooing the Dean.   10
The Dean never stops,
When he opens his chops;
I'm quite over-run
With rebus and pun.

Before he came here
To spunge for good cheer,
I sat with delight,
From morning till night,
With two bony thumbs
Could rub my own gums,   20
Or scratching my nose,
And jogging my toes;
But at present, forsooth,
I must not rub a tooth:
When my elbows he sees
Held up by my knees,
My arms, like two props,
Supporting my chops,
And just as I handle 'em
Moving all like a pendulum;   30
He trips up my props,
And down my chin drops,
From my head to my heels,
Like a clock without wheels;
I sink in the spleen,
An useless machine.

If he had his will,
I should never sit still:
He comes with his whims,

I must move my limbs;   40
I cannot be sweet
Without using my feet;
To lengthen my breath
He tires me to death.
By the worst of all Squires,
Thro' bogs and thro' briers,
Where a cow would be startled,
I'm in spite of my heart led:
And, say what I will,
Haul'd up every hill;   50
'Till, daggled and tatter'd,
My spirit's quite shatter'd,
I return home at night,
And fast out of spite:
For I'd rather be dead,
Than it e'er should be said
I was better for him,
In stomach or limb.

.   But, now to my diet,
No eating in quiet,   60
He's still finding fault,
Too sour or too salt:
The wing of a chick
I hardly can pick,
But trash without measure
I swallow with pleasure.

Next, for his diversion,
He rails at my person:
What court-breeding this is?
He takes me to pieces.   70
From shoulder to flank
I'm lean and am lank;
My nose, long and thin,
Grows down to my chin;

My chin will not stay,
But meets it half way:
My fingers, prolix,
Are ten crooked sticks:
He swears my el—bows
Are two iron crows,   80
Or sharp pointed rocks,
And wear out my smocks:
To 'scape them, Sir Arthur
Is forced to lie farther,
Or his sides they would gore,
Like the tusks of a boar.

Now, changing the scene,
But still to the Dean:
He loves to be bitter at
A lady illiterate;   90
If he sees her but once,
He'll swear she's a dunce;
Can tell her by looks
A hater of books:
Thro' each line of her face
Her folly can trace;
Which spoils ev'ry feature
Bestow'd by her nature,
But sense gives a grace
To the homeliest face: 100
Wise books and reflection
Will mend the complexion.
(A civil Divine!
I suppose meaning mine.)
No Lady who wants them
Can ever be handsome.

I guess well enough
What he means by this stuff:

167

He haws and he hums,
At last out it comes.   110

What, Madam? No walking,
No reading, nor talking?
You're now in your prime,
Make use of your time.
Consider, before
You come to threescore,
How the hussies will fleer
Where'er you appear:
That silly old puss
Would fain be like us,   120
What a figure she made
In her tarnish'd brocade?

And then he grows mild:
Come, be a good child:
If you are inclin'd
To polish your mind,
Be ador'd by the men
'Till threescore and ten,
And kill with the spleen
The jades of sixteen,   130
I'll shew you the way:
Read six hours a-day.
The wits will frequent ye,
And think you but twenty.

Thus was I drawn in,
Forgive me my sin.
At breakfast he'll ask
An account of my task.
Put a word out of joint,
Or miss but a point,   140
He rages and frets,
His manners forgets;

And, as I am serious,
Is very imperious.
No book for delight
Must come in my sight:
But, instead of new plays,
Dull Bacon's Essays,
And pore ev'ry day on
That nasty Pantheon. 150
If I be not a drudge,
Let all the world judge,
'Twere better be blind,
Than thus be confin'd.

But, while in an ill tone,
I murder poor Milton,
The Dean, you will swear,
Is at study or pray'r.
He's all the day saunt'ring,
With labourers bant'ring, 160
Among his colleagues,
A parcel of Teagues,
(Whom he brings in among us
And bribes with mundungus.)
Hail fellow, well met,
All dirty and wet:
Find out, if you can,
Who's master, who's man;
Who makes the best figure,
The Dean or the digger; 170
And which is the best
At cracking a jest.
How proudly he talks
Or zigzags and walks;
And all the day raves
Of cradles and caves;
And boasts of his feats,
His grottos and seats;

169

Shews all his gew-gaws
And gapes for applause?   180
A fine occupation
For one in his station!
A hole where a rabbit
Would scorn to inhabit,
Dug out in an hour,
He calls it a bow'r.

But, Oh, how we laugh,
To see a wild calf
Come, driven by heat,
And foul the green seat;   190
Or run helter skelter
To his arbor for shelter,
Where all goes to ruin
The Dean has been doing.
The girls of the village
Come flocking for pillage,
Pull down the fine briers,
And thorns, to make fires;
But yet are so kind
To leave something behind: 200
No more need be said on't,
I smell where I tread on't.

Dear friend, Doctor Jenny,
If I could but win ye,
Or Walmsley or Whaley,
To come hither daily,
Since fortune, my foe,
Will needs have it so,
That I'm, by her frowns,
Condemn'd to black gowns;   210
No Squire to be found
The neighbourhood round,
(For, under the rose,

```
            I would rather chuse those:)
            If your wives will permit ye,
            Come here out of pity,
            To ease a poor Lady,
            And beg her a play-day.
            So may you be seen
            No more in the spleen:              220
            May Walmsley give wine,
            Like a hearty divine;
            May Whaley disgrace
            Dull Daniel's whey-face;
            And may your three spouses
            Let you lie at friends houses.
                              1728/1765
```

On Cutting Down the Old Thorn
at Market-Hill

AT *Market-Hill*, as well appears
   By Chronicle of ancient Date,
There stood for many a Hundred Years,
   A spacious Thorn before the Gate.

Hither came every Village-Maid,
   And on the Boughs her Garland hung;
And here, beneath the spreading Shade,
   Secure from Satyrs, sat and sung.

[1]Sir *Archibald*, that val'rous Knight,
   Then Lord of all the fruitful Plain,   10
Would come to listen with Delight,
   For he was fond of rural Strain.

---

[1] *Sir* Archibald Acheson, *Secretary of State for* Scotland.

171

(Sir *Archibald* whose fav'rite Name
   Shall stand for Ages on Record,
By *Scottish* Bards of highest Fame,
   [1]Wise *Hawthorden* and *Sterling*'s Lord.)

But Time, with Iron Teeth, I ween,
   Has canker'd all its Branches round;
No Fruit or Blossom to be seen,
   Its Head reclining tow'rds the Ground.   20

This aged, sickly, sapless Thorn,
   Which must alas no longer stand;
Behold! the cruel Dean in Scorn
   Cuts down with sacrilegious Hand.

Dame Nature, when she saw the Blow,
   Astonish'd gave a dreadful Shriek;
And Mother *Tellus* trembled so,
   She scarce recover'd in a Week.

The *Sylvan* Pow'rs with Fear perplex'd,
   In Prudence and Compassion sent,   30
(For none could tell whose Turn was next)
   Sad Omens of the dire Event.

The Magpye, lighting on the Stock,
   Stood chatt'ring with incessant Din;
And with her Beak gave many a Knock
   To rouze and warn the Nymph within.

The Owl foresaw in pensive Mood,
   The ruin of her antient Seat;
And fled in Haste with all her Brood,
   To seek a more secure Retreat.   40

[1] Drummond *of* Hawthorden, *and Sir* William Alexander, *Earl of* Sterling, *both famous for their Poetry, who were Friends to Sir* Archibald.

Last trotted forth the gentle Swine,
    To ease her Itch against the Stump,
And dismally was heard to whine,
    All as she scrubb'd her meazly Rump.

The Nymph who dwells in every Tree,
    (If all be true that Poets chant)
Condemn'd by Fate's supreme Decree,
    Must die with her expiring Plant.

Thus, when the gentle *Spina* found
    The Thorn committed to her Care,   50
Receiv'd its last and deadly Wound,
    She fled and vanish'd into Air.

But from the Root a dismal Groan
    First issuing, struck the Murd'rer's Ears;
And in a shrill revengeful Tone,
    This Prophecy he trembling hears.

'Thou chief Contriver of my Fall,
    'Relentless Dean! to Mischief born,
'My Kindred oft thine Hide shall gall;
    'Thy Gown and Cassock oft be torn.   60

'And thy confed'rate Dame who brags
    'That she condemn'd me to the Fire,
'Shall rent her Petticoats to Rags,
    'And wound her Legs with ev'ry Bri'r.

'Nor thou, Lord [1]*Arthur*, shalt escape,
    'To thee I often call'd in vain,
'Against that Assassin in Crape,
    'Yet thou couldst tamely see me slain.

---

[1] *Sir* Arthur Acheson.

'Nor, when I felt the dreadful Blow,
   'Or chid the Dean, or pinch'd thy Spouse;
'Since you could see me treated so;   71
   'An old Retainer to your House.

'May that fell Dean, by whose Command
   'Was form'd this *Machi'vilian* Plot,
'Not leave a Thistle on thy Land;
   'Then who will own thee for a *Scot*?

'Pigs and Fanaticks, Cows, and Teagues,
   'Through all thy Empire I foresee,
'To tear thy Hedges join in Leagues,
   'Sworn to revenge my Thorn and me.   80

'And thou, the Wretch ordain'd by Fate
   '*Neal Gaghagan*, *Hibernian* Clown,
'With Hatchet blunter than thy Pate,
   'To hack my hallow'd Timber down;

'When thou, suspended high in Air,
   'Dy'st on a more ignoble Tree,
'(For thou shalt steal thy Landlord's Mare)
   'Then, bloody *Caitif*, think on me.'
                        1728/1732

Upon a Very Old Glass

The Following Lines were Wrote upon a Very
Old Glass of Sir Arthur Acheson's

FRAIL Glass, thou Mortal art, as well as I,
Tho' none can tell, which of us first shall dye.

174

ANSWERED EXTEMPORE BY DR. SWIFT

WE both are Mortal; but thou, frailer Creature,
May'st dye like me by Chance; but not by Nature.
                                    1728/1746

To Janus on New-Year's Day

    Two fac'd *Janus*, God of Time,
Be my *Phœbus* while I rhyme,
To oblige your Crony S[*wif*]*t*,
Bring our Dame a New-Year's Gift:
She has got but half a Face:
Janus, since thou hast a Brace,
To my Lady once be kind;
Give her half thy Face behi**nd.**

    God of Time, if you be wise,
Look not with your future Eyes: 10
What imports thy forward Sight?
Well, if you could lose it quite.
Can you take Delight in viewing
This poor Isle's approaching Ruin?
When thy Retrospection vast,
Sees the glorious Ages past.

    Happy Nation were we blind,
Or, had only Eyes behind.—

    Drown your Morals, Madam cryes;
I'll have none but forward Eyes: 20
Prudes decay'd about may tack,
Strain their Necks with looking back:
Give me *Time* when coming on;
Who regards him when he's gone?

By the D[ea]n though gravely told,
New Years help to make me old;
Yet I find, a New-Year's Lace
Burnishes an old Year's Face.
Give me Velvet and Quadrille.
I'll have Youth and Beauty still.   30
                                    1729/1735

[SECOND VISIT]

The Grand Question Debated: Whether Hamilton's [1]Bawn should be turned into a Barrack or a Malt-house

THUS spoke to my Lady, the Knight full of Care,
Let me have your Advice in a weighty Affair.
This [2]HAMILTON'S *Bawn*, while it sticks on my Hand,
I lose by the House what I get by the Land;
But how to dispose of it to the best Bidder,
For a [3]*Barrack* or *Malt-house*, we now must consider.

First, let me suppose, I make it a *Malt-house*:
Here I have computed the Profit will fall t'us,
There's nine hundred Pounds for Labour and Grain,
I increase it to twelve, so three hundred remain: 10
A handsome Addition for Wine and good Chear,
Three Dishes a Day, and three Hogsheads a Year.
With a dozen large Vessels my Vault shall be stor'd,

[1] A BAWN was a Place near the House inclosed with Mud or Stone Walls, to keep Cattle from being stolen in the Night. They are now little used.
[2] *A large House two Miles from Sir* A[rthur] A[cheson]'*s Seat.*
[3] *The Army in Ireland is lodged in strong Buildings over the whole Kingdom, called* Barracks.

No little scrub Joint shall come on my Board:
And you and the *Dean* no more shall combine,
To stint me at Night to one Bottle of Wine;
Nor shall I, for his Humour, permit you to purloin
A Stone and a Quarter of Beef from my Sirloin.
If I make it a *Barrack*, the Crown is my Tenant,
My Dear, I have ponder'd again and again on't: 20
In Poundage and Drawbacks, I lose half my Rent,
Whatever they give me I must be content,
Or join with the Court in ev'ry Debate,
And rather than that, I would lose my Estate.

   Thus ended the Knight: Thus began his *meek* Wife:
It *must*, and it *shall* be a *Barrack*, my Life.
I'm grown a meer Mopus; no Company comes;
But a Rabble of Tenants, and rusty dull [1]*Rums*;
With *Parsons*, what Lady can keep herself clean?
I'm all over dawb'd when I sit by the *Dean*.   30
But, if you will give us a *Barrack*, my Dear,
The *Captain*, I'm sure, will always come here;
I then shall not value his Deanship a Straw,
For the Captain, I warrant, will keep him in Awe;
Or should he pretend to be brisk and alert,
Will tell him, that Chaplains should not be so pert;
That Men of his Coat should be minding their Pray'rs,
And not among Ladies to give themselves Airs.

   Thus argu'd my Lady, but argu'd in vain;
The Knight his Opinion resolv'd to maintain.   40

   But, [2]*Hannah*, who listen'd to all that was past,
And could not endure so vulgar a Taste;
As soon as her Ladyship call'd to be drest,
Cry'd, Madam, why surely my Master's possest;
Sir *Arthur the Malster!* how fine it will sound?

---

[1] *A Cant Word in* Ireland *for a poor Country Clergyman.*
[2] *My Lady's Waiting Woman.*

I'd rather the *Bawn* were sunk under Ground.
But, Madam, I guess'd there would never come Good,
When I saw him so often with ¹*Darby* and *Wood*.
And now my Dream's out: For I was a-dream'd
That I saw a huge Rat; O dear, how I screamed!   50
And after, methought, I had lost my new Shoes;
And *Molly*, she said, I should hear some ill News.

Dear Madam, had you but the Spirit to teaze,
You might have a *Barrack* whenever you please:
And, Madam, I always believ'd you so stout,
That for twenty Denials you wou'd not give out.
If I had a Husband like him, I *purtest*,
'Till he gave me my Will, I would give him no Rest:
And rather than come in the same Pair of Sheets
With such a Cross Man, I would lie in the Streets. 60
But, Madam, I beg you contrive and invent,
And worry him out, till he gives his Consent.

Dear Madam, whene'er of a *Barrack* I think,
An I were to be hang'd, I can't sleep a Wink:
For, if a new Crotchet comes into my Brain,
I can't get it out, tho' I'd never so fain,
I fancy already a *Barrack* contriv'd
At *Hamilton*'s *Bawn*, and the Troop is arriv'd:
Of this, to be sure, Sir *Arthur* has Warning,
And waits on the Captain betimes the next morning. 70

Now, see, when they meet, how their Honours be-
    have;
Noble *Captain*, your Servant,—Sir *Arthur* your Slave;
You honour me much—the Honour is mine—
'Twas a sad rainy Night—but the Morning is fine—
Pray, how does my Lady?—My Wife's at your ser-
    vice—
I think I have seen her Picture by *Jervis*.

¹ *Two of Sir* A[rthur]'s *Managers.*

178

Good morrow, good *Captain*,—I'll wait on you
    down—
You shan't stir a Foot.—You'll think me a Clown.—
For all the World, *Captain*, not half an Inch
    farther—
You must be obey'd—your Servant, Sir *Arthur*,   80
My humble Respects to my Lady unknown—
I hope you will use my House as your own.

    'Go, bring me my Smock, and leave off your Prate,
'Thou hast certainly gotten a Cup in thy Pate.'
Pray, Madam, be quiet; what was it I said?—
You had like to have put it quite out of my Head.

    Next Day, to be sure, the *Captain* will come
At the Head of his Troop, with Trumpet and Drum,
Now, Madam, observe, how he marches in State:
The Man with the Kettle-drum enters the Gate;   90
Dub, *dub*, *a-dub*, *dub*. The Trumpeters follow,
Tantara, *tantara*, while all the Boys halloo.
See, now comes the *Captain*, all dawb'd with Gold-
    lace:
O law! the sweet Gentleman, look in his Face;
And see how he rides like a Lord of the Land,
With the fine flaming Sword that he holds in his
    Hand;
And his Horse, the dear *Creter*, it prances and rears,
With Ribbons in Knots, at its Tail and its Ears,
At last comes the Troop, by the Word of Command
Drawn up in our Court, when the *Captain* cries,
    Stand.   100
Your *Ladyship* lifts up the Sash to be seen,
(For sure I had *dizen'd* you out like a Queen)
The *Captain*, to shew he is proud of the Favour,
Looks up to your *Window*, and cocks up his Beaver.
(His Beaver is cock'd; pray, Madam, mark that,
For, a *Captain* of Horse never takes off his Hat;

Because he has never a Hand that is idle;
For, the Right holds the Sword, and the Left holds
    the Bridle.)
Then flourishes thrice his Sword in the Air,
As a Compliment due to a Lady so fair;   110
How I tremble to think of the Blood it hath spilt!
Then he low'rs down the point, and kisses the Hilt.
Your *Ladyship* smiles, and thus you begin;
Pray, *Captain*, be pleas'd to light, and walk in:
The *Captain* salutes you with Congee profound;
And your *Ladyship* curchyes half way to the Ground.

   Kit, run to your Master, and bid him come to us,
I'm sure he'll be proud of the Honour you do us;
And, *Captain*, you'll do us the Favour to stay,
And take a short Dinner here with us To-day: 120
You're heartily welcome: But as for good Cheer,
You come in the very worst time of the Year;
If I had expected so worthy a Guest:—
Lord! Madam! your Ladyship sure is in Jest;
You *banter* me, Madam, the Kingdom must grant—
You Officers, *Captain*, are so complaisant.

   'Hist, Huzzy, I think I hear some Body coming—'
No, Madam; 'tis only Sir *Arthur* a humming.

   To shorten my Tale, (for I hate a long Story,)
The *Captain* at Dinner appears in his Glory;   130
The *Dean* and the [1]*Doctor* have humbled their Pride,
For the *Captain*'s entreated to sit by your Side;
And, because he's their Betters, you carve for him
    first,
The *Parsons*, for Envy, are ready to burst:
The Servants amaz'd, are scarce ever able
To keep off their Eyes, as they wait at the Table;

[1] *Doctor* Jenny, *a Clergyman in the Neighbourhood.*

And, *Molly* and I have thrust in our Nose,
To peep at the *Captain*, in all his fine *Clo'es*:
Dear Madam, be sure he's a fine spoken Man,
Do but hear on the Clergy how glib his Tongue
    ran;   140
'And, Madam, says he, if such Dinners you give,
'You'll never want *Parsons* as long as you live;
'I ne'er knew a *Parson* without a good Nose,
'But the Devil's as welcome wherever he goes:
'G— d— me, they bid us reform and repent,
'But, Z—s, by their Looks, they never keep Lent:
'Mister *Curate*, for all your grave Looks, I'm afraid,
'You cast a Sheep's Eye on her Ladyship's Maid;
'I wish she wou'd lend you her pretty white Hand,
'In mending your Cassock, and smoothing your
    Band:'   150
(For the *Dean* was so shabby, and look'd like a
    Ninny,
That the *Captain* suppos'd he was *Curate* to *Jenny*.)
'Whenever you see a Cassock and Gown,
'A Hundred to One, but it covers a Clown;
'Observe how a *Parson* comes into a Room,
'G— d— me, he hobbles as bad as my Groom;
'A *Scholard*, when just from his College broke loose,
'Can hardly tell how to cry *Bo* to a Goose;
'Your [1]*Noveds*, and *Blutracks*, and *Omurs* and Stuff,
'By G— they don't signify this Pinch of Snuff.   160
'To give a young Gentleman right Education,
'The Army's the only good School in the Nation;
'My School-Master call'd me a Dunce and a Fool,
'But at Cuffs I was always the Cock of the School;
'I never cou'd take to my Book for the Blood o'me,
'And the Puppy confess'd, he expected no Good
    o'me,
'He caught me one Morning coquetting his Wife,
'But he maul'd me, I ne'er was so maul'd in my Life:

[1] *Ovids, Plutarchs, Homers.*

'So, I took to the Road, and what's very odd,
'The first Man I robb'd was a Parson by G— 170
'Now Madam, you'll think it a strange thing to say,
'But, the Sight of a Book makes me sick to this Day.'

    Never since I was born did I hear so much Wit,
And, Madam, I laugh'd till I thought I shou'd split.
So, then you look'd scornful, and snift at the *Dean*,
As, who shou'd say, *Now am I* [1]*Skinny and Lean?*
But, he durst not so much as once open his Lips,
And, the *Doctor* was plaguily down in the Hips.

    Thus, merciless *Hannah*, ran on in her Talk,
Till she heard the *Dean* call, *Will your Ladyship
    walk?* 180
Her *Ladyship* answers, *I'm just coming down*;
Then, turning to *Hannah*, and forcing a Frown,
Altho' it was plain, in her Heart she was glad,
Cry'd, Huzzy, why sure the *Wench* is gone mad:
How cou'd these *Chimera's* get into your Brains?—
Come hither, and take this old Gown for your Pains.
But the *Dean*, if this Secret shou'd come to his Ears,
Will never have done with his Gibes and his Jeers:
For your Life, not a Word of the Matter, I charge ye;
Give me but a *Barrack*, a Fig for the *Clergy*. 190
                        1729/1732

Drapier's Hill

    WE give the World to understand,
Our thriving D[ea]n has purchas'd Land;
A Purchase, which will bring him clear,
Above his Rent four Pounds a Year;
Provided, to improve the Ground,

         [1] *Nick-Names for my Lady.*

He will but add two Hundred Pound,
And from his endless hoarded Store,
To build a House five Hundred more.
[1]Sir *Arthur* too shall have his Will,
And call the Mansion *Drapier*'s Hill;   10
That when a Nation long enslav'd,
Forgets by whom it once was sav'd;
When none the DRAPIER's praise shall sing;
His Signs aloft no longer swing;
His Medals and his Prints forgotten,
And all his [2]Handkerchiefs are rotten;
His famous LETTERS made waste Paper;
This Hill may keep the Name of DRAPIER:
In Spight of Envy flourish still,
And DRAPIER's vye with COOPER's Hill.   20

                                    1729/1729

To Dean Swift
by Sir Arthur Acheson

GOOD cause have I to sing and vapour,
For I am landlord to the Drapier:
He, that of ev'ry ear's the charmer,
Now condescends to be my farmer,
And grace my villa with his strains;
Lives such a Bard on British plains?
No, not in all the British Court;
For none but witlings there resort,
Whose names and works (tho' dead) are
          made
Immortal by the Dunciad;   10
And sure, as monuments of brass,

---

[1] *The Gentleman of whom the Purchase was made.*
[2] *Medals were cast; many Signs hung up; and Handkerchiefs made with Devices in Honour of the Author, under the Name of* M. B. Drapier.

Their fame to future times shall pass,
How, with a weakly warbling tongue,
Of brazen Knight they vainly sung:
A subject for their genius fit;
He dares defy both sense and wit.
What dares he not? He can, we know it,
A laureat make that is no poet;
A judge, without the least pretence
To common law, or common sense;   20
A bishop that is no divine;
And coxcombs in red ribbons shine:
Nay, he can make what's greater far,
A middle-state 'twixt peace and war;
And say, there shall, for years together,
Be peace and war, and both, and neither.
Happy, O Market-hill! at least,
That court and courtiers have no taste:
You never else had known the Dean,
But, as of old, obscurely lain;   30
All things gone on the same dull track,
And Drapier's-hill been still Drumlack;
But now your name with Penshurst vies,
And wing'd with fame shall reach the skies.

1729/1765

Robin and Harry

ROBIN, to beggars, with a curse,
Throws the last shilling in his purse;
And, when the coachman comes for pay,
The rogue must call another day.

Grave Harry, when the poor are pressing,
Gives them a penny, and God's blessing;

But, always careful of the main,
With two-pence left, walks home in rain.

Robin, from noon to night, will prate,
Runs out in tongue, as in estate;   10
And, ere a twelvemonth and a day,
Will not have one new thing to say.
Much talking is not Harry's vice;
He need not tell a story twice;
And, if he always be so thrifty,
His fund may last to five and fifty.

It so fell out, that cautious Harry,
As soldiers use, for love must marry,
And, with his Dame, the ocean crost,
All for Love, or the World well Lost.   20
Repairs a cabin gone to ruin,
Just big enough to shelter two in;
And in his house, if any body come,
Will make them welcome to his modicum.
Where Goody Julia milks the cows,
And boils potatoes for her spouse;
Or darns his hose, or mends his breeches,
While Harry's fencing up his ditches.

Robin, who ne'er his mind could fix
To live without a coach and six,   30
To patch his broken fortunes, found
A mistress worth five thousand pound;
Swears he could get her in an hour,
If Gaffer Harry would endow her;
And sell, to pacify his wrath,
A birth-right for a mess of broth.

Young Harry, as all Europe knows,
Was long the quintessence of beaux;
But, when espoused, he ran the fate

That must attend the marry'd state; 40
From gold brocade and shining armour,
Was metamorphos'd to a farmer;
His grazier's coat with dirt besmear'd,
Nor twice a week will shave his beard.

Old Robin, all his youth a sloven,
At fifty-two, when he grew loving,
Clad in a coat of paduasoy,
A flaxen wig, and waistcoat gay,
Powder'd from shoulder down to flank,
In courtly style addresses Frank; 50
Twice ten years older than his wife,
Is doom'd to be a beau for life:
Supplying those defects by dress,
Which I must leave the world to guess.

1729/1765

A Pastoral Dialogue

DERMOT, SHEELAH

A Nymph and Swain, *Sheelah* and *Dermot* hight,
Who *wont* to weed the Court of [1]*Gosford Knight*,
While each with stubbed Knife remov'd the Roots
That rais'd between the Stones their daily Shoots;
As at their Work they sat in counterview,
With mutual Beauty smit, their Passion grew.
Sing heavenly Muse in sweetly flowing Strain,
The soft Endearments of the Nymph and Swain.

---

[1] *Sir* Arthur Acheson, *whose great Grand Father was Sir* Archibald *of* Gosford *in* Scotland.

DERMOT

My love to *Sheelah* is more firmly fixt,
Than strongest Weeds that grow these Stones
    betwixt,   10
My *Spud* these Nettles from the Stones can part;
No Knife so keen to weed thee from my Heart.

SHEELAH

My Love for gentle *Dermot* faster grows,
Than yon tall Dock that rises to thy Nose.
Cut down the Dock, 'twill sprout again; but O!
Love rooted out, again will never grow.

DERMOT

No more that Bry'r thy tender Leg shall rake:
(I spare the Thistles for ¹Sir *Arthur*'s Sake.)
Sharp are the Stones, take thou this rushy Mat;
The hardest Bum will bruse with sitting squat.   20

SHEELAH

Thy Breeches torn behind, stand gaping wide,
This Petticoat shall save thy dear Back-side;
Nor need I blush, although you see it wet;
Dermot, I vow, 'tis nothing else but Sweat.

DERMOT

At an old stubborn Root I chanc'd to tug,
When the Dean threw me this Tobacco-plug:
A longer Half-p'orth never did I see;
This, dearest *Sheelah*, thou shalt share with me.

SHEELAH

In at the Pantry-door this Morn I slipt,
And from the Shelf a charming Crust I whipt: 30

---

¹ *Who is a great Lover of* Scotland.

¹*Dennis* was out, and I got hither safe:
And thou, my *Dear*, shalt have the bigger Half.

DERMOT

When you saw *Tady* at Long-bullets play,
You sat and lous'd him all a Sun-shine Day.
How could you, *Sheelah*, listen to his Tales,
Or crack such Lice as his betwixt your Nails?

SHEELAH

When you with *Oonah* stood behind a Ditch,
I peept, and saw you kiss the dirty Bitch.
Dermot, how could you touch those nasty Sluts;
I almost wish't this *Spud* were in your Guts.　　40

DERMOT

If *Oonah* once I kiss'd, forbear to chide;
Her Aunt's my Gossip by my Father's Side:
But, if I ever touch her Lips again,
May I be doom'd for Life to weed in Rain.

SHEELAH

Dermot, I swear, tho' *Tady*'s Locks could hold
Ten Thousand Lice, and ev'ry Louse was Gold,
Him on my Lap you never more should see;
Or may I lose my Weeding-Knife—and thee.

DERMOT

O, could I earn for thee, my lovely Lass,
A Pair of Brogues to bear thee dry to Mass!　　50
But see, where *Norah* with the Sowins comes—
Then let us rise, and rest our weary Bums.
                                        1729/1732

---

¹ *Sir* Arthur's *Butler*.

The Revolution at Market-Hill

FROM distant Regions, Fortune sends
An odd Triumvirate of Friends;
Where *Phœbus* pays a scanty Stipend,
Where never yet a Codling ripen'd:
Hither the frantick Goddess draws
Three Suff'rers in a ruin'd Cause.
By Faction banish't here unite,
A D[ea]n, a [1]*Spaniard*, and a Knight.
Unite; but on Conditions cruel;
The D[ea]n and *Spaniard* find it too well: 10
Condemn'd to live in Service hard;
On either Side his Honour's Guard:
The D[ea]n, to guard his Honour's Back,
Must build a Castle at [2]*Drumlack*,
The *Spaniard*, sore against his Will,
Must raise a Fort at *Market-Hill*.
And thus, the Pair of humble Gentry,
At *North* and *South* are posted Centry;
While in his lordly Castle fixt,
The Knight triumphant reigns betwixt: 20
And, what the Wretches most resent,
To be his Slaves must pay him Rent;
Attend him daily as their *Chief*,
Decant his Wine, and carve his Beef.

O Fortune, 'tis a Scandal for thee,
To smile on those who are least worthy.

---

[1] *Col.* Harry Leslie, *who served and lived long in Spain.*
[2] *The* Irish *Name of a Farm the D[ea]n took, and was to build on, but changed his Mind. He called it* Drapier's-Hill. Vide *that Poem.*

Weigh but the Merits of the three,
His Slaves have ten times more than he.

Proud Baronet of *Nova Scotia*,
The D[ea]n and *Spaniard* must reproach
    ye;   30
Of *their* two Fames the World enough
    rings;
Where are *thy* Services and Suff'rings?
What, if for nothing once you kiss't,
Against the Grain, a M[onarch]'s Fist?
What, if among the courtly Tribe,
You lost a Place, and sav'd a Bribe?
And, then in surly Mood came here
To Fifteen Hundred Pounds a Year,
And fierce against the Whigs harangu'd;
You never ventur'd to be hang'd.   40
How dare you treat your Betters thus?
Are you to be compar'd to Us?

Come, *Spaniard*, let us from our Farms
Call forth our Cottagers to Arms;
Our Forces let us both unite,
Attack the Foe at Left and Right;
From [1]*Market-Hill*'s exalted Head
Full Northward let your Troops be led:
While I from *Drapier*'s-*Mount* descend,
And to the South my Squadrons bend: 50
New River-walk with friendly Shade,
Shall keep my Host in Ambuscade;
While you, from where the Basin stands,
Shall scale the Rampart with your Bands.
Nor need we doubt the Fort to win;
I hold Intelligence within.
True, Lady *Anne* no Danger fears,
Brave as the *Upton* Fan she wears:

[1] *A Village near Sir* A[rthur] A[cheson]'*s Seat.*

190

Then, lest upon our first Attack
Her valiant Arm should force us back,   60
And we of all our Hopes depriv'd;
I have a Stratagem contriv'd;
By these embroider'd high Heel Shoes,
She shall be caught as in a Noose:
So well contriv'd her Toes to pinch,
She'll not have Pow'r to stir an Inch:
These gaudy Shoes must [1]*Hannah* place
Direct before her Lady's Face.
The Shoes put on; our faithful Portress
Admits us in, to storm the Fortress;   70
While tortur'd Madam bound remains,
Like *Montezume* in golden Chains:
Or, like a Cat with Walnuts shod,
Stumbling at ev'ry Step she trod.
Sly Hunters thus, in *Borneo's* Isle,
To catch a Monkey by a Wile,
The mimick Animal amuse;
They place before him Gloves and Shoes;
Which when the Brute puts aukward on,
All his Agility is gone;   80
In vain to frisk or climb he tries;
The Huntsmen seize the grinning Prize.

But, let us on our first Assault
Secure the Larder, and the Vault:
The valiant [2]*Dennis* you must fix on,
And, I'll engage with [3]*Peggy Dixon*:
Then, if we once can seize the Key,
And Chest, that keeps my Lady's Tea,
They must surrender at Discretion,
And soon as we have got Possession,   90
We'll act as *other* Conqu'rors do;
Divide the Realm between us two.

[1] *My Lady's Waiting-Maid.*   [2] *The Butler.*
[3] *The House-keeper.*

Then, (let me see) we'll make the Knight
Our Clerk, for he can read and write;
But, must not think, I tell him that,
Like ¹*Lorimer*, to wear his Hat.
Yet, when we dine without a Friend,
We'll place him at the lower End.
Madam, whose Skill does all in Dress lye,
May serve to wait on Mrs. *Leslie*:   100
But, lest it might not be so proper,
That her own Maid should overtop her;
To mortify the *Creature* more,
We'll take her Heels five Inches lower.

For *Hannah*; when we have no need of
    her,
'Twill be our Interest to get rid of her;
And when we execute our Plot,
'Tis best to hang her on the Spot;
As all your Politicians wise
Dispatch the Rogues by whom they Rise. 110
                    1730/1735

A Panegyrick on the Dean

in the Person of a Lady in the North

RESOLV'D my Gratitude to show,
Thrice Rev'rend D[ea]n for all I owe;
Too long I have my Thanks delay'd;
Your Favours left too long unpay'd;
But now in all our Sexes Name,
My artless Muse shall sing your Fame.

Indulgent you to Female Kind,
To all their weaker Sides are blind;

¹ *The Agent.*

Nine more such Champions as the D[ea]n,
Would soon restore our ancient Reign.   10
How well to win the Ladies Hearts,
You celebrate their Wit and Parts!
How have I felt my Spirits rais'd,
By you so oft, so highly prais'd!
Transform'd by your convincing Tongue,
To witty, beautiful, and young.
I hope, to quit that awkward Shame
Affected by each vulgar Dame;
To Modesty a weak Pretence;
And soon grow pert on Men of Sense;   20
To show my Face with scornful Air;
Let others match it if they dare.

    Impatient to be out of Debt,
O, may I never once forget
The Bard, who humbly deigns to chuse
Me for the subject of his Muse.
Behind my Back, before my Nose,
He sounds my Praise in Verse and Prose.

    My Heart with Emulation burns,
To make you suitable Returns;   30
My Gratitude the World shall know:
And, see, the Printer's Boy below:
Ye Hawkers all, your Voices lift;
A Panegyrick on D[ea]n *S[wift]*.
And then to mend the Matter still;
By Lady *Anne* of [1]*Market-Hill*.

    I thus begin. My grateful Muse
Salutes the D[ea]n in diff'rent Views;
D[ea]n, Butler, Usher, Jester, Tutor;

---

[1] *A Village near Sir* A[rthur] A[cheson]'*s House, where the Author passed two Summers.*

¹*Robert* and *Darby*'s Coadjutor: 40
And, as you in Commission sit,
To rule the Dairy next to ²*Kit*.

    In each Capacity I mean
To sing your Praise, and first as D[ea]n:
Envy must own, you understand your
Precedence, and support your Grandeur:
Nor, of your Rank will bate an Ace,
Except to give D[ea]n D[anie]l place.
In you such Dignity appears;
So suited to your State, and Years!   50
With Ladies what a strict Decorum!
With what Devotion you adore 'um!
Treat me with so much Complaisance,
As fits a Princess in Romance.
By your Example and Assistance,
The *Fellows* learn to know their Distance,
Sir A[rthu]r, since you set the Pattern,
No longer calls me *Snipe* and *Slattern*;
Nor dares he though he were a Duke,
Offend me with the least Rebuke.   60

    Proceed we to your ³preaching next;
How nice you split the hardest Text!
How your superior Learning shines
Above our neighbouring dull Divines!
At *Beggar*'s-*Op'ra* not so full Pit
Is seen, as when you mount our Pulpit.

    Consider now your Conversation;
Regardful of your Age and Station,
You ne'er was known, by Passion stirr'd,
To give the least offensive Word;   70
But still, whene'er you Silence break,

---

¹ *The Names of two Overseers.*   ² *My Lady's Footman.*
³ *The Author preached but once while he was there.*

Watch ev'ry Syllable you speak:
Your Style so clear, and so concise,
We never ask to hear you twice.
But then, a Parson so genteel,
So nicely clad from Head to Heel;
So fine a Gown, a Band so clean,
As well become St. P[atrick]'s D[ea]n;
Such reverential Awe express,
That Cow-boys know you by your Dress!   80
Then, if our neighb'ring Friends come here,
How proud are we when you appear!
With such Address, and graceful Port,
As clearly shews you bred at Court!

Now raise your Spirits, Mr. D[ea]n:
I lead you to a nobler Scene;
When to the Vault you walk in State,
In Quality of ¹Butler's Mate;
You, next to *Dennis* bear the Sway:
To you we often trust the Key: 90
Nor, can he judge with all his Art
So well, what Bottle holds a Quart:
What Pints may best for Bottles pass,
Just to give ev'ry Man his Glass:
When proper to produce the best;
And, what may serve a common Guest.
With ²*Dennis* you did ne'er combine,
Not you, to steal your Master's Wine;
Except a Bottle now and then,
To welcome *Brother* Serving-men;   100
But, that is with a good Design,
To drink Sir A[rthu]r's Health and mine:
Your Master's Honour to maintain,
And get the like Returns again.

¹ *He sometimes used to direct the Butler.*
² *The Butler.*

Your [1]Usher's Post must next be handled:
How bless't am I by such a Man led!
Under whose wise and careful Guardship,
I now despise Fatigue and Hardship:
Familiar grown to Dirt and Wet,
Though daggled round, I scorn to fret: 110
From you my Chamber-Damsels learn
My broken Hose to patch and dearn.

Now, as a Jester, I accost you;
Which never yet one Friend has lost you.
You judge so nicely to a Hair,
How far to go, and when to spare:
By long Experience grown so wise,
Of ev'ry Taste to know the Size;
There's none so ignorant or weak
[2]To take Offence at what you speak.   120
Whene'er you joke, 'tis all a Case;
Whether with *Dermot*, or *His Grace*;
With *Teague O'Murphy*, or an Earl;
A Dutchess or a Kitchen Girl.
With such Dexterity you fit
Their sev'ral Talents to your Wit,
That *Moll* the Chamber-maid can smoak,
And *Gaghagan* take ev'ry Joke.

I now become your humble Suitor,
To let me praise you as my [3]Tutor.   130
Poor I, a Savage bred and born,
By you instructed ev'ry Morn,
Already have improv'd so well,
That I have almost learn't to spell:
The Neighbours who come here to dine,

[1] *He sometimes used to walk with the Lady.*
[2] *The neighbouring Ladies were no great Understanders of Raillery.*
[3] *In bad Weather the Author used to direct my Lady in her Reading.*

Admire to hear me speak so *fine*.
How enviously the Ladies look,
When they surprize me at my Book!
And, sure as they're alive, at Night;
As soon as gone, will shew their Spight: 140
Good Lord! what can my Lady mean,
Conversing with that rusty D[ea]n!
She's grown so nice, and so ¹*penurious*,
With *Socratus* and *Epicurius*.
How could she sit the live-long Day;
Yet never ask us once to play?

But, I admire your Patience most;
That, when I'm duller than a Post,
Nor can the plainest Word pronounce,
You neither fume, nor fret, nor flounce;   150
Are so indulgent, and so mild,
As if I were a darling Child.
So gentle is your whole Proceeding,
That I could spend my Life in reading.

You merit new Employments daily:
Our Thatcher, Ditcher, Gard'ner, Baily.
And, to a Genius so extensive,
No Work is grievous or offensive.
Whether, your fruitful Fancy lies
To make for Pigs convenient Styes: 160
Or, ponder long with anxious Thought,
To banish Rats that haunt our Vault.
Nor have you grumbled, Rev'rend D[ea]n,
To keep our Poultry sweet and clean;
To sweep the Mansion-house they dwell in;
And cure the rank unsav'ry Smelling.

¹ *Ignorant Ladies often mistake the Word* Penurious *for* nice,
and dainty.

Now, enter as the Dairy Hand-maid:
Such charming ¹Butter never Man made.
Let others with Fanatick Face,
Talk of their *Milk* for *Babes of Grace*;   170
From *Tubs* their snuffling Nonsense utter:
Thy *Milk* shall make us *Tubs* of Butter.
The Bishop with his *Foot* may burn it;
But, with his *Hand*, the D[ea]n can churn it.
How are the Servants overjoy'd
To see thy D[ea]nship thus employ'd!
Instead of poring on a Book,
Providing Butter for the Cook.
Three Morning-Hours you toss and shake
The Bottle, till your Fingers ake: 180
Hard is the Toil, nor small the Art,
The Butter from the Whey to part:
Behold; a frothy Substance rise;
Be cautious, or your Bottle flies.
The Butter comes; our Fears are ceas't;
And, out you squeeze an Ounce at least.

Your Rev'rence thus, with like Success,
Nor is your Skill, or Labour less,
When bent upon some smart Lampoon,
You toss and turn your Brain till Noon;   190
Which, in its Jumblings round the Skull,
Dilates, and makes the Vessel full;
While nothing comes but Froth at first,
You think your giddy Head will burst:
But, squeezing out four Lines in Rhime,
Are largely paid for all your time.

But, you have rais'd your gen'rous Mind
To Works of more exalted Kind.
Palladio was not half so skill'd in

---

¹ *A Way of making Butter for Breakfast, by filling a Bottle with
Cream, and shaking it till the Butter comes.*

The Grandeur or the Art of Building.   200
Two Temples of magnifick Size,
Attract the curious Trav'llers Eyes,
That might be envy'd by the *Greeks*;
Rais'd up by you in twenty Weeks:
Here, gentle Goddess *Cloacine*
Receives all Off'rings at her Shrine:
In sep'rate Cells the He's and She's
Here pay their Vows with *bended Knees*:
(For, 'tis prophane when Sexes mingle;
And ev'ry Nymph must enter single;   210
And when she feels an *inward Motion*,
Comes fill'd with *Rev'rence* and Devotion.)
The bashful Maid, to hide her Blush,
Shall creep no more behind a Bush;
Here unobserv'd she boldly goes,
As who should say, to *pluck a Rose*.

Ye, who frequent this hallow'd Scene,
Be not ungrateful to the D[ea]n;
But, duly e'er you leave your Station,
Offer to him a pure Libation;   220
Or, of his own, or [1]*Smedley*'s Lay,
Or Billet doux, or Lock of Hay:
And, O! may all who hither come,
Return with unpolluted Thumb.

Yet, when your lofty Domes I praise,
I sigh to think of antient Days.
Permit me then to raise my Style,
And sweetly moralize a while.

Thee bounteous Goddess *Cloacine*,
To Temples why do we confine?   230
Forbid in open Air to breath;
Why are thine Altars fix'd beneath?

[1] *See his Character hereafter.*

199

When *Saturn* rul'd the Skies alone,
That *golden Age*, to *Gold* unknown;
This earthly Globe to thee assign'd,
Receiv'd the Gifts of all Mankind.
Ten thousand Altars *smoaking* round
Were built to thee, with Off'rings crown'd:
And here thy daily Vot'ries plac'd
Their Sacrifice with Zeal and Haste: 240
The Margin of a purling Stream,
Sent up to thee a grateful Steam.
(Though sometimes thou wer't pleas'd to wink,
If *Nayads* swept them from the Brink)
Or, where appointing Lovers rove,
The Shelter of a shady Grove:
Or, offer'd in some flow'ry Vale,
Were wafted by a gentle Gale.
There, many a Flow'r abstersive grew,
Thy fav'rite Flow'rs of yellow Hue;   250
The Crocus and the Daffodil,
The Cowslip soft, and sweet Jonquil.

But, when at last usurping *Jove*
Old *Saturn* from his Empire drove;
Then *Gluttony* with greasy Paws,
Her Napkin pinn'd up to her Jaws,
With wat'ry Chaps, and wagging Chin,
Brac'd like a Drum her oily Skin;
Wedg'd in a spacious Elbow-Chair,
And on her Plate a treble Share,   260
As if she ne'er could have enough;
Taught harmless Man to cram and stuff.
She sent her Priests in wooden Shoes
From haughty *Gaul* to make Ragous.
Instead of wholesome Bread and Cheese,
To dress their Soupes and Fricassyes;

And for our home-bred *British* Chear,
Botargo, Catsup, and Caveer.

This bloated Harpy, sprung from Hell,
Confin'd thee, Goddess, to a Cell: 270
Sprung from her Womb that impious Line,
Contemners of thy Rites divine.
First, lolling *Sloth* in Woollen Cap,
Taking her After-dinner Nap:
Pale *Dropsy* with a sallow Face,
Her Belly burst, and slow her Pace,
And, lordly *Gout* wrapt up in Furr,
And, wheezing *Asthma*, loath to stir:
Voluptuous *Fase*, the Child of *Wealth*,
Infecting thus our Hearts by Stealth: 280
None seek thee now in open Air;
To thee no verdant Altars rear;
But, in their Cells and Vaults obscene,
Present a Sacrifice unclean;
From whence unsav'ry Vapours rose,
Offensive to thy nicer Nose.

Ah! who in our degen'rate Days
As Nature prompts, his Off'ring pays?
Here, Nature never Diff'rence made
Between the Scepter and the Spade.   290

Ye Great ones, why will ye disdain
To pay your Tribute on the Plain?
Why will you place in lazy Pride
Your Altars near your Couches Side?
[1]When from the homeliest Earthen Ware
Are sent up Off'rings more sincere,
Than where the haughty Dutchess locks
Her Silver Vase in Cedar-Box.

---

[1] *Vide* Virgil *and* Lucretius.

Yet, some Devotion still remains
Among our harmless Northern Swains;   300
Whose Off'rings plac'd in golden Ranks,
Adorn our chrystal Rivers Banks:
Nor seldom grace the flow'ry Downs,
With spiral Tops and Copple-Crowns:
Or gilding in a sunny Morn
The humble Branches of a Thorn.
(So Poets sing, with [1]golden Bough
The *Trojan* Hero paid his Vow.)

Hither by luckless Error led,
The crude Consistence oft I tread,   310
Here, when my Shoes are out of Case,
Unweeting gild the tarnish'd Lace:
Here, by the sacred Bramble ting'd,
My Petticoat is doubly fring'd.

Be Witness for me, Nymph divine,
I never robb'd thee with Design:
Nor will the zealous *Hannah* pout,
To wash thy injur'd Off'rings out.

But, stop ambitious Muse, in time:
Nor dwell on Subjects too sublime.   320
In vain on lofty Heels I tread,
Aspiring to exalt my Head:
With Hoop expanded wide and light,
In vain I tempt too high a Flight.

Me [2]*Phœbus* in a Midnight [3]Dream
Accosting; said, [4]*Go shake your Cream.*
Be humble minded; know your Post;
Sweeten your Tea, and watch your Toast.
Thee best befits a lowly Style:

[1] Virg. lib 6.   [2] *Cynthius aurem vellis.* Hor.
[3] *Cum somnia vera.* Hor.   [4] *In the Bottle to make Butter.*

Teach *Dennis* how to stir the Guile: 330
With ¹*Peggy Dixon* thoughtful sit,
Contriving for the Pot and Spit,
Take down thy proudly swelling Sails,
And rub thy Teeth, and pare thy Nails.
At nicely carving shew thy Wit:
But ne'er presume to eat a Bit:
Turn ev'ry Way thy watchful Eye;
And ev'ry Guest be sure to ply;
Let never at your Board be known
An empty Plate except your own.   340
²Be these thy Arts; nor higher aim
Than what befits a rural Dame.

But, *Cloacina*, Goddess bright,
Sleek —— claims her as his Right:
And ³*Smedley*, Flow'r of all Divines,
Shall sing the D[ea]n in *Smedley*'s Lines.
                1730/1735

The Dean's Reasons
for not Building at Drapier's Hill

I WILL not build on yonder mount:
And, should you call me to account,
Consulting with myself, I find,
It was no levity of mind.
Whate'er I promised or intended,
No fault of mine, the scheme is ended:
Nor can you tax me as unsteady,
I have a hundred causes ready:

¹ *Mrs.* Dixon *the Housekeeper.*
² *Hae tibi erunt artes.* Virg.
³ *A very stupid, insolent, factious, deformed, conceited Parson; a vile Pretender to Poetry, preferred by the D. of* Grafton *for his Wit.*

All risen since that flatt'ring time,
When Drapier's-hill appear'd in rhyme.   10

    I am, as now too late I find,
The greatest cully of mankind:
The lowest boy in Martin's school
May turn and wind me like a fool.
How could I form so wild a vision,
To seek, in desarts, Fields Elysian?
To live in fear, suspicion, variance,
With Thieves, Fanaticks, and Barbarians?

    But here my Lady will object;
Your Deanship ought to recollect,   20
That, near the Knight of Gosford plac't,
Whom you allow a man of taste,
Your intervals of time to spend
With so conversible a friend,
It would not signify a pin
Whatever climate you were in.

    'Tis true, but what advantage comes
To me from all a us'rer's plums;
Though I should see him twice a day,
And am his neighbour cross the way;   30
If all my rhetorick must fail
To strike him for a pot of ale?

    Thus, when the learned and the wise
Conceal their talents from our eyes,
And, from deserving friends, with-hold
Their gifts, as misers do their gold;
Their knowledge, to themselves confin'd,
Is the same avarice of mind:
Nor makes their conversation better,
Than if they never knew a letter.   40
Such is the fate of Gosford's Knight,

Who keeps his wisdom out of sight;
Whose uncommunicative heart,
Will scarce one precious word impart:
Still rapt in speculations deep,
His outward senses fast asleep;
Who, while I talk, a song will hum,
Or, with his fingers, beat the drum;
Beyond the skies transports his mind,
And leaves a lifeless corpse behind.   50

    But, as for me, who ne'er could clamber
      high,
To understand Malebranche or Cambray;
Who send my mind (as I believe) less
Than others do, on errands sleeveless;
Can listen to a tale humdrum,
And, with attention, read Tom Thumb;
My spirits with my body progging,
Both hand in hand together jogging;
Sunk over head and ears in matter,
Nor can of metaphysics smatter;   60
Am more diverted with a quibble
Than dreams of worlds intelligible;
And think all notions too abstracted
Are like the ravings of a crackt head;
What intercourse of minds can be
Betwixt the Knight sublime and me?
If when I talk, as talk I must,
It is but prating to a bust.

    Where friendship is by Fate design'd,
It forms an union in the mind: 70
But, here I differ from the Knight
In every point, like black and white:
For, none can say that ever yet
We both in one opinion met:
Not in philosophy, or ale,

205

In state-affairs, or planting cale;
In rhetoric, or picking straws;
In roasting larks, or making laws:
In public schemes, or catching flies,
In parliaments, or pudding-pies.   80

    The neighbours wonder why the Knight
Should in a country life delight,
Who not one pleasure entertains
To chear the solitary scenes:
His guests are few, his visits rare,
Nor uses time, nor time will spare;
Nor rides, nor walks, nor hunts, nor fowls,
Nor plays at cards, or dice, or bowls;
But, seated in an easy chair,
Despises exercise and air.   90
His rural walks he ne'er adorns;
Here poor Pomona sits on thorns:
And there neglected Flora settles
Her bum upon a bed of nettles.

    Those thankless and officious cares
I use to take in friends affairs,
From which I never could refrain,
And have been often chid in vain:
From these I am recover'd quite,
At least in what regards the Knight.   100
Preserve his health, his store increase;
May nothing interrupt his peace.
But now, let all his tenants round
First milk his cows, and after, pound:
Let ev'ry cottager conspire
To cut his hedges down for fire;
The naughty boys about the village
His crabs and sloes may freely pillage;
He still may keep a pack of knaves
To spoil his work, and work by halves: 110

His meadows may be dug by swine,
It shall be no concern of mine.
For, why should I continue still
To serve a friend against his will?

1730/1765

Daphne

DAPHNE knows, with equal ease,
How to vex and how to please;
But, the folly of her sex
Makes her sole delight to vex.
Never woman more devis'd
Surer ways to be despis'd:
Paradoxes weakly wielding,
Always conquer'd, never yielding.
To dispute, her chief delight,
With not one opinion right: 10
Thick her arguments she lays on,
And with cavils combats reason:
Answers in decisive way,
Never hears what you can say:
Still her odd perverseness shows
Chiefly where she nothing knows.
And where she is most familiar,
Always peevisher and sillier:
All her spirits in a flame
When she knows she's most to blame.   20

Send me hence ten thousand miles,
From a face that always smiles:
None could ever act that part,
But a fury in her heart.
Ye who hate such inconsistence,
To be easy keep your distance;

Or in folly still befriend her,
But have no concern to mend her.
Lose not time to contradict her,
Nor endeavour to convict her.   30
Never take it in your thought,
That she'll own, or cure a fault.
Into contradiction warm her,
Then, perhaps, you may reform her:
Only take this rule along,
Always to advise her wrong;
And reprove her when she's right;
She may then grow wise for spight.

No—that scheme will ne'er succeed,
She has better learnt her creed: 40
She's too cunning and too skilful,
When to yield and when be willful.
Nature holds her forth two mirrors,
One for truth, and one for errors:
That looks hideous, fierce, and frightful;
This is flatt'ring, and delightful:
That she throws away as foul;
Sits by this, to dress her soul.

Thus you have the case in view,
Daphne, 'twixt the Dean and you,   50
Heav'n forbid he should despise thee;
But will never more advise thee.
                                    1730/1765

IMPERSONAL SATIRES

A Quiet Life and a Good Name

To a Friend who Married a Shrew

Nell scolded in so loud a Din,
That *Will* durst hardly venture in:
He mark't the Conjugal Dispute;
Nell roar'd incessant, *Dick* sat mute:
But when he saw his Friend appear,
Cry'd bravely, Patience, good my Dear.
At Sight of *Will* she bawl'd no more,
But hurry'd out, and clapt the Door.

Why *Dick !* the Devil's in thy *Nell*,
Quoth *Will*; thy House is worse than Hell: 10
Why, what a Peal the Jade has rung!
Damn her, why don't you slit her Tongue?
For nothing else will make it cease:
Dear *Will*, I suffer this for Peace;
I never quarrel with my Wife;
I bear it for a quiet Life.
Scripture, you know, exhorts us to it;
Bids us to *seek Peace and ensue it.*

Will went again to visit *Dick*;
And ent'ring in the very Nick,   20
He saw Virago *Nell* belabour,
With *Dick*'s own Staff, his peaceful
        Neighbour.
Poor *Will*, who needs must interpose,
Receiv'd a Brace or two of Blows.

But, now, to make my Story short;
Will drew out *Dick* to take a Quart.
Why *Dick*, thy Wife has dev'lish Whims;
Od's-buds, why don't you break her Limbs?

If she were mine, and had such Tricks,
I'd teach her how to handle Sticks: 30
Z—ds, I would ship her to *Jamaica*,
And truck the Carrion for *Tobacco*;
I'd send her far enough away—
Dear *Will*; but, what would People say?
Lord! I should get so ill a Name,
The Neighbours round would cry out, *Shame*.

   Dick suffer'd for his Peace and Credit;
But, who believ'd him when he said it?
Can he who makes himself a Slave,
Consult his Peace, or Credit save?   40
Dick found it by his ill Success,
His Quiet small, his Credit less.
She serv'd him at the usual Rate;
She stun'd, and then she broke his Pate.
And, what he thought the hardest Case,
The Parish jeer'd him to his Face;
Those Men who wore the Breeches least,
Call'd him a Cuckold, Fool, and Beast.
At home, he was pursu'd with Noise;
Abroad, was pester'd by the Boys.   50
Within, his Wife would break his Bones,
Without, they pelted him with Stones:
The 'Prentices procur'd a Riding,
To act his Patience and her Chiding.

   False Patience and mistaken Pride!
There are ten thousand *Dicks* beside;
Slaves to their Quiet and good Name,
Are us'd like *Dick*, and bear the Blame.
1719/1735

Phyllis;
or, the Progress of Love

DESPONDING Phyllis was endu'd
With ev'ry Talent of a Prude:
She trembled, when a Man drew near;
Salute her, and she turn'd her Ear;
If o'er against her you were plac'd,
She durst not look above your Waist:
She'd rather take you to her Bed,
Than let you see her dress her Head:
In Church you heard her, thro' the Crowd,
Repeat the *Absolution* loud;   10
In Church, secure behind her Fan,
She durst behold that Monster, *Man*:
There practis'd how to place her Head,
And bit her Lips, to make them red;
Or, on the Mat devoutly kneeling,
Wou'd lift her Eyes up to the Ceiling,
And heave her Bosom, unaware,
For neighb'ring Beaux to see it bare.

    At length, a lucky Lover came,
And found admittance to the Dame.   20
Suppose all Parties now agreed,
The Writings drawn, the Lawyer fee'd,
The Vicar and the Ring bespoke:
Guess, how could such a Match be broke?
See then, what Mortals place their Bliss in!
Next Morn, betimes, the Bride was missing.
The Mother scream'd, the Father chid;
Where can this idle Wench be hid?
No News of *Phyl!* The Bridegroom came,
And thought his Bride had skulk'd for
        Shame;   30

213

Because her Father us'd to say,
The Girl *had such a bashful Way*.

Now *John*, the Butler, must be sent,
To learn the Road that *Phyllis* went.
The Groom was *wish'd* to saddle *Crop*;
For, *John* must neither light, nor stop,
But find her wheresoe'er she fled,
And bring her back, alive or dead.

See here again, the Dev'l to do!
For, truly, *John* was missing too.   40
The Horse and Pillion both were gone!
Phyllis, it seems, was fled with *John*.

Old Madam, who went up to find
What Papers *Phyl* had left behind,
A Letter on the Toylet sees,
To my much honour'd Father—These.
('Tis always done, Romances tell us,
When Daughters run away with Fellows)
Fill'd with the choicest Common-Places,
By others us'd in the like Cases;   50
'That, long ago, a *Fortune-teller*
'Exactly said what now befel her;
'And in a *Glass* had made her see
'A *Serving-Man of low Degree*.
'It was *her Fate*, must be forgiven,
'For *Marriages were made in Heaven*:
'His Pardon begg'd; but, to be plain,
'She'd *do't*, if '*twere to do again*.
'Thank GOD, 'twas *neither Shame nor Sin*;
'For *John* was come of *honest Kin*.   60
'Love never thinks of Rich and Poor,
'*She'd beg with* John *from Door to Door*.
'Forgive her, if it be a Crime,
'She'll never do't *another Time*.

214

'She ne'er before in all her Life
'Once disobey'd him, *Maid nor Wife*.'
One Argument she summ'd all up in,
'The *Thing was done*, and *past recalling*;
'And therefore hop'd she should recover
'His Favour, when his *Passion's over!*   70
'She valu'd not what others thought her,
'And was—his *most obedient Daughter*.'

    Fair Maidens all, attend the Muse,
Who now the wand'ring Pair pursues.
Away they rode in homely Sort,
Their Journey long, their Money short;
The loving Couple well bemir'd;
The Horse and both the Riders tir'd:
Their Victuals bad, their Lodging worse;
Phyl cry'd, and *John* began to curse;   80
Phyl wish'd, that she had strain'd a Limb,
When first she ventur'd out with him:
John wish'd, that he had broke a Leg,
When first for her he quitted *Peg*.

    But what Adventures more befel 'em,
The Muse hath now no Time to tell 'em.
How *Johny* wheedled, threatned, fawn'd,
Till *Phyllis* all her Trinkets pawn'd:
How oft she broke her Marriage Vows,
In Kindness, to maintain her Spouse,   90
Till Swains unwholesome spoil'd the Trade;
For now the Surgeon must be paid,
To whom those Perquisites are gone,
In Christian Justice due to *John*.

    When Food and Rayment now grew
        scarce,
Fate put a Period to the Farce,
And with exact poetick Justice;

For, *John* is Landlord, *Phyllis* Hostess:
They keep, at *Staines*, the *old blue Boar*,   99
Are Cat and Dog, and Rogue and Whore.
                                        1719/1727

The Progress of Beauty

WHEN first *Diana* leaves her Bed,
   Vapours and Steams her Looks disgrace,
A frowzy dirty-colour'd Red
   Sits on her cloudy wrinkled Face.

But, by Degrees, when mounted high,
   Her artificial Face appears
Down from her Window in the Sky,
   Her Spots are gone, her Visage clears.

'Twixt earthly Females and the Moon,
   All Parallels exactly run;   10
If *Celia* should appear too soon,
   Alas, the Nymph would be undone!

To see her from her Pillow rise,
   All reeking in a cloudy Steam;
Crack'd Lips, foul Teeth, and gummy Eyes;
   Poor *Strephon*, how would he blaspheme!

Three Colours, Black, and Red, and White,
   So graceful in their proper Place,
Remove them to a different Light,
   They form a frightful hideous Face.   20

For instance, when the Lilly skips
   Into the Precincts of the Rose,

And takes Possession of the Lips
   Leaving the Purple to the Nose.

So, *Celia* went entire to Bed,
   All her Complexions safe and sound;
But, when she rose, White, Black, and Red,
   Tho' still in sight, had chang'd their Ground.

The Black, which would not be confin'd,
   A more inferior Station seeks,   30
Leaving the fiery Red behind,
   And mingles in her muddy Cheeks.

But *Celia* can with Ease reduce,
   By Help of Pencil, Paint, and Brush,
Each Colour to its Place and Use,
   And teach her Cheeks again to Blush.

She knows her *early* self no more;
   But fill'd with Admiration stands,
As *other* Painters oft adore
   The Workmanship of their own Hands.   40

Thus, after four important Hours,
   Celia's the Wonder of her Sex:
Say, which among the heav'nly Powers
   Could cause such marvellous Effects?

Venus, indulgent to her Kind,
   Gave Women all their Hearts could wish,
When first she taught them where to find
   White-Lead and [1]*Lusitanian* Dish.

Love with white Lead cements his Wings;
   White Lead was sent us to repair   50

[1] Portugal.

Two brightest, brittlest, earthly Things,
   A Lady's Face, and *China*-Ware.

She ventures now to lift the Sash,
   The Window is her proper Sphere:
Ah, lovely Nymph! be not too rash,
   Nor let the Beaux approach too near.

Take Pattern by your *Sister* Star;
   Delude at once, and bless our Sight;
When you are seen, be seen from far;
   And chiefly chuse to shine by Night.   60

But, Art no longer can prevail,
   When the Materials all are gone;
The best Mechanick Hand must fail,
   Where nothing's left to work upon.

Matter, as wise Logicians say,
   Cannot without a *Form* subsist;
And *Form*, say I, as well as they,
   Must fail, if *Matter* brings no Grist.

And this is fair *Diana*'s Case;
   For all Astrologers maintain,   70
Each Night, a Bit drops off her Face,
   When Mortals say she's in her Wane.

While *Partrige* wisely shews the Cause
   Efficient, of the Moon's Decay,
That *Cancer* with his pois'nous Claws,
   Attacks her in the *milky Way*.

But *Gadbury*, in Art profound,
   From her pale Cheeks pretends to show,
That Swain *Endymion* is not found;
   Or else, that *Mercury*'s her Foe.   80

But, let the Cause be what it will,
   In half a Month she looks so thin,
That *Flamstead* can, with all his Skill,
   See but her Forehead and her Chin.

Yet, as she wastes, she grows discreet,
   'Till Midnight never shews her Head:
So rotting *Celia* stroles the Street,
   When sober Folks are all a-bed.

For, sure if this be *Luna*'s Fate,
   Poor *Celia*, but of mortal Race,   90
In vain expects a longer Date
   To the Materials of *her* Face.

When *Mercury* her Tresses mows,
   To think of black Lead-Combs is vain;
No Painting can restore a *Nose*,
   Nor will her *Teeth* return again.

Ye Pow'rs, who over Love preside!
   Since mortal Beauties drop so soon,
If you would have us well supply'd,   99
   Send us *new* Nymphs with each *new* Moon.
              1719/1727

The Progress of Marriage

  ÆTATIS suæ fifty-two,
A rich Divine began to woo
A handsome, young, imperious girl,
Nearly related to an Earl.
Her parents and her friends consent,
The couple to the temple went:
They first invite the Cyprian Queen;

219

'Twas answer'd, she would not be seen:
The Graces next, and all the Muses
Were bid in form, but sent excuses.   10
Juno attended at the porch,
With farthing candle for a torch,
While Mistress Iris held her train,
The faded bow distilling rain.
Then Hebe came, and took her place,
But shew'd no more than half her face.

Whate'er those dire forebodings meant,
In mirth the wedding-day was spent;
The wedding-day, you take me right,
I promise nothing for the night.   20
The bridegroom drest, to make a figure
Assumes an artificial vigour;
A flourisht night-cap on, to grace
His ruddy, wrinkled, smiling face;
Like the faint red upon a pippin,
Half wither'd by a winter's keeping.

And, thus set out, this happy pair,
The Swain is rich, the Nymph is fair;
But, what I gladly would forget,
The Swain is old, the Nymph coquette.   30
Both from the goal together start;
Scarce run a step before they part;
No common ligament that binds
The various textures of their minds;
Their thoughts, and actions, hopes and
     fears,
Less corresponding than their years.
Her spouse desires his coffee soon,
She rises to her tea at noon.
While he goes out to cheapen books,
She at the lass consults her looks;   40

While Betty's buzzing in her ear,
Lord, what a dress these parsons wear!
So odd a choice how could she make?
Wisht him a Col'nel for her sake.
Then, on her fingers ends, she counts,
Exact, to what his age amounts.
The Dean, she heard her uncle say,
Is sixty, if he be a day;
His ruddy cheeks are no disguise;
You see the crows feet round his eyes.   50

   At one she rambles to the shops,
To cheapen tea, and talk with fops;
Or calls a council of her maids,
And tradesmen, to compare brocades.
Her weighty morning bus'ness o'er,
Sits down to dinner just at four;
Minds nothing that is done or said,
Her ev'ning work so fills her head,
The Dean, who us'd to dine at one,
Is maukish, and his stomach gone;   60
In thread-bare gown, would scarce a louse
   hold,
Looks like the chaplain of his houshold,
Beholds her from the chaplain's place
In French brocades and Flanders lace;
He wonders what employs her brain,
But never asks, or asks in vain;
His mind is full of other cares,
And, in the sneaking parson's airs,
Computes, that half a parish dues
Will hardly find his wife in shoes.   70

   Can'st thou imagine, dull Divine,
'Twill gain her love to make her fine?
Hath she no other wants beside?
You raise desire as well as pride,

Enticing coxcombs to adore,
And teach her to despise thee more.

   If in her coach she'll condescend
To place him at the hinder end
Her hoop is hoist above his nose,
His odious gown would soil her cloaths,   80
And drops him at the church, to pray,
While she drives on to see the Play.
He, like an orderly divine,
Comes home a quarter after nine,
And meets her hasting to the ball:
Her chairmen push him from the wall.
He enters in, and walks up stairs,
And calls the family to pray'rs;
Then goes alone to take his rest
In bed, where he can spare her best.   90
At five the footmen make a din,
Her Ladyship is just come in,
The masquerade began at two,
She stole away with much ado;
And shall be chid this afternoon
For leaving company so soon:
She'll say, and she may truly say't,
She can't abide to stay out late.

   But now, though scarce a twelvemonth
      marry'd,
Poor Lady Jane has thrice miscarry'd: 100
The cause, alas, is quickly guest,
The town has whisper'd round the jest.
Think on some remedy in time,
You find his Rev'rence past his prime,
Already dwindled to a lath;
No other way but try the Bath.

For Venus rising from the ocean,
Infus'd a strong prolifick potion,
That mixt with Achelaus' spring,
The *horned* flood, as poets sing,   110
Who, with an English beauty smitten,
Ran underground from Greece to Britain;
The genial virtue with him brought,
And gave the Nymph a plenteous draught;
Then fled, and left his horn behind
For husbands past their youth to find:
The Nymph, who still with passion burn'd,
Was to a boiling fountain turn'd,
Where childless wives croud ev'ry morn
To drink in Achelaus' horn.   120
And here the father often gains
That title by another's pains.

Hither, though much against the grain,
The Dean has carry'd Lady Jane.
He, for a while, would not consent,
But vow'd his money all was spent:
His money spent! a clownish reason!
And must my Lady slip her season?
The Doctor, with a double fee,
Was brib'd to make the Dean agree.   130

Here all diversions of the place
Are proper in my Lady's case:
With which she patiently complies,
Merely because her friends advise;
His money and her time employs
In Musick, raffling-rooms and toys;
Or, in the *Cross-bath*, seeks an heir,
Since others oft have found one there:
Where, if the Dean by chance appears,
It shames his cassock and his years.   140
He keeps his distance in the gallery

'Till banish'd by some coxcomb's raillery;
For, 'twould his character expose
To bathe among the belles and beaux.

So have I seen, within a pen,
Young ducklings foster'd by a hen;
But, when let out, they run and muddle,
As instinct leads them, in a puddle:
The sober hen, not born to swim,
With mournful note clucks round the
    brim.   150

The Dean, with all his best endeavour,
Gets not an heir, but gets a fever,
A victim to the last essays
Of vigor in declining days,
He dies, and leaves his mourning mate
(What could he less?) his whole estate.

The widow goes through all her forms:
New Lovers now will come in swarms.
Oh, may I see her soon dispensing
Her favours to some broken ensign!   160
Him let her marry, for his face,
And only coat of tarnisht lace;
To turn her naked out of doors,
And spend her jointure on his whores:
But, for a parting present, leave her
A rooted pox to last for ever.
                    1722/1765

Pethox the Great

FROM *Venus* born, thy Beauty shows;
But who thy Father, no Man knows;

Nor can the skilful Herald trace
The Founder of thy ancient Race.
Whether thy Temper, full of Fire,
Discovers *Vulcan* for thy Sire;
The God who made *Scamander* boil,
And round his Margin sing'd the Soil;
(From whence Philosophers agree,
An equal Pow'r descends to thee.)   10
Whether from dreadful *Mars* you claim
The high Descent from whence you came,
And, as a Proof, shew num'rous Scars,
By fierce Encounters made in Wars;
(Those honourable Wounds you bore
From Head to Foot, and *all before*;)
And still the bloody Field frequent,
Familiar in each Leader's Tent.
Or whether, as the Learn'd contend,
You from the neighb'ring *Gaul* descend;   20
Or from ¹*Parthenope* the Proud,
Where numberless thy Vot'ries crowd.
Whether thy great Forefathers came
From Realms, that bear *Vesputio*'s Name;
For so Conjectors would obtrude,
And from thy painted Skin conclude.
Whether, as *Epicurus* shows
The World from jostling Seeds arose;
Which, mingling with prolifick Strife
In Chaos, kindled into Life;   30
So your Production was the same,
And from contending Atoms came.

   Thy fair indulgent Mother crown'd
Thy Head with sparkling Rubies round;
Beneath thy decent Steps, the Road
Is all with precious Jewels strow'd.

¹ Naples.

225

The [1]Bird of *Pallas* knows his Post,
Thee to attend, where-e'er thou go'st.

Byzantians boast, that on the Clod,   39
Where once their *Sultan*'s Horse hath trod,
Grows neither Grass, nor Shrub, nor Tree,
The same thy Subjects boast of Thee.

The greatest Lord, when you appear,
Will deign your Livery to wear,
In all thy various Colours seen,
Of Red, and Yellow, Blue, and Green.

With half a Word, when you require,
The Man of Bus'ness must retire.

The haughty Minister of State,
With Trembling must thy Leisure wait;   50
And while his Fate is in thy Hands,
The Bus'ness of the Nation stands.

Thou dar'st the greatest Prince attack,
Can'st hourly set him on the Rack,
And, as an Instance of thy Pow'r,
Inclose him in a wooden Tow'r,
With pungent Pains on ev'ry Side;
So *Regulus* in Torments dy'd.

From thee our Youth all Virtues learn;
Dangers with Prudence to discern;   60
And well thy Scholars are endu'd
With Temp'rance, and with Fortitude;
With Patience, which all Ills supports;
And Secrecy, the Art of Courts.

[1] Bubo, *the Owl.*

226

The glitt'ring Beau could hardly tell,
Without your Aid, to read or spell;
But, having long convers'd with you,
Knows how to scrawl a Billet-doux.

With what Delight, methinks, I trace
Thy Blood in ev'ry noble Race!　　　70
In whom thy Features, Shape, and Mien,
Are to the Life distinctly seen.

The *Britons*, once a savage Kind,
By you were brighten'd and refin'd:
Descendants of the barb'rous *Huns*,
With Limbs robust, and Voice that stuns;
But you have molded them afresh,
Remov'd the tough superfluous Flesh,
Taught them to modulate their Tongues,
And speak without the Help of Lungs.　　　80

Proteus on you bestow'd the Boon
To change your Visage like the Moon;
You sometimes half a Face produce,
Keep t'other Half for private Use.

How fam'd thy Conduct in the Fight,
With [1]*Hermes*, Son of *Pleias* bright:
Out-number'd, half encompass'd round,
You strove for ev'ry Inch of Ground;
Then, by a soldierly Retreat,
Retired to your Imperial Seat.　　　90
The Victor, when your Steps he trac'd,
Found all the Realms before him waste.
You, o'er the high triumphal Arch
Pontifick, made your glorious March:
The wond'rous Arch behind you fell,
And left a Chasm profound as Hell:

[1] Mercury.

You, in your Capitol secur'd,
A Siege as long as *Troy* endur'd.

1723/1727

The Furniture of a Woman's Mind

A SET of Phrases learn't by Rote;
A Passion for a Scarlet-Coat;
When at a Play to laugh, or cry,
Yet cannot tell the Reason why:
Never to hold her Tongue a Minute;
While all she prates has nothing in it.
While Hours can with a Coxcomb sit,
And take his Nonsense all for Wit;
Her Learning mounts to read a Song;
But, half the Words pronouncing wrong; 10
Has ev'ry Repartee in Store,
She spoke ten Thousand Times before.
Can ready Compliments supply
On all Occasions, cut and dry.
Such Hatred to a Parson's Gown,
The Sight will put her in a Swoon.
For Conversation well endu'd;
She calls it witty to be rude;
And, placing Raillery in Railing,
Will tell aloud your greatest Failing;   20
Nor make a Scruple to expose
Your bandy Leg, or crooked Nose.
Can at her Morning Tea, run o'er
The Scandal of the Day before,
Improving hourly in her Skill,
To cheat and wrangle at Quadrille.

In chusing Lace a Critick nice,
Knows to a Groat the lowest Price;

228

Can in her Female Clubs dispute
What Lining best the Silk will suit;   30
What Colours each Complexion match,
And where with Art to place a Patch.

If chance a Mouse creeps in her Sight,
Can finely counterfeit a Fright;
So, sweetly screams if it comes near her,
She ravishes all Hearts to hear her.
Can dext'rously her Husband teize,
By taking Fits whene'er she please:
By frequent Practice learns the Trick
At proper Seasons to be sick;   40
Thinks nothing gives one Airs so pretty;
At once creating Love and Pity.
If *Molly* happens to be careless,
And but neglects to warm her Hair-Lace,
She gets a Cold as sure as Death;
And vows she scarce can fetch her Breath:
Admires how modest Woman can
Be so *robustious* like a Man.

In Party, furious to her Power:
A bitter Whig, or Tory sow'r.   50
Her Arguments directly tend
Against the Side she would defend:
Will prove herself a Tory plain,
From Principles the Whigs maintain;
And, to defend the Whiggish Cause,
Her Topicks from the Tories draws.

O yes! If any Man can find
More Virtues in a Woman's Mind,
Let them be sent to Mrs. ¹*Harding*
She'll pay the Charges to a Farthing: 60
Take Notice, she has my Commission

¹ *A Printer.*

To add them to the next Edition:
They may out-sell a better Thing;
So, Halloo Boys! God save the King.

1727/1735

The Journal of a Modern Lady

IT was a most unfriendly Part
In you who ought to know my Heart,
Are well acquainted with my Zeal
For all the Female Common-weal:
How cou'd it come into your Mind,
To pitch on me, of all Mankind,
Against the Sex to write a Satyr,
And brand me for a Woman-Hater?
On me, who think them all so fair,
They rival *Venus* to a Hair;   10
Their Virtues never ceas'd to sing,
Since first I learn'd to tune a String.
Methinks I hear the Ladies cry,
Will he his Character belye?
Must never our Misfortunes end?
And have we lost our only Friend?
Ah lovely Nymphs, remove your Fears,
No more let fall those precious Tears.
Sooner shall, &c.

[*Here several Verses are omitted.*

The Hound be hunted by the Hare,   20
Than I turn Rebel to the Fair.

'Twas you engag'd me first to write,
Then gave the Subject out of Spite:
The *Journal of a modern Dame*
Is by my Promise what you claim:

My Word is past, I must submit;
And yet perhaps you may be bit.
I but transcribe, for not a Line
Of all the Satyr shall be mine.

Compell'd by you to tag in Rhimes,⠀⠀⠀30
The common Slanders of the Times,
Of modern Times, the Guilt is yours,
And me my Innocence secures.

Unwilling Muse begin thy Lay,
The Annals of a Female Day.

By Nature turn'd to play the Rake-well,
(As we shall shew you in the Sequel)
The modern Dame is wak'd by Noon,
Some Authors say, not quite so soon:
Because, though sore against her Will,⠀⠀⠀40
She sat all Night up at *Quadrill*.
She stretches, gapes, unglues her Eyes,
And asks, if it be time to rise;
Of Head-ach, and the Spleen complains;
And then to cool her heated Brains,
(Her Night-Gown and her Slippers brought
⠀⠀⠀her,)
Takes a large Dram of *Citron-Water*.
Then to her Glass; and 'Betty, pray
'Don't I look frightfully To-day?
'But, was it not confounded hard?⠀⠀⠀50
'Well, if I ever touch a Card:
'Four *Mattadores*, and lose *Codill!*
'Depend upon't, I never will:
'But run to *Tom*, and bid him fix
'The Ladies here To-night by Six.'
Madam, the Goldsmith waits below;
He says, his Business is to know
If you'll redeem the Silver Cup

He keeps in Pawn?—'Why, shew him up.'
Your Dressing-Plate, he'll be content   60
To take, for Interest *Cent. per Cent.*
And, Madam, there's my Lady *Spade*
Hath sent this Letter by her Maid.
'Well, I remember what she won:
'And hath she sent so soon to dun?
'Here, carry down those ten Pistoles
'My Husband left to pay for Coals:
'I thank my Stars they all are light;
'And I may have Revenge To-night.'
Now, loit'ring o'er her Tea and Cream,   70
She enters on her usual Theme;
Her last night's ill Success repeats;
Calls Lady *Spade* a Hundred Cheats:
She slipt *Spadillo* in her Breast,
Then thought to turn it to a Jest.
There's Mrs. *Cut* and she combine,
And to each other give the Sign.
Through every Game pursues her Tale,
Like Hunters o'er their Evening Ale.

     Now to another Scene give Place,   80
Enter the Folks with Silks and Lace:
Fresh Matter for a World of Chat;
Right *Indian* this, right *Macklin* that;
Observe this Pattern; there's a Stuff!
I can have Customers enough.
Dear Madam, you are grown so hard,
This Lace is worth twelve Pounds a Yard;
Madam, if there be Truth in Man,
I never sold so cheap a Fan.

     This Business of Importance o'er,   90
And Madam almost dress'd by Four;
The Footman, in his usual Phrase,
Comes up with, 'Madam, Dinner stays;'

She answers in her usual Style,
'The Cook must keep it back a while;
'I never can have time to dress,
'No Woman breathing takes up less;
'I'm hurry'd so, it makes me sick,
'I wish the Dinner at *Old Nick*.'
At Table now she acts her Part,   100
Has all the Dinner-Cant by Heart:
'I thought we were to dine alone,
'My Dear, for sure if I had known
'This Company would come to Day—
'But really, 'tis my Spouse's Way,
'He's so unkind, he never sends
'To tell when he invites his Friends;
'I wish you may but have enough.'
And while, with all this paultry Stuff,
She sits tormenting every Guest,   110
Nor gives her Tongue one Moment's Rest,
In Phrases batter'd, stale, and trite,
Which *modern* Ladies call polite;
You see the Booby Husband sit
In Admiration at her Wit!

But let me now a while survey
Our Madam o'er her Ev'ning Tea;
Surrounded with her noisy Clans
Of Prudes, Coquets, and Harridans;
When frighted at the clam'rous Crew,   120
Away the God of *Silence* flew,
And fair *Discretion* left the Place,
And *Modesty* with blushing Face:
Now enters over-weening *Pride*,
And *Scandal*, ever gaping wide,
Hypocrisy with Frown severe,
Scurrility with gibing Air;
Rude *Laughter* seeming like to burst;
And *Malice* always judging worst;

233

And *Vanity* with Pocket-Glass;   130
And *Impudence* with Front of Brass;
And studied *Affectation* came,
Each Limb and Feature out of Frame:
While *Ignorance*, with Brain of Lead,
Flew hov'ring o'er each Female Head.

Why should I ask of thee, my Muse,
An hundred Tongues, as Poets use,
When, to give ev'ry Dame her Due,
An Hundred Thousand were too few!
Or how should I, alas! relate,   140
The Sum of all their senseless Prate;
Their Innuendo's, Hints, and Slanders,
Their Meanings lewd, and *double Entendres*.
Now comes the gen'ral Scandal Charge;
What some invent, the rest enlarge:
And, 'Madam, if it be a Lye,
'You have the Tale as cheap as I:
'I must conceal my Author's Name,
'But now 'tis known to common Fame.'

Say, foolish Females, bold and blind;   150
Say, by what fatal Turn of Mind,
Are you on Vices most severe,
Wherein yourselves have greatest Share?
Thus ev'ry Fool herself deludes;
The Prude condemns the absent Prudes;
Mopsa, who stinks her Spouse to Death,
Accuses *Chloe*'s tainted Breath;
Hercina rank with Sweat, presumes
To censure *Phillis* for Perfumes;
While crooked *Cynthia* sneering says,   160
That *Florimel* wears Iron Stays;
Chloe of ev'ry Coxcomb jealous,
Admires how Girls can talk with Fellows;
And full of Indignation frets

That Women should be such Coquets:
Iris, for Scandal most notorious,
Cries, 'Lord, the World is so censorious!'
And *Rufa*, with her Combs of Lead,
Whispers that *Sappho*'s Hair is red:
Aura, whose Tongue you hear a Mile hence,
Talks half a Day in Praise of Silence; 171
And *Silvia*, full of inward Guilt,
Calls *Amoret* an arrant Jilt.

   Now Voices over Voices rise,
While each to be the loudest vies;
They contradict, affirm, dispute;
No single Tongue one Moment mute;
All mad to speak, and none to hearken,
They set the very Lap-Dog barking:
Their Chattering makes a louder Din 180
Than Fish-Wives o'er a Cup of Gin:
Not School-Boys, at a Barring out,
Rais'd ever such incessant Rout:
The jumbling Particles of Matter
In Chaos made not such a Clatter;
Far less the Rabble roar and rail,
When drunk with sour Election Ale.

   Nor do they trust their Tongue alone,
But speak a Language of their own;
Can read a Nod, a Shrug, a Look, 190
Far better than a printed Book:
Convey a Libel in a Frown,
And wink a Reputation down;
Or, by the Tossing of the Fan,
Describe the Lady and the Man.

   But see, the Female Club disbands,
Each, twenty Visits on her hands.
Now, all alone, poor Madam sits,

In Vapours and Hysterick Fits:
'And was not *Tom* this Morning sent?   200
'I'd lay my Life he never went.
'Past Six, and not a living Soul!
'I might, by this, have won a Vole.'
A dreadful Interval of Spleen!
How shall we pass the Time between?
'Here, *Betty*, let me take my Drops,
'And feel my Pulse, I know it stops:
'This Head of mine, Lord, how it swims!
'And such a Pain in all my Limbs.'
Dear Madam, try to take a Nap—   210
But now they hear a Foot-man's Rap:
'Go run, and light the Ladies up:
'It must be One before we sup.'

    The Table, Cards, and Counters set,
And all the Gamester Ladies met,
Her Spleen and Fits recover'd quite,
Our Madam can sit up all Night,
'Whoever comes, I'm not within—'
Quadrill the Word, and so begin.

    How can the Muse her Aid impart,   220
Unskill'd in all the Terms of Art?
Or in harmonious Numbers put
The Deal, the Shuffle, and the Cut?
The superstitious Whims relate,
That fill a Female Gamester's Pate?
What Agony of Soul she feels
To see a Knave's inverted Heels?
She draws up Card by Card, to find
Good Fortune peeping from behind:
With panting Heart, and earnest Eyes,   230
In hope to see *Spadillo* rise;
In vain, alas! her Hope is fed;
She draws an Ace, and sees it red.

In ready Counters never pays,
But pawns her Snuff-Box, Rings and Keys,
Ever with some new Fancy struck,
Tries twenty Charms to mend her Luck.
'This Morning when the *Parson* came,
'I said, I should not win a Game.
'This odious Chair, how came I stuck in't?
'I think, I never had good Luck in't,   241
'I'm so uneasy in my Stays;
'Your Fan a Moment, if you please.
'Stand further, Girl, or get you gone.
'I always lose when you look on.'
Lord, Madam, you have lost *Codill*;
I never saw you play so ill.
'Nay, Madam, give me leave to say,
''Twas you that threw the Game away;
'When Lady *Tricksy* play'd a Four,   250
'You took it with a Mattadore;
'I saw you touch your Wedding Ring,
'Before my Lady call'd a King.
'You spoke a Word began with H,
'And I know whom you mean to teach,
'Because you held the King of Hearts:
'Fie, Madam, leave these little Arts.'
That's not so bad as one that rubs
Her Chair to call the King of Clubs,
And makes her Partner understand   260
A Mattadore is in her Hand.
'Madam, you have no Cause to flounce,
'I swear, I saw you thrice renounce.'
And truly, Madam, I know when
Instead of five you scor'd me Ten.
Spadillo here has got a Mark,
A Child may know it in the Dark:
I guess the Hand it seldom fails,
I wish some Folks would pare their Nails.

While thus they rail, and scold, and storm,
It passes but for common Form;   271
And conscious that they all speak true,
They give each other but their Due;
It never interrupts the Game,
Or makes 'em sensible of Shame.

The Time too precious now to waste,
And Supper gobbled up in haste;
Again a-fresh to Cards they run,
As if they had but just begun.
But I shall not again repeat   280
How oft they squabble, snarl and cheat,
At last they hear the Watchman knock,
A frosty Morn—Past four o'Clock.
The Chair-men are not to be found,
'Come, let us play another Round.'

Now, all in haste they huddle on
Their Hoods, and Cloaks, and get them
    gone:
But, first, the Winner must invite
The Company to-morrow Night.

Unlucky Madam, left in Tears,   290
(Who now again *Quadrill* forswears,)
With empty Purse, and aching Head,
Steals to her sleeping Spouse to Bed.
              1729/1729

Death and Daphne

To an agreeable young Lady, but extremely lean

DEATH went upon a solemn Day,
At *Pluto*'s Hall, his Court to pay:

The Phantom, having humbly kiss't
His griesly Monarch's sooty Fist,
Presented him the Weekly Bills
Of Doctors, Fevers, Plagues, and Pills.
Pluto observing, since the Peace,
The Burial Article decrease;
And, vext to see Affairs miscarry,
Declar'd in Council, *Death* must marry: 10
Vow'd, he no longer could support
Old Batchelors about his Court:
The Int'rest of his Realm had need
That *Death* should get a num'rous Breed;
Youth *Deathlings*, who, by Practice made
Proficients in their Father's Trade,
With Colonies might stock around
His large Dominions under Ground.

   A Consult of Coquets below
Was call'd, to rig him out a Beau: 20
From her own Head, *Megæra* takes
A Perriwig of twisted Snakes;
Which in the nicest Fashion curl'd,
Like ¹*Toupets* of this upper World;
With Flour of Sulphur powder'd well,
(That graceful on his Shoulders fell)
An Adder of the sable Kind,
In Line direct, hung down behind,
The Owl, the Raven, and the Bat,
Club'd for a Feather to his Hat; 30
His Coat, an Us'rers Velvet Pall,
Bequeath'd to *Pluto*, Corps and all.
But, loth his Person to expose
Bare, like a Carcase pick'd by Crows,
A Lawyer o'er his Hands and Face,
Stuck artfully a Parchment Case.
No new-flux'd Rake shew'd fairer Skin;

¹ *The Perriwigs now in Fashion are so called.*

Not *Phyllis* after lying in.
With Snuff was fill'd his Ebon-Box,
Of Shin-Bones rotted by the Pox.   40
Nine Spirits of Blaspheming Fops,
With Aconite anoint his Chops:
And give him Words of dreadful Sounds,
G—d—n his Blood, and Bl— and W—ds.

   Thus, furnish'd out, he sent his Train,
To take a House in *Warwick*-Lane:
The *Faculty*, his humble Friends,
A complimental Message sends:
Their President in scarlet Gown,
Harangu'd and welcom'd him to Town.   50

   But, *Death* had Bus'ness to dispatch:
His Mind was running on his Match.
And, hearing much of *Daphne*'s Fame,
His *Majesty of Terrors* came,
Fine as a Col'nel of the Guards,
To visit where she sat at Cards:
She, as he came into the Room,
Thought him *Adonis* in his Bloom.
And now her Heart with Pleasure jumps,
She scarce remembers what is Trumps.   60
For, such a Shape of Skin and Bone
Was never seen, except her own:
Charm'd with his Eyes, and Chin, and
    Snout,
Her Pocket-Glass drew slily out;
And, grew enamour'd with her Phiz,
As just the Counter-Part of his.
She darted many a private Glance,
And freely made the first Advance:
Was of her Beauty grown so vain,
She doubted not to win the *Swain*.   70
Nothing she thought could sooner gain him,

Than with her Wit to entertain him,
She ask't about her Friends below;
This meagre Fop, that batter'd Beau:
Whether some late departed Toasts
Had got Gallants among the Ghosts?
If *Chloe* were a Sharper still,
As great as ever, at Quadrille?
(The Ladies there must needs be Rooks,
For, Cards we know, are *Pluto*'s Books)   80
If *Florimel* had found her Love
For whom she hang'd herself above?
How oft a Week was kept a Ball
By *Proserpine*, at *Pluto*'s Hall?
She fancy'd, those *Elysian* Shades
The sweetest Place for Masquerades:
How pleasant on the Banks of *Styx*,
To troll it in a Coach and Six!

    What Pride a Female Heart enflames!
How endless are Ambition's Aims!   90
Cease, haughty Nymph; the Fates decree,
Death must not be a Spouse for thee:
For, when by chance the meagre Shade
Upon thy Hand his Finger laid;
Thy Hand as dry and cold as Lead,
His matrimonial Spirit fled;
He felt about his Heart a Damp,
That quite extinguish'd *Cupid*'s Lamp:
Away the frighted Spectre scuds,
And leaves my Lady in the Suds.   100
1730/1735

To Betty the Grizette

QUEEN of Wit and Beauty, *Betty*,
Never may the Muse forget ye:
How thy Face charms ev'ry Shepherd,
Spotted over like a Le'pard!
And, thy freckled Neck display'd,
Envy breeds in ev'ry Maid,
Like a Fly-blown Cake of Tallow,
Or, on Parchment, Ink turn'd yellow;
Or, a tawny speckled Pippin,
Shrivel'd with a Winter's keeping.   10

And, thy Beauty thus dispatch't;
Let me praise thy Wit unmatch't.

Sets of Phrases, cut and dry,
Evermore thy Tongue supply.
And, thy Memory is loaded
With old Scraps from Plays exploded.
Stock't with Repartees and Jokes,
Suited to all Christian Folks:
Shreds of Wit, and senseless Rhimes,
Blunder'd out a thousand Times.   20
Nor, wilt thou of Gifts be sparing,
Which can ne'er be worse for wearing,
Picking Wit among Collegions,
In the Play-House upper Regions;
Where, in Eighteen-penny Gall'ry,
Irish Nymphs learn *Irish* Raillery:
But, thy Merit is thy Failing,
And, thy Raillery is Railing.

Thus, with Talents well endu'd
To be scurrilous and rude;   30
When you pertly raise your Snout,

Fleer, and gibe, and laugh, and flout;
This, among *Hibernian* Asses,
For sheer Wit, and Humour passes!
Thus, indulgent *Chloe* bit,
Swears you have a World of Wit.

1730/1735

The Lady's Dressing-Room

FIVE Hours, (and who can do it less in?)
By haughty *Cælia* spent in Dressing;
The Goddess from her Chamber issues,
Array'd in Lace, Brocade and Tissues:
Strephon, who found the Room was void,
And *Betty* otherwise employ'd,
Stole in, and took a strict Survey
Of all the Litter, as it lay:
Whereof to make the Matter clear,
An *Inventory* follows here.   10

And first, a dirty Smock appear'd,
Beneath the Arm-pits well besmear'd;
Strephon, the Rogue, display'd it wide,
And turn'd it round on ev'ry Side:
In such a Case, few Words are best,
And *Strephon* bids us guess the rest;
But swears how damnably the Men lye,
In calling *Cælia* sweet and cleanly.

Now listen, while he next produces
The various Combs for various Uses;   20
Fill'd up with Dirt so closely fixt,
No Brush cou'd force a Way betwixt;
A Paste of Composition rare,
Sweat, Dandriff, Powder, Lead and Hair,

243

A Forehead-Cloath with Oil upon't,
To smooth the Wrinkles on her Front:
Here, Alum Flour to stop the Steams,
Exhal'd from sour unsav'ry Streams;
There, Night-Gloves made of *Tripsey*'s Hide,
Bequeath'd by *Tripsey* when she dy'd;⠀⠀⠀30
With Puppy-Water, Beauty's Help,
Distill'd from *Tripsey*'s darling Whelp,
Here Gally-pots and Vials plac'd,
Some fill'd with Washes, some with Paste;
Some with Pomatums, Paints, and Slops,
And Ointments good for scabby Chops,
Hard by, a filthy Bason stands,
Foul'd with the scow'ring of her Hands;
The Bason takes whatever comes,
The Scrapings from her Teeth and Gums,⠀⠀40
A nasty Compound of all Hues,
For here she spits, and here she spues.

⠀⠀But O! it turn'd poor *Strephon*'s Bowels,
When he beheld and smelt the Towels:
Begumm'd, bematter'd, and beslim'd;
With Dirt, and Sweat, and Ear-wax grim'd.
No Object *Strephon*'s Eye escapes;
Here Petticoats in frowzy Heaps.
Nor be the Handkerchiefs forgot,
All varnish'd o'er with Snuff and Snot.⠀⠀50
The Stockings, why should I expose,
Stain'd with the Moisture of her Toes;
Or greasy Coifs, and Pinners reeking,
Which *Cælia* slept at least a week in.
A pair of Tweezers next he found,
To pluck her Brows in Arches round,
Or, Hairs that sink the Forehead low,
Or, on her Chin like Bristles grow.

The Virtues we must not let pass
Of *Cælia*'s magnifying Glass: 60
When frighted *Strephon* cast his Eye on't,
It shew'd the Visage of a Giant:
A Glass that can to Sight disclose
The smallest Worm in *Cælia*'s Nose,
And faithfully direct her Nail,
To squeeze it out from Head to Tail;
For, catch it nicely by the Head,
It must come out, alive or dead.

Why, *Strephon*, will you tell the rest?
And must you needs describe the Chest?   70
That careless Wench! No Creature warn her,
To move it out from yonder Corner,
But leave it standing full in Sight,
For you to exercise your Spight!
In vain the Workman shew'd his Wit,
With Rings and Hinges counterfeit,
To make it seem in this Disguise,
A Cabinet to vulgar Eyes;
Which *Strephon* ventur'd to look in,
Resolv'd to go thro' *thick and thin*,   80
He lifts the Lid: There need no more,
He smelt it all the Time before.

As, from within *Pandora*'s Box,
When *Epimetheus* op'd the Locks,
A sudden universal Crew
Of human Evils upward flew;
He still was comforted to find,
That *Hope* at last remain'd behind.

So, *Strephon*, lifting up the Lid,
To view what in the Chest was hid,   90
The Vapours flew out from the Vent;
But *Strephon*, cautious, never meant

The Bottom of the *Pan* to grope,
And foul his Hands in search of *Hope.*

O! ne'er may such a vile Machine
Be once in *Cælia*'s Chamber seen!
O! may she better learn to keep
Those *Secrets of the hoary Deep*![1]

As Mutton-Cutlets, [2]*Prime of Meat,*
Which, tho' with Art you salt and beat,   100
As Laws of Cookery require,
And roast them at the clearest Fire;
If from [3]*adown* the hopeful Chops,
The Fat upon a Cinder drops,
To stinking Smoak it turns the Flame,
Pois'ning the Flesh from whence it came,
And up exhales a greazy Stench,
For which you curse the careless Wench:
So, Things which must not be exprest,
When *plumpt* into the reeking Chest,   110
Send up an excremental Smell,
To taint the Parts from whence they fell:
The Petticoats and Gown perfume,
And waft a Stink round ev'ry Room.

Thus finishing his grand Survey,
The Swain disgusted slunk away,
Repeating in his am'rous Fits,
Oh! *Cælia, Cælia, Cælia*, sh—

But *Vengeance*, Goddess, never sleeping,
Soon punish'd *Strephon* for his peeping.   120
His foul Imagination links
Each Dame he sees with all her Stinks;
And, if unsavoury Odours fly,

---

[1] Milton.   [2] *Prima Virorum.*
[3] *Vide* D—n D—s *Works, and* N. P—y's.

Conceives a Lady standing by.
All Women his Description fits,
And both Ideas jump like Wits,
By vicious Fancy coupled fast,
And still appearing in *Contrast*.

   I pity wretched *Strephon*, blind
To all the Charms of Woman-kind.   130
Should I the *Queen of Love* refuse,
Because she rose from stinking Ooze?
To him that looks behind the Scene,
Satira's but some pocky Quean.

   When *Cælia* all her Glory shows,
If *Strephon* would but stop his Nose,
Who now so impiously blasphemes
Her Ointments, Daubs, and Paints, and
      Creams;
Her Washes, Slops, and ev'ry Clout,
With which he makes so foul a Rout;   140
He soon would learn to think like me,
And bless his ravish'd Eyes to see,
Such Order from Confusion sprung,
Such gaudy *Tulips* rais'd from *Dung*.
                1730/1732

A Beautiful Young Nymph Going to Bed

   Corinna, Pride of *Drury-Lane*,
For whom no Shepherd sighs in vain;
Never did *Covent-Garden* boast
So bright a batter'd, stroling Toast;
No drunken Rake to pick her up,
No Cellar where on Tick to sup;
Returning at the Midnight Hour;

Four Stories climbing to her Bow'r;
Then, seated on a three-leg'd Chair,
Takes off her artificial Hair: 10
Now, picking out a Chrystal Eye,
She wipes it clean, and lays it by.
Her Eye-brows from a Mouse's Hyde,
Stuck on with Art on either Side,
Pulls off with Care, and first displays 'em,
Then in a Play-book smoothly lays 'em.
Now dext'rously her Plumpers draws,
That serve to fill her hollow Jaws.
Untwists a Wire; and from her Gums
A Set of Teeth compleatly comes.   20
Pulls out the Rags, contriv'd to prop
Her flabby Dugs, and down they drop.
Procéeding on, the lovely Goddess,
Unlaces next her Steel-ribb'd Bodice;
Which by the Operator's Skill,
Press down the Lumps, the Hollows fill.
Up goes her Hand, and off she slips
The Bolsters that supply her Hips.
With gentlest Touch, she next explores
Her Shankers, Issues, running Sores;   30
Effects of many a sad Disaster,
And then to each applies a Plaister.
But must, before she goes to Bed,
Rub off the Dawbs of White and Red;
And smooth the Furrows in her Front,
With greasy Paper stuck upon't.
She takes a *Bolus* e'er she sleeps;
And then between two Blankets creeps.
With Pains of Love tormented lies;
Or, if she chance to close her Eyes,   40
Of *Bridewell* and the *Compter* dreams,
And feels the Lash, and faintly screams;
Or, by a faithless Bully drawn,
At some Hedge-Tavern lies in Pawn.

Or, to *Jamaica* seems transported,
[1]Alone, and by no Planter courted.
Or, near *Fleet-Ditch*'s oozy Brinks,
Surrounded with a Hundred Stinks:
Belated, seems on Watch to lye,
And snap some Cully passing by.   50
Or, struck with Fear, her Fancy runs
On Watchmen, Constables, and Duns,
From who she meets with frequent Rubs;
But never from religious Clubs;
Whose Favour she is sure to find,
Because she pays them all in Kind.

Corinna wakes. A dreadful Sight!
Behold the Ruins of the Night!
A wicked Rat her Plaister stole,
Half eat, and dragg'd it to his Hole.   60
The Chrystal Eye, alas, was miss't;
And Puss had on her Plumpers p—st.
A Pidgeon pick't her Issue-Peas;
And *Shock* her Tresses fill'd with Fleas.

The Nymph, though in this mangled
    Plight,
Must ev'ry Morn her Limbs unite;
But, how shall I describe her Arts
To recollect the scatter'd Parts?
Or, shew the Anguish, Toyl, and Pain,
Of gathering up her self again.   70
The bashful Muse will never bear,
In such a scene to interfere.
Corinna in the Morning dizen'd,
Who sees will spew; who smells, be poison'd.
                                        1731/1734

[1] *—Et longam incomitata videtur*
    Ire viam.—

Strephon and Chloe

OF *Chloe* all the Town has rung;
By ev'ry Size of Poets sung.
So beautiful a Nymph appears
But once in Twenty Thousand Years.
By Nature form'd with nicest Care,
And, faultless to a single Hair;
Her graceful Mien, her Shape, and Face,
Confess't her of no mortal Race:
And then, so nice, and so genteel;
Such Cleanliness from Head to Heel: 10
No Humours gross, or frowzy Steams,
No noisome Whiffs, or sweaty Streams,
Before, behind, above, below,
Could from her taintless Body flow.
Would so discreetly Things dispose,
None ever saw her pluck a Rose.
Her dearest Comrades never caught her
Squat on her Hams, to make Maid's Water.
You'd swear, that so divine a Creature
Felt no Necessities of Nature.   20
In Summer, had she walk't the Town,
Her Arm-pits would not stain her Gown:
At Country-Dances, not a Nose
Could in the Dog-Days smell her Toes.
Her Milk-white Hands, both Palms and
    Backs,
Like Iv'ry dry, and soft as Wax.
Her Hands, the softest ever felt,
[1]Though cold would burn, though dry
    would melt.

Dear *Venus*, hide this Wond'rous Maid,
Nor let her loose to spoil your Trade.   30

[1] *Though deep, yet clear*, &c. Denham.

While she engrosseth ev'ry Swain,
You but o'er half the World can reign.
Think what a Case all Men are now in,
What ogling, sighing, toasting, vowing!
What powder'd Wigs! What Flames and
    Darts!
What Hampers full of bleeding Hearts!
What Sword-knots! What poetick Strains!
What Billet-doux, and clouded Canes!

But, *Strephon* sigh'd so loud and strong,
He blew a Settlement along: 40
And, bravely drove his Rivals down
With Coach and Six, and House in Town.
The bashful Nymph no more withstands,
Because her dear Papa commands.
The charming Couple now unites:
Proceed we to the Marriage Rites.

Imprimis, at the Temple Porch
Stood *Hymen* with a flaming Torch:
The smiling *Cyprian* Goddess brings
Her infant Loves with purple Wings: 50
And Pidgeons billing, Sparrows treading,
Fair Emblems of a fruitful Wedding.
The Muses next in Order follow,
Conducted by their Squire, *Apollo*:
Then *Mercury* with Silver Tongue,
And *Hebe*, Goddess ever young.
Behold the Bridegroom and his Bride,
Walk Hand in Hand, and Side by Side;
She, by the tender Graces drest,
But, he by *Mars*, in Scarlet Vest.   60
The Nymph was cover'd with her [1]*Flammeum,*

[1] *A Veil which the* Roman *Brides covered themselves with when they were going to be married.*

And *Phœbus* sung th' ¹*Epithalamium*.
And, last, to make the Matter sure,
Dame *Juno* brought a Priest demure.
²*Luna* was absent, on Pretence
Her Time was not till Nine Months hence.

    The Rites perform'd, the Parson paid,
In State return'd the grand Parade;
With loud Huzza's from all the Boys,
That, now the Pair must *crown their Joys*.   70

    But, still the hardest Part remains,
Strephon had long perplex'd his Brains,
How with so high a Nymph he might
Demean himself the Wedding-Night:
For, as he view'd his Person round,
Meer mortal Flesh was all he found:
His Hand, his Neck, his Mouth, and Feet
Were duly washt, to keep them sweet;
(With other Parts that shall be nameless,
The Ladies else might think me shameless.)
The Weather and his Love were hot;   81
And should he struggle; I know what—
Why let it go, if I must tell it—
He'll sweat, and then the Nymph may smell
    it.
While she a Goddess dy'd in Grain
Was unsusceptible of Stain:
And, *Venus*-like, her fragrant Skin
Exhal'd *Ambrosia* from within:
Can such a Deity endure
A mortal human Touch impure?   90
How did the humbled Swain detest
His prickled Beard, and hairy Breast!
His Night-cap border'd round with Lace
Could give no Softness to his Face.

¹ *A Marriage-Song at Weddings.*   ² Diana, *Goddess of Midwives.*

Yet, if the Goddess could be kind,
What endless Raptures must he find!
And, Goddesses have now and then
Come down to visit mortal Men:
To visit, and to court them too:
A certain Goddess, God knows who,   100
(As in a Book he heard it read)
Took Col'nel *Peleus* to her Bed.
But, what if he should leave his Life
By vent'ring *on* his heavenly Wife?
For, *Strephon* could remember well,
That, once he heard a School-boy tell,
How *Semele* of mortal Race,
By Thunder dy'd in *Jove's* Embrace,
And, what if daring *Strephon* dyes
By Lightning shot from *Chloe's* Eyes?   110

    While these Reflections fill'd his Head,
The Bride was put in Form to Bed:
He follow'd, stript, and in he crept,
But, awfully his Distance kept.

    Now, *Ponder well ye Parents dear*;
Forbid your Daughter guzzling Beer:
And, make them ev'ry Afternoon
Forbear their Tea, or drink it soon;
That, e're to Bed they venture up,
They may discharge it ev'ry Sup: 120
If not; they must in evil Plight
Be often forc'd to rise at Night;
Keep them to wholsome Food confin'd,
Nor let them taste what causes Wind;
[1]('Tis this the Sage of *Samos* means,
Forbidding his Disciples Beans)
O, think what Evils must ensue;
Miss *Moll* the Jade will burn it blue:

[1] *A well known Precept of* Pythagoras, *not to eat Beans.*

And, when she once hath got the Art,
She cannot help it for her Heart;   130
But, out it flies, ev'n when she meets
Her Bridegroom in the Wedding-Sheets.
¹*Carminative* and ²*Diuretick*,
Will damp all Passion Sympathetick:
And, Love such Nicety requires,
One *Blast* will put out all his Fires.
Since Husbands get behind the Scene,
The Wife should study to be clean;
Nor give the smallest Room to guess
The Time when wants of Nature press;   140
But, after Marriage, practise more
Decorum than she did before;
To keep her Spouse deluded still,
And make him fancy what she will.

In Bed we left the married Pair:
'Tis Time to shew how Things went there.
Strephon, who had been often told,
That Fortune still assists the Bold,
Resolv'd to make his first Attack:
But, *Chloe* drove him fiercely back.   150
How could a Nymph so chaste as *Chloe*,
With Constitution cold and snowy,
Permit a brutish Man to touch her;
Ev'n Lambs by Instinct fly the Butcher.
Resistence on the Wedding-night
Is what our Maidens claim by Right:
And, *Chloe*, 'tis by all agreed,
Was Maid in Thought, and Word, and Deed.
Yet some assign a diff'rent Reason;
That *Strephon* chose no proper Season.   160

Say, fair Ones, must I make a Pause?
Or freely tell the secret Cause.

¹ *Medicines to break Wind.*   ² *Medicines to provoke Urine.*

Twelve Cups of Tea, (with Grief I speak,)
Had now constrain'd the Nymph to leak.
This Point must needs be settled first:
The Bride must either void or burst.
Then, see the dire Effect of Pease,
Think what can give the Cholick ease.
The Nymph opprest before, behind,
As Ships are toss't by Waves and Wind,   170
Steals out her Hand, by Nature led,
And brings a Vessel into Bed:
Fair Utensil, as smooth and white
As *Chloe*'s skin, almost as bright.

Strephon who heard the fuming Rill,
As from a mossy Cliff distill;
Cry'd out, ye Gods, what Sound is this?
Can *Chloe*, heav'nly *Chloe* —?
But, when he smelt a noysome Steam
Which oft attends that luke-warm Stream;
[1](*Salerno* both together joins;   181
As sov'reign Med'cines for the Loyns)
And, though contriv'd, we may suppose
To slip his Ears, yet struck his Nose:
He found her, while the Scent increast,
As *mortal* as himself at least.
But, soon with like Occasions prest,
He boldly sent his Hand in quest,
(Inspir'd with Courage from his Bride)
To reach the Pot on t'other Side.   190
And as he filled the reeking Vase,
Let fly a Rouzer in her Face.

The little *Cupids* hov'ring round,
(As Pictures prove) with Garlands crown'd,

---

[1] *Vide Schol.* Salern. Rules of Health, written by the School of **Salernum**. *Mingere cum bumbis res est saluberrima lumbis.*

Abash't at what they saw and heard,
Flew off, nor ever more appear'd.

Adieu to ravishing Delights,
High Raptures, and romantick Flights;
To Goddesses so heav'nly sweet;
Expiring Shepherds at their Feet;   200
To silver Meads, and shady Bow'rs,
Drest up with *Amaranthine* Flow'rs.

How great a Change! how quickly made!
They learn to call a Spade, a Spade.
They soon from all Constraint are freed;
Can see each other *do their Need*.
On Box of Cedar sits the Wife,
And makes it warm for *Dearest Life*.
And, by the beastly Way of Thinking,
Find great Society in Stinking.   210
Now, *Strephon* daily entertains
His *Chloe* in the homeli'st Strains:
And, *Chloe* more experienc'd grown,
With Int'rest pays him back his own.
No Maid at Court is less asham'd,
Howe'er for selling Bargains fam'd,
Than she, to name her Parts behind,
Or, when a-bed, to let out Wind.

Fair *Decency*, celestial Maid,
Descend from Heav'n to Beauty's Aid,   220
Though Beauty may beget Desire,
'Tis thou must fan the Lover's Fire:
For, Beauty, like supreme Dominion,
Is best supported by Opinion:
If Decency bring no Supplies,
Opinion falls, and Beauty dies.

To see some radiant Nymph appear
In all her glitt'ring Birth-day Gear,
You think some Goddess from the Sky
Descended, ready cut and dry: 230
But e'er you sell your self to Laughter,
Consider well what may come after;
For fine Ideas vanish fast,
While all the gross and filthy last.

O *Strephon*, e'er that fatal Day
When *Chloe* stole your Heart away,
Had you but through a Cranny spy'd
On House of Ease your future Bride,
In all the Postures of her Face,
Which Nature gives in such a Case;   240
Distortions, Groanings, Strainings, Heavings;
'Twere better you had lick't her Leavings,
Than from Experience find too late
Your Goddess grown a filthy Mate.
Your Fancy then had always dwelt
On what you saw, and what you smelt;
Would still the same Ideas give ye,
As when you spy'd her on the Privy.
And, spight of *Chloe*'s Charms divine,
Your Heart had been as whole as mine.   250

Authorities both old and recent,
Direct, that Women must be decent;
And, from the Spouse each Blemish hide
More than from all the World beside.

Unjustly all our Nymphs complain,
Their Empire holds so short a Reign;
Is after Marriage lost so soon,
It hardly holds the Honey-moon:
For, if they keep not what they caught,
It is entirely their own Fault.   260

They take Possession of the Crown,
And then throw all their Weapons down:
Though by the Politician's Scheme,
Whoe'er arrives at Pow'r supream,
Those Arts by which at first they gain it,
They still must practise to maintain it.

What various ways our Females take,
To pass for Wits before a Rake!
And, in the fruitless Search, pursue
All other Methods but the true.   270

Some try to learn polite Behaviour,
By reading Books against their Saviour.
Some call it witty, to reflect
On ev'ry natural Defect;
Some shew, they never want explaining,
To comprehend a double Meaning.
But, sure a Tell-tale out of School,
Is, of all Wits, the greatest Fool:
Whose rank Imagination fills
Her Heart, and from her Lips distils;   280
You'd think she utter'd from behind,
Or, at her Mouth, were breaking Wind.

Why is a handsome Wife ador'd
By ev'ry Coxcomb, but her Lord?
From yonder Puppet-man inquire,
Who wisely hides his Wood and Wire:
Shews *Sheba*'s Queen compleatly dress't,
And *Solomon* in Royal Vest:
But, view them litter'd on the Floor,
Or, strung on Pegs behind the Door;   290
Punch is exactly of a Piece
With *Lorrin*'s Duke, and Prince of *Greece*.

A Prudent Builder should forecast
How long the Stuff is like to last;
And, carefully observe the Ground,
To build on some Foundation sound:
What House, when its Materials crumble,
Must not inevitably tumble?
What Edifice can long endure,
Rais'd on a Basis unsecure?   300
Rash Mortals, e'er you take a Wife,
Contrive your Pile to last for Life:
Since Beauty scarce endures a Day,
And Youth so swiftly glides away;
Why will you make your self a Bubble
To build on Sand, with Hay and Stubble?

On Sense and Wit your Passion found,
By Decency cemented round;
Let Prudence with good Nature strive,
To keep Esteem and Love alive.   310
Then come old Age whene'er it will,
Your Friendship shall continue still:
And, thus a mutual gentle Fire,
Shall never but with Life expire.

                                    1731/1734

Cassinus and Peter

A Tragical Elegy

Two College Sophs of *Cambridge* Growth,
Both special Wits, and Lovers both,
Conferring, as they us'd to meet,
On Love, and Books, in Rapture sweet;
(Muse, find me Names to fit my Metre,
Cassinus this, and t'other *Peter*)
Friend *Peter* to *Cassinus* goes,

To chat a while, and warm his Nose:
But, such a Sight was never seen,
The Lad lay swallow'd up in Spleen;   10
He seem'd as just crept out of Bed;
One greasy Stocking round his Head,
The other he sat down to darn
With Threads of diff'rent colour'd Yarn.
His Breeches torn, exposing wide
A ragged Shirt, and tawny Hyde.
Scorch't were his Shins, his Legs were bare,
But, well embrown'd with Dirt and Hair.
A Rug was o'er his Shoulders thrown;
A Rug; for Night-gown he had none.   20
His Jordan stood in Manner fitting
Between his Legs, to spew or spit in.
His antient Pipe in Sable dy'd,
And half unsmoak't, lay by his Side.

Him, thus accoutr'd, *Peter* found,
With Eyes in Smoak, and Weeping drown'd:
The Leavings of his last Night's Pot
On Embers plac't, to drink it hot.

Why *Cassy*, thou wilt doze thy Pate:
What makes thee lie a-bed so late?   30
The Finch, the Linnet, and the Thrush,
Their Mattins chant in ev'ry Bush:
And, I have heard thee oft salute
Aurora with thy early Flute.
Heaven send thou hast not got the Hypps.
How? Not a Word come from thy Lips?

Then, gave him some familiar Thumps,
A College Joke, to cure the Dumps.

The Swain at last, with Grief oppress't,
Cry'd *Celia* thrice, and sigh'd the rest.   40

Dear *Cassy*, though to ask I dread,
Yet, ask I must. Is *Celia* dead?

How happy I, were that the worst:
But I was fated to be curst.

Come, tell us, has she play'd the Whore?

Oh *Peter*, wou'd it were no more!

Why, Plague confound her sandy Locks:
Say, has the small or greater Pox
Sunk down her Nose, or seam'd her Face?
Be easy, 'tis a common Case.   50

O *Peter!* Beauty's but a Varnish,
Which Time and Accidents will tarnish:
But, *Celia* has contriv'd to blast
Those Beauties that might ever last.
Nor, can Imagination guess,
Nor Eloquence Divine express,
How that ungrateful charming Maid,
My purest Passion has betray'd.
Conceive the most invenom'd Dart,
To pierce an injur'd Lover's Heart.   60

Why, hang her; though she seem'd so coy,
I know she loves the Barber's Boy.

Friend *Peter*, this I could excuse;
For, ev'ry Nymph has Leave to chuse;
Nor, have I Reason to complain:
She loves a more deserving Swain.
But, oh! how ill hast thou divin'd
A Crime that shocks all human Kind;
A Deed unknown to Female Race,
At which the Sun should hide his Face.   70

Advice in vain you would apply—
Then, leave me to despair and dye.
Yet, kind *Arcadians*, on my Urn
These Elegies and Sonnets burn,
And on the Marble grave these Rhimes,
A Monument to after-Times:
'Here *Cassy* lies, by *Celia* slain,
'And dying, never told his Pain.'

Vain empty World farewel. But, hark,
The loud *Cerberian* triple Bark,   80
And there—behold *Alecto* stand,
A Whip of Scorpions in her Hand.
Lo, *Charon* from his leaky Wherry,
Beck'ning to waft me o'er the Ferry.
I come, I come,—*Medusa*, see,
Her Serpents hiss direct at me.
Begone; unhand me, hellish Fry:
[1]Avaunt—ye cannot say 'twas I.

Dear *Cassy*, thou must purge and bleed;
I fear thou wilt be mad indeed.   90
But now, by Friendship's sacred Laws,
I here conjure thee, tell the Cause;
And *Celia*'s horrid Fact relate:
Thy Friend would gladly share thy Fate.

To force it out, my Heart must rend:
Yet, when conjur'd by such a Friend—
Think *Peter*, how my Soul is rack't.
These Eyes, these Eyes beheld the Fact.
Now, bend thine Ear; since out it must:
But, when thou seest me laid in Dust,   100
The Secret thou shalt ne'er impart;
Not to the Nymph that keeps thy Heart;
(How would her Virgin Soul bemoan,

[1] *See* Macbeth.

A Crime to all her Sex unknown!)
Nor whisper to the tattling Reeds,
The blackest of all Female Deeds.
Nor blab it on the lonely Rocks,
Where *Echo* sits, and list'ning, mocks.
Nor let the Zephyr's treach'rous Gale,
Through *Cambridge* waft the direful Tale. 110
Nor to the chatt'ring feather'd Race,
Discover *Celia's* foul Disgrace.
But, if you fail; my Spectre dread,
Attending nightly round your Bed;
And yet, I dare confide in you;
So, take my Secret, and adieu.

Nor, wonder how I lost my Wits:
Oh! *Celia, Celia, Celia,* sh—
1731/1734

Apollo:
or, a Problem solved

Apollo, God of Light and Wit,
Could Verse inspire, but seldom writ:
Refin'd all Metals with his Looks,
As well as Chymists by their Books:
As handsome as my Lady's Page;
Sweet Five and Twenty was his Age.
His Wig was made of sunny Rays,
He crown'd his youthful Head with Bays:
Not all the Court of Heav'n could shew
So nice and so compleat a Beau. 10
No Heir upon his first Appearance,
With Twenty Thousand Pounds a Year Rents,
E'er drove, before he sold his Land,
So fine a Coach along the Strand;

The Spokes, we are by *Ovid* told,
Were Silver, and the Axel Gold.
(I own, 'twas but a Coach and Four,
For *Jupiter* allows no more.)

Yet, with his Beauty, Wealth, and Parts,
Enough to win ten Thousand Hearts;   20
No vulgar Deity above
Was so unfortunate in Love.

Three weighty Causes were assign'd,
That mov'd the Nymphs to be unkind.
Nine Muses always waiting round him,
He left them Virgins as he found 'em.
His Singing was another Fault;
For he could reach to *B*. in *alt:*
And, by the Sentiments of *Pliny*,
Such Singers are like [1]*Nicolini*.   30
At last, the Point was fully clear'd;
In short; *Apollo* had no Beard.

                                          1731/1735

[1]*A famous* Italian *Singer*.

TRIFLES BY SWIFT
AND HIS FRIENDS

On Dan Jackson's Picture cut in Paper

To fair Lady *Betty*, *Dan* sat for his Picture,
And defy'd her to draw him so oft as he *piqu'd* her.
He knew she'd no Pencil or Colouring by her,
And therefore he thought he might safely defy her.
Come, sit, says my Lady, then whips up her Scissar,
And cuts out his Coxcomb in Silk in a trice, Sir.
Dan sat with Attention, and saw with Surprise,
How she lengthen'd his Chin, how she hollow'd his
    Eyes;
But flatter'd himself with a secret Conceit,
That his thin leathern Jaws all her Art would defeat.
Lady *Betty* observ'd it, then pulls out a Pin,   11
And varied the Grain of the Stuff to his Grin,
And to make roasted Silk to resemble his Raw-Bone,
She rais'd up a Thread to the Jet of his Jaw-Bone;
'Till at length in exactest Proportion he rose,
From the Crown of his Head to the Arch of his Nose.
And if Lady *Betty* had drawn him with Wig and all,
'Tis certain the Copy had outdone the Original.
Well, that's but my Outside, says *Dan*, with a Vapour,
Say you so? said my Lady; I've lin'd it with Paper.   20
          P[ATRICK] D[ELANY] *sculpsit.*
                    1718/1735

On the Same

IF you say this was made for friend Dan, you belie it,
I'll swear he's so like it that he was made by it.
          THO. SHERIDAN, *sculp.*
                  1718/1735

Another

CLARISSA draws her Scissars from the Case,
To draw the Lines of poor *Dan Jackson*'s Face.
One sloping Cut made Forehead, Nose, and Chin, ⎱
A Nick produc'd a Mouth and made him grin, ⎬
Such as in Taylor's Measure you have seen. ⎰
But still were wanting his grimalkin Eyes,
For which grey worsted Stockings Paint supplies.
Th' unravell'd Thread thro' Needle's Eye convey'd,
Transferr'd itself into his Pasteboard Head.
How came the Scissars to be thus out-done?   10
The Needle had an Eye, and they had none.
O wond'rous Force of Art! Now look at *Dan*——
You'd swear the Pasteboard was the better Man.
The Dev'l, sayš he, the Head is not so full—
Indeed it is, behold the Paper Scull.

THO. S[HERIDA]N *sculp.*
1718/1735

Another

DAN's evil Genius, in a trice,
Had stript him of his Coin at Dice:
Chloe observing this Disgrace,
On *Pam* cut out his rueful Face.
By G—, says *Dan*, 'tis very hard,
Cut out at Dice, cut out at Card!

G. R[OCHFOR]D *sculp.*
1718/1735

Dan. Jackson's Answer

My Verse little better you'll find than my Face is,
A Word to the Wise, ut Pictura poesis.

THREE merry Lads with Envy stung,
Because *Dan*'s Face is better hung,
Combin'd in Verse to rhyme it down,
And in its Place set up their own;
As if they'd run it down much better
By Number of their Feet in Metre,
Or, that its red did cause their Spite,
Which made them draw in black and white.
Be that as 'twill, this is most true,
They were inspir'd by what they drew.   10
Let then such Critics know my Face,
Gives them their Comeliness and Grace:
Whilst ev'ry Line of Face does bring
A Line of Grace to what they sing.
But yet methinks, tho' with Disgrace
Both to the Picture and the Face,
I name the Men who do rehearse
The Story of the Picture-Farce;
The 'Squire in *French* as hard as Stone,
Or, strong as Rock, that's all as one,   20
On Face, on Cards, is very brisk, Sirs,
Because on them you play at Whisk, Sirs.
But much I wonder why my Crany
Should envy'd be by De-el-any;
And yet much more than Half-name-sake
Should join a Party in the Freak.
For sure I am it was not safe
Thus to abuse his better Half,
As I shall prove you *Dan* to be,
Divisim and conjunctively.   30
For, if *Dan* love not *Sherry,* can
Sherry be any Thing to *Dan?*

This is the Case, whene'er you see
[That] *Dan* makes nothing of *Sherry*;
Or, should *Dan* be by *Sherry* o'erta'n,
Then *Dan* would be poor *Sherridane*;
'Tis hard then he should be decry'd
By *Dan* with *Sherry* by his Side.
But, if the Case must be so hard,
That Faces suffer by a Card,   40
Let Critics censure, what care I?⎫
Backbiters only we defy,   ⎬
Faces are free from Injury.   ⎭

         1718/1735

Answer

BY DR. DELANY

Assist me, my Muse, while I labour to limn him.
Credite Pisones isti tabulæ persimilem.
You look and you write with so different a Grace,
That I envy your Verse, though I didn't your Face.
And to him that thinks rightly, there's Reason enough,
'Cause one is as smooth as the other is rough.
But much I'm amazed you should think my ⎫
 Design   ⎪
Was to rhyme down your Nose, or your Harlequin ⎬
 Grin,   ⎪
Which you yourself wonder the De'il should ⎪
 malign.   ⎭
And, if 'tis so strange, that your Monstership's
 Crany   10
Should be env'yd by him, much less by *Delany*.
Though I own to you, when I consider it stricter,
I envy the Painter, although not the Picture.
And justly she's envy'd since a Fiend of Hell

Was never drawn right but by her [and] *Raph'el*.
   Next as to the Charge which you tell us is true,
That we were inspir'd by the Subject we drew:
Inspir'd we were, and well, Sir, you knew it,
Yet not by your Nose, but the Fair-one that drew it;
Had your Nose been the Muse, we had ne'er been
     inspir'd,   20
Though perhaps it might justly've been said we were
     fir'd.
   As to the Division of Words in your Staves,
Like my Countryman's Horn-Comb, into three Halves
I meddle not with't, but presume to make merry,
You call'd *Dan* one Half, and t'other Half *Sherry*:
Now if *Dan*'s a Half, as you call't o'er and o'er,
Then it can't be deny'd that *Sherry*'s two more.
For pray give me leave to say, Sir, for all you,
That *Sherry*'s at least of double the Value.
But, perhaps, Sir, you did it to fill up the Verse, ⎫
So Crouds in a Concert (like Actors in Farce) ⎬ 30
Play two Parts in one, when Scrapers are scarce. ⎭
But be that as 'twill, you'll know more anon, Sir,
When *Sheridan* sends to *merry Dan* Answer.
                             1718/1735

Answer to Dan. Jackson

BY MR. GEORGE ROCHFORT

YOU say your Face is better hung
Than ours—by what? by Nose or Tongue?
In not explaining you are wrong
               to us, Sir.

Because we thus must state the Case,
That you have got a hanging Face,
Th' untimely End's a damn'd Disgrace
                    of Noose, Sir.

But, yet be not cast down, I see
A Weaver will your Hangman be;   10
You'll only hang in Tapestry,
                    with many;

And then the Ladies I suppose,
Will praise your Longitude of Nose,
For latent Charms within your Clothes,
                    dear *Danny*.

Thus will the Fair of ev'ry Age
From all Parts make their Pilgrimage,
Worship thy Nose with pious Rage
                    of Love, Sir.   20

All their Religion will be spent
About thy woven Monument,
And not one Orison be sent
                    to *Jove*, Sir.

You the fam'd Idol will become,
As Gardens grac'd in antient *Rome*,
By Matrons worshipp'd in the Gloom
                    of Night.

O happy *Dan!* thrice happy sure;
Thy Fame for ever shall endure,   30
Who after Death can Love secure
                    at Sight.

So far I thought it was my **Duty**
To dwell upon thy boasted **Beauty**;
Now I'll proceed a Word or two t'ye,
                            in Answer.

To that Part where you carry on
This Paradox, that Rock and Stone,
In your Opinion, all are one,
                    How can, Sir,   40

A Man of Reas'ning so profound,
So stupidly be run a-ground,
As Things so different to confound
                        t'our Senses?

Except you judg'd 'em by the Knock
Of near an equal hardy Block:
Such an experimental Stroke
                        convinces.

Then might you be, by Dint of Reason,
A proper Judge on this Occasion;   50
'Gainst Feeling there's no Disputation,
                        is granted.

Therefore to thy Superior Wit,
Who made the Trial we submit;
Thy Head to prove the Truth of it
                        we wanted.

In one Assertion you're to blame,
Where *Dan* and *Sherry*'s made the same,
Endeavouring to have your Name
                        refin'd, Sir.   60

You'll see most grossly you mistook,
If you consult your Spelling-Book,
(The better Half you say you took),
> you'll find, Sir,

S, H, E, *she*—and R, I, *ri*,
Both put together make *Sherry*,
D, A, N, *Dan*, makes up the three
> Syllables.

Dan is but one, and *Sherry* two,
Then, Sir, your Choice will never do;   70
Therefore I've turn'd, my Friend, on you
> the Tables.
>
> 1718/1735

Answer

BY DR. SHERIDAN

THREE merry Lads you own we are;
'Tis very true, and free from Care,
But envious we cannot bear,
> believe, Sir,

For were all Forms of Beauty thine,
Were you like *Nereus*, soft and fine,
We should not in the least repine,
> or grieve, Sir.

Then know from us, most beauteous *Dan*,
That Roughness best becomes a Man;   10
'Tis Women should be pale and wan,
> and taper.

And all your trifling Beaux and Fops,
Who comb their Brows and sleek their Chops,
Are but the Offspring of Toy-shops,
                              mere Vapour.

We know your Morning Hours you pass
To cull and gather out a Face;
Is this the Way you take your Glass?
                              Forbear it.   20

Those Loads of Paint upon your Toilet,
Will never mend your Face, but spoil it,
It looks as if ye did parboil it,
                              Drink Claret.

Your Cheeks, by sleeking, are so lean,
That they're like *Cynthia* in the Wain,
Or Breast of Goose when 'tis pick'd clean,
                              or Pullet.

See what by Drinking you have done,
You've made your Phiz a Skeleton,   30
From the long Distance of your Crown,
                              t'your Gullet!
                                    1718/1735

On the Foregoing Picture

WHILST you three merry Poets traffic
To give us a Description Graphic
Of *Dan*'s large Nose in modern Sapphic,

I spend my Time in making Sermons,
Or, writing Libels on the *Germans*,
Or, murmuring at Whigs Preferments.

275

But when I would find Rhyme for *Rochfort*,
And look in *English*, *French*, and *Scotch* for't,
At last I'm fairly forc'd to botch for't.

Bid Lady *Betty* recollect her,   10
And tell who was it could direct her
To draw the Face of such a Spectre.

I must confess, that as to me, Sirs,
Though I ne'er saw her hold her Scissars,
I now could safely swear it is hers.

'Tis true no Nose could come in better,
'Tis a vast Subject stuff'd with Matter,
Which all may handle, none can flatter.

Take Courage, *Dan*, this plainly shews,
That not the wisest Mortal knows   20
What Fortune may befal his Nose.

Shew me the brightest *Irish* Toast,
Who from her Lover e'er could boast,
Above a Song or two at most:

For thee three Poets now are drudging all,
To praise the Cheeks, Chin, Nose, the Bridge and all
Both of the Picture and Original.

Thy Nose's Length and Fame extend
So far, dear *Dan*, that ev'ry Friend
Tries who shall have it by the End.   30

And future Poets as they rise,
Shall read with Envy and Surprise,
Thy Nose outshining *Cælia*'s Eyes. SWIFT.
1718/1745

Dan. Jackson's Reply

WRITTEN BY THE DEAN IN THE NAME OF
DAN. JACKSON

WEARIED with Grace and saying Pray'r,
I hasten'd down to Country-Air,
To read your Answer, and prepare
              Reply to't.

But your fair Lines so grossly flatter,
Pray do they praise me or bespatter?
I much suspect you mean the latter,
              ah Sly-boot!

It must be so, what else, alas!
Can mean my culling of a Face,   10
And all that Stuff of Toilet, Glass,
            and Box-Comb?

But, be't as 'twill, this you must grant,
That you're a Dawb, whilst I but paint;
Then which of us two are the quaint-
            er Coxcomb?

I value not your Jokes of Noose,
Your Gibes and all your foul Abuse,
More than the Dirt beneath my Shoes,
           nor fear it.   20

Yet one Thing vexes me, I own,
Thou sorry Scarecrow, Skin and Bone,
To be call'd lean by a Skeleton,
            who'd bear it?

'Tis true indeed, to curry Friends,
You seem to praise to make amends,
And yet before your Stanza ends,
                              you flout me

'Bout latent Charms beneath my Cloaths;
For every one that knows me knows   30
That I have nothing like my Nose
                              about me.

I pass now where you fleer and laugh,
'Cause I call *Dan* my better Half!
Oh, there you think you have me safe!
                              but hold, Sir,

Is not a Penny often found
To be much greater than a Pound?
By your good Leave, my most profound
                              and bold, Sir,   40

Dan's noble Mettle, *Sherry* base;
So *Dan*'s the better though the less,
An Ounce of Gold's worth ten of Brass,
                              dull Pedant.

As to your Spelling let me see,
If *SHE* makes *sher*, and *RI* makes *ry*,
Good Spelling-Master your Crany,
                              has lead in't.
                              1718–1735

Another Reply

BY THE DEAN IN DAN. JACKSON'S NAME

THREE Days for Answer I have waited,
I thought an Ace you'd ne'er have bated,
And art thou forc'd to yield, ill-fated
    Poetaster?

Henceforth acknowledge that a Nose
Of thy Dimension's fit for Prose;
But every one that knows *Dan* knows
    thy Master.

Blush for ill Spelling, for ill Lines,
And fly with Hurry to *Rathmines*:   10
Thy Fame, thy Genius now declines,
    proud Boaster.

I hear with some Concern your Roar,
And flying think to quit the Score,
By clapping Billets on your Door
    and Posts, Sir.

Thy Ruin, *Tom*, I never meant,
I'm griev'd to hear your Banishment,
But pleas'd to find you do relent
    and cry on.   20

I maul'd you when you look'd so bluff;
But now I'll secret keep your Stuff;
For know, Prostration is enough
    to th' Lion.
     1718/1735

Sheridan's Submission

WRITTEN BY THE DEAN

Cedo jam, miseræ cognoscens præmia rixæ,
Si rixa est, ubi tu pulsas, ego vapulo tantum.

POOR *Sherry* inglorious,
To *Dan* the victorious,
Presents, as 'tis fitting,
Petition and Greeting.

To you victorious and brave,
Your now subdu'd and suppliant Slave
    Most humbly sues for Pardon.
Who when I fought, still cut me down,
And when I vanquish'd, fled the Town,
    Pursu'd and laid me hard on.   10

Now lowly crouch'd, I cry *Peccavi*,
And prostrate, supplicate *pour ma vie*;
    Your Mercy I rely on.
For you my Conqu'ror and my King,
In pard'ning, as in punishing,
    Will shew yourself a Lion.

Alas, Sir, I had no Design,
But was unwarily drawn in:
    For Spite I ne'er had any.
'Twas the damn'd 'Squire with the hard Name;
The De'il too that ow'd me a Shame,   21
    The Devil and *Delany*;

They tempted me t'attack your Highness,
And then with wonted Wile and Slyness,
    They left me in the Lurch.

Unhappy Wretch! for now I ween,
I've nothing left to vent my Spleen
      But Ferula and Birch;

And they, alas! yield small Relief,
Seem rather to renew my Grief,   30
      My Wounds bleed all anew:
For ev'ry Stroke goes to my Heart,
And at each Lash I feel the Smart
      Of Lash laid on by you.
                  1718/1735

The Pardon

DAN JACKSON TO SHERIDAN

THE suit which humbly you have made,
Is fully and maturely weigh'd;
      And as 'tis your petition,
I do forgive, for well I know,
Since you're so bruis'd, another blow
      Would break the head of Priscian.

'Tis not my purpose or intent
That you should suffer banishment;
      I pardon, now you've courted;
And yet I fear this clemency   10
Will come too late to profit thee,
      For you're with grief transported.

However, this I do command,
That you your birch do take in hand,
      Read concord and syntax on;
The bays, you own, are only mine,

Do you then still your nouns decline,
Since you've declin'd Dan Jackson.

1718/1735

To the Rev. Mr. Daniel Jackson

to be humbly presented by Mr. Sheridan in
Person, with Respect, Care and Speed

To be delivered by and with Mr. Sheridan

DEAR Dan,
Here I return my Trust, nor ask
    One Penny for Remittance;
If I have well perform'd my Task,
    Pray send me an Admittance.

Too long I bore this weighty Pack,
    As *Hercules* the Sky;
Now take him you, *Dan Atlas*, back,
    Let me be Stander-by.

Not all the witty Things you speak,
    In Compass of a Day;   10
Not half the Puns you make a Week,
    Should bribe his longer Stay.

With me you left him out at Nurse,
    Yet are you not my Debtor?
For as he hardly can be worse,
    I ne'er could make him better.

He rhimes and puns, and puns and rhimes,
    Just as he did before,
And when he's lash'd an hundred Times,
    He rhimes and puns the more.   20

When Rods are laid on School-Boys Bums,
    The more they frisk and skip:
The School-Boy's Top but louder hums,
    The more they use the Whip.

Thus, a lean Beast beneath a Load,
    (A Beast of *Irish* Breed)
Will in a tedious, dirty Road,
    Outgo the prancing Steed.

You knock him down and down in vain,
    And lay him flat before ye,   30
For, soon as he gets up again,
    He'll strut and cry, *Victoria!*

At ev'ry Stroke of mine, he fell,
    'Tis true he roar'd and cry'd;
But his impenetrable Shell
    Could feel no Harm beside.

The Tortoise thus, with Motion slow,
    Will clamber up a Wall;
Yet, senseless to the hardest Blow,
    Gets nothing but a Fall.   40

Dear *Dan*, then why should you, or I
    Attack his Pericrany?
And since it is [in] vain to try,
    We'll send him to *Delany*.

POSTSCRIPT.

Lean *Tom*, when I saw him, last Week, on his Horse,
    awry,
Threat'n'd loudly to turn me to Stone with his
    Sorcery.

But I think, little *Dan*, that in Spight of what our Foe
    says,
He will find I read *Ovid*, and his Metamorphoses.
For omitting the first (where I make a Comparison,
With a Sort of Allusion to *Putland* or *Harrison*,)   50
Yet by my Description, you'll find he in short is
A Pack and a Garran, a Top and a Tortoise.
So I hope from hence forward you ne'er will ask, can
    I maul
This teazing, conceited, rude, insolent, Animal?
And, if this Rebuke might turn to his Benefit,
(For I pity the Man) I should be then glad of it.
                            1718/1762

The Last Speech and Dying Words
of Daniel Jackson

MY DEAR COUNTRYMEN,

    —Mediocribus esse poetis
Non funes, non gryps, non concessere columnæ.

To give you a short translation of these two lines
from Horace's Art of Poetry, which I have chosen for
my neck-verse, before I proceed to my speech, you will
find they fall naturally into this sense:

    For poets who can't tell [high] rocks from stones,
    The rope, the hangman, and the gallows groans,

I was born in a fen near the foot of Mount Parnas- 10
sus, commonly called the Logwood Bog. My mother,
whose name was Stanza, conceived me in a dream,
and was delivered of me in her sleep. Her dream was,
that Apollo, in the shape of a gander, with a prodigious long bill, had embraced her; upon which she con-

284

sulted the Oracle of Delphos, and the following answer
was made:

> You'll have a gosling, call it Dan,
> And do not make your goose a swan.
> 'Tis true, because the God of Wit   20
> To get him in that shape thought fit,
> He'll have some glowworm sparks of it.
> Venture you may to turn him loose,
> But let it be to another goose.
> The time will come, the fatal time,
> When he shall dare a swan to rhyme;
> The tow'ring swan comes sousing down,
> And breaks his pinions, cracks his crown.
> From that sad time, and sad disaster,
> He'll be a lame, crack'd poetaster.   30
> At length for stealing rhymes and triplets,
> He'll be content to hang in giblets.

You see now, Gentlemen, this is fatally and literally
come to pass; for it was my misfortune to engage with
that Pindar of the times, Tom Sheridan, who did so
confound me by sousing on my crown, and did so
batter my pinions, that I was forced to make use of
borrowed wings, though my false accusers have de-
posed that I stole my feathers from Hopkins, Stern-
hold, Silvester, Ogilby, Durfey, &c. for which I now   40
forgive them and all the world. I die a poet; and this
ladder shall be my Gradus ad Parnassum; and I hope
the critics will have mercy on my works.

> Then lo, I mount as slowly as I sung,
> And then I'll make a line for every rung;
> There's nine, I see,—the Muses, too, are nine.
> Who would refuse to die a death like mine!

> 1. Thou first rung, Clio, celebrate my name;
> 2. Euterp, in tragic numbers do the same.

3. This rung, I see, Terpsichore's thy flute;   50
4. Erato, sing me to the Gods; ah, do't:
5. Thalia, don't make me a comedy;
6. Urania, raise me tow'rds the starry sky;
7. Calliope, to ballad-strains descend,
8. And, Polyhymnia, tune them for your friend;
9. So shall Melpomene mourn my fatal end.

POOR DAN JACKSON.

1718/1735

The Reverend Dr. Sheridan to J.S.D.D.D.S.P.D.

DEAR Dean, since in *Cruxes* and *Puns* you and I deal,
Pray why is a Woman a Sieve and a Riddle?
'Tis a Thought that came into my Noddle this Morning,
In bed as I lay, Sir, a tossing and turning.
You'll find, if you read but a few of your Histories,
All Women, as *Eve*, all Women are Mysteries.
To find out this Riddle, I know you'll be eager,
And make every one of the Sex a *Bell-phagor*.
But that will not do, for I mean to come-mend 'em,
I swear without Jest, I an Honour intend 'em,   10
In a Sieve, Sir, their ancient Extraction I quite tell,
In a Riddle I give you their Power and their Title.
This I told you before, do you know what I mean, Sir?
[1]*Not I, by my Troth, Sir.*—Then read it again, Sir.
The Reason I send you these Lines of Rhymes double,
Is purely through pity, to save you the Trouble
Of thinking two Hours for a Rhyme, as you did last;
When your *Pegasus* canter'd in triple, and rid fast.

[1] *The Dean's Answer.*

286

As for my little Nag, which I keep at *Parnassus*
With *Phœbus*'s Leave, to run with his Asses,   20
He goes slow and sure, and he never is jaded,
While your fiery Steed is whipp'd, spurr'd, bastinaded.

                           1718/1735

Dean Swift's Answer to the Reverend Doctor Sheridan

SIR,
  In reading your Letter alone in my Hackney,
Your damnable Riddle, my poor Brains did rack
    nigh.
And when with much Labour the Matter I crackt,
I found you mistaken in Matter of Fact,

  A WOMAN's no Sieve (for with that you begin)
Because she let's out more, than e'er she takes in.
And that she's a Riddle, can never be right,
For a Riddle is dark, but a Woman is *light*.
But grant her a Sieve, I can say something archer,
Pray what is a Man? he's a fine-Linen *Searcher*.   10

  Now tell me a Thing that wants Interpretation,
What Name for a [1]Maid, was the first Man's Damna-
    tion?
If your Worship will please to explain me this *Rebus*,
I swear from henceforward you shall be my *Phœbus*.

  From my Hackney-Coach,
    Sept. 11, 1718. *Past* 12
    at Noon.

                           1718/1735

[1] *Vir Gin.*

Dr. Sheridan's Reply to the Dean

DON'T think these few lines which I send, a
  reproach,
From my muse in a car, to your muse in a coach.
The great God of poems delights in a car,
Which makes him so bright that we see him from far;
For were he mew'd up in a coach, 'tis allow'd
We'd see him no more than we see thro' a cloud.
  You know to apply this—I do not disparage
Your lines, but I say they're the worse for the
  carriage.
  Now, first, you deny that a woman's a sieve;
I say that she is: What reason d'ye give?   10
Because she let's out more than she takes in.
Is't that you advance for't? you are still to begin.
Your major and minor I both can refute,
I'll teach you hereafter with whom to dispute.
A sieve keeps in half, deny't if you can.
D. 'Adzucks, I mistook it, who thought of the bran?'
I tell you in short, Sir, you should ¹have a pair o'
  stocks
For thinking to palm on your friend such a paradox.
Indeed, I confess, at the close you grew better,
But you light from your coach when you finish'd your
  letter.   20
Your thing which you say wants interpretation,
What's name for a maiden—the first man's damna-
  tion?
A damsel—Adam's hell—ay, there I have hit it,
Just as you conceiv'd it, just so have I writ it.
Since this I've discover'd, I'll make you to know it,
That now I'm your Phœbus, and you are my poet.
But if you interpret the two lines that follow,
I'll again be your poet, and you my Apollo.

¹ Begging pardon for the expression to a dignitary of the
church.

Why a noble lord's dog, and my school-house this
    weather,
Make up the best catch when they're coupled
    together? 30

    From my Ringsend car, Sept. 12,
      1718, past 5 in the morning,
      on a repetition day.

                1718/1789

To the Same

BY DR. SHERIDAN

              12 o'Clock at Noon,
              [Sept. 12, 1718.]

SIR,
   Perhaps you may wonder, I send you so soon
Another epistle; consider 'tis noon.
For all his acquaintance well know that friend Tom is,
Whenever he makes one, as good as his promise.
Now Phœbus exalted, sits high on his throne,
Dividing the heav'ns, dividing my crown,
Into poems and business, my skull's split in two,
One side for the lawyers, and t'other for you.
With my left eye I see you sit snug in your stall,
With my right I'm attending the lawyers that scrawl.
With my left I behold your bellower a cur chase; 11
With my right I'm a reading my deeds for a purchase.
My left ear's attending the hymns of the choir,
My right ear is stunn'd with the noise of the crier.
My right hand's inditing these lines to your reverence,
My left is indenting for me and heirs ever-hence.
Although in myself I'm divided in two,
Dear Dean, I shall ne'er be divided from you.
                1718/1789

The Dean of St. Patrick's to Thomas Sheridan

SIR,

 I cannot but think that we live in a bad age,
O tempora, O mores! as 'tis in the adage.
My foot was but just set out from my cathedral,
When into my hands comes a letter from the droll.
I can't pray in quiet for you and your verses;
But now let us hear what the Muse from your car says
  Hum—excellent good—your anger was stirr'd;
Well, punners and rhymers must have the last word.
But let me advise you when next I hear from you,
To leave off this passion which does not become you;
For we who debate on a subject important,   11
Must argue with calmness, or else will come short
  on't.
For myself, I protest, I care not a fiddle,
For a riddle and sieve, or a sieve and a riddle;
And think of the sex as you please, I'd as lieve
You call them a riddle, as call them a sieve.
Yet still you are out, (tho' to vex you I'm loth,)
For I'll prove it impossible they can be both;
A school-boy knows this, for it plainly appears
That a sieve dissolves riddles by help of the shears; 20
For you can't but have heard of a trick among
  wizards,
To break open riddles with shears or with scissars.
 Think again of the sieve, and I'll hold you a wager,
You'll dare not to question my minor or major.[1]
A sieve keeps half in, and therefore, no doubt,
Like a woman, keeps in less than it lets out.
Why sure, Mr. Poet, your head got a-jar,
By riding this morning too long on your car:

---

[1] Ut tu perperàm argumentaris.

And I wish your few friends, when they next see your
    car go,
For the sake of your senses would lay an embargo. 30
You threaten the stocks; I say you are scurrilous,
And you durst not talk thus, if I saw you at our ale-
    house.
But as for your threats, you may do what you can,
I despise any poet that truckled to Dan.
But keep a good tongue, or you'll find to your smart,
From rhyming in cars, you may swing in a cart.
You found out my rebus with very much modesty;
But thanks to the lady; I'm sure she's too good to ye:
Till she lent you her help, you were in a fine twitter;
You hit it, you say;—you're a delicate hitter.   40
How could you forget so ungratefully a lass,
And if you be my Phœbus, pray who was your Pallas?
   As for your new rebus, or riddle, or crux,
I will either explain, or repay it by trucks:
Tho' your lords, and your dogs, and your catches,
    methinks,
Are harder than ever were put by the Sphinx.
And thus I am fully reveng'd for your late tricks,
Which is all at present from the
                DEAN OF ST. PATRICK'S.

From my closet, Sept. 12, 1718,
    just 12 at noon.

                        1718/1808

To the Dean of St. Patrick's

SIR,
   Your Billingsgate Muse methinks does begin
With much greater noise than a conjugal din.
A pox of her bawling, her *tempora et mores*!
What are times now to me! an't I one of the Tories?

You tell me my verses disturb you at prayers;
Oh, oh, Mr. Dean, are you there with your bears?
You pray, I suppose, like a Heathen, to Phœbus,
To give his assistance to make out my rebus:
Which I don't think so fair; leave it off for the future;
When the combat is equal, this God should be neuter.
I'm now at the tavern, where I drink all I can,   11
To write with more spirit; I'll drink no more Helicon;
For Helicon is water, and water is weak;
'Tis wine on the gross lee, that makes your Muse
      speak.
This I know by her spirit and life; but I think
She's much in the wrong to scold in her drink.
Her damn'd pointed tongue pierced almost to my
      heart;
Tell me of a cart,—tell me of a ——,
I'd have you to tell on both sides her ears,
If she comes to my house, that I'll kick her down
      stairs: 20
Then home she shall limping go, squalling out, O my
      knee!
You shall soon have a crutch to buy for your
      Melpomene.
You may come as her bully, to bluster and swagger:
But my ink is my poison, my pen is my dagger.
Stand off, I desire, and mark what I say to you,
If you come I will make your Apollo shine thro' you.
Don't think, Sir, I fear a Dean, as I would fear a dun;
Which is all at present from yours,
                              THOMAS SHERIDAN.
                                    1718/1808

The Dean to Thomas Sheridan

SIR,
   When I saw you to-day, as I went with Lord
      Anglesey,
Lord, said I, who's that parson, how awkwardly
      dangles he!
When whip you trot up, without minding your betters,
To the very coach side, and threaten your letters.
   Is the poison [and dagger] you boast in your jaws,
      trow?
Are you still in your cart with *convitia ex plaustro?*
But to scold is your trade, which I soon should be
      foil'd in,
For scolding is just *quasi diceres*—school-din:
And I think I may say, you could many good shillings
      get,
Were you drest like a bawd, and sold oysters at
      Billingsgate: 10
But coach it or cart it, I'd have you know, sirrah,
I'll write, tho' I'm forc'd to write in a wheel-barrow:
Nay, hector and swagger, you'll still find me stanch,
And you and your cart shall give me *carte blanche.*
Since you write in a cart, keep it *tecta et sarta,*
'Tis all you have for it; 'tis your best Magna Carta;
And I love you so well, as I told you long ago,
That I'll ne'er give my vote for *Delenda Cart-ago.*
Now you write from your cellar, I find out your art,
You rhyme as folks fence, in *tierce* and in *cart*:   20
Your ink is your poison,[1] your pen is what not;
Your ink is your drink,[2] your pen is your pot.
To my goddess Melpomene, pride of her sex,
I gave, as you beg, your most humble respects:
The rest of your compliment I dare not tell her,
For she never descends so low as the cellar;

---

[1] Viz. ut tu prædicas.   [2] Viz. ut ego assero verius.

But before you can put yourself under her banners,
She declares from her throne, you must learn better
    manners.
If once in your cellar my Phœbus should shine,
I tell you I'd not give a fig for your wine;   30
So I'll leave him behind, for I certainly know it.
What he ripens above ground, he sours below it.
But why should we fight thus, my partner so dear,
With three hundred and sixty-five poems a-year?
Let's quarrel no longer, since Dan and George
    Rochfort
Will laugh in their sleeves: I can tell you they watch
    for't.
Then George will rejoice, and Dan will sing high-day:
Hoc Ithacus velit, et magni mercentur Atridæ.

JON. SWIFT.

Written, signed and sealed, five
    minutes and eleven seconds after
    the receipt of yours, allowing
    seven seconds for sealing and
    superscribing, from my bed-side,
    just eleven minutes after eleven,
    Sept. 15, 1718.

Erratum in your last, l. antepenult, pro 'fear a *Dun*,'
    lege 'fear a *Dan*:' ita omnes MSS. quos ego legi, et
    ita magis congruum tam sensui quam veritati.

1718/1808

A Left-Handed Letter to Dr. Sheridan[1]

DELANY reports it, and he has a shrewd Tongue.
That we both act the Part of the Clown and the Cow-
    dung;
We lye cramming ourselves, and are ready to burst,

---

[1] All the Humour of this Poem is lost, by the impossibility of
printing it Left-handed, as it was wrote.—Faulkner.

Yet still are no wiser than we were at first.
Pudet hæc opprobria, I freely must tell ye,
Et diu potuisse et non potuisse refelli.
Tho' DELANY advis'd you to plague me no longer,
You reply and rejoin like HOADLY of Bangor.
I must now, at one Sitting, pay off my old Score:
How many to answer? One, two, three, four.   10
But because the three former are long ago past,
I shall, for Method Sake, begin with the last.
You treat me like a Boy, that knocks down his Foe,
Who, 'ere t'other gets up demands the rising Blow.
Yet I know a young Rogue that thrown flat on the
      Field,
Would, as he lay under, cry out, Sirrah, yield:
So, the *French*, when our Generals soundly did pay
      'em,
Went triumphant to Church, and sang stoutly Te
      Deum:
So the famous TOM LEIGH, when quite run a-ground,
Comes off by out-laughing the Company round.   20
In ev'ry vile Pamphlet you'll read the same Fancies,
Having thus overthrown all our further Advances.
My Offers of Peace you ill understood.
Friend SHERIDAN, when will you know your own
      Good?
'Twas to teach you in modester Language your Duty:
For, were you a Dog, I could not be rude t'ye.
As a good quiet Soul, who no Mischief intends
To a quarrelsome Fellow, cries let us be Friends.
But we like ANTEUS and HERCULES fight,
The oft'ner you fall, the oft'ner you write;   30
And I'll use you as he did that over-grown Clown,
I'll first take you up, and then take you down:
And, 'tis your own Case, for you never can wound
The worst Dunce in the School, 'till he's heav'd to the
      Ground.

I beg your Pardon for using my Left-hand, but I was in great Haste, and the other Hand was employed at the same Time in writing some Letters of Business.

September 20, 1718.

I Will send you the rest when I have Leisure, but pray come to Dinner with the Company you met here last.

1718/1762

To the Dean of St. Patrick's in answer to his left-handed letter

SINCE your poetic prancer is turn'd into Cancer,
I'll tell you at once, Sir, I'm now not your man, Sir;
For pray, Sir, what pleasure in fighting is found
With a coward, who studies to traverse his ground?
When I drew forth my pen, with your pen you ran
    back;
But I found out the way to your den by its track:
From thence the black monster I drew, o' my
    conscience,
And so brought to light what before was stark
    nonsense.
When I with my right hand did stoutly pursue,
You turn'd to your left, and you writ like a Jew;   10
Which, good Mister Dean, I can't think so fair,
Therefore turn about to the right, as you were;
Then if with true courage your ground you maintain,
My fame is immortal, when Jonathan's slain:
Who's greater by far than great Alexander,
As much as a teal surpasses a gander;
As much as a game-cock's excell'd by a sparrow;
As much as a coach is below a wheelbàrrow:

As much and much more as the most handsome man
Of all the whole world is exceeded by Dan.   20

T. SHERIDAN

This was written with that hand which in others is commonly
called the left-hand.

Oft have I been by poets told,
That, poor Jonathan, thou grow'st old.
Alas, thy numbers falling all,
Poor Jonathan, how they do fall!
Thy rhymes, which whilom made thy pride swell,
Now jingle like a rusty bridle:
Thy verse, which ran both smooth and sweet,
Now limp upon their gouty feet:
Thy thoughts, which were the true sublime,
Are humbled by the tyrant, Time: 30
Alas! what cannot Time subdue?
Time has reduc'd my wine and you;
Emptied my casks, and clipp'd your wings,
Disabled both in our main springs;
So that of late we two are grown
The jest and scorn of all the town.
But yet, if my advice be ta'en,
We two may be as great again;
I'll send you wings, and send me wine:
Then you will fly, and I shall shine.   40

This was written with my right-hand, at the same time with the
other.

How does Melpy like this? I think I have vext her:
Little did she know, I was *ambidexter*.

T. SHERIDAN.
1718/1808

To the Dean of St. Patrick's

DEAR Dean, I'm in a sad condition,
    I cannot see to read or write;
Pity the darkness of thy Priscian,
    Whose days are all transform'd to night.

My head, tho' light, 's a dungeon grown,
    The windows of my soul are clos'd;
Therefore to sleep I lay me down,
    My verse and I are both compos'd.

Sleep, did I say? that cannot be;
    For who can sleep, that want's his eyes?   10
My bed is useless then to me,
    Therefore I lay me down to rise.

Unnumber'd thoughts pass to and fro
    Upon the surface of my brain;
In various maze they come and go,
    And come and go again.

So have you seen in sheet burnt black,
    The fiery sparks at random run;
Now here, now there, some turning back,
    Some ending where they just begun.   20
                THOMAS SHERIDAN.
                    1718/1808

An Answer, by Delany

DEAR Sherry, I'm sorry for your bloodsheded sore
    eye,
And the more I consider your case, still the more I
Regret it, for see how the pain on't has wore ye.

Besides; the good Whigs, who strangely adore ye,
In pity cry out, 'he's a poor blinded Tory.'
But listen to me, and I'll soon lay before ye
A sovereign cure well attested in Gory.
First wish it with *ros*, that makes dative *rori*,
Then send for three leeches, and let them all gore ye;
Then take a cordial dram to restore ye,   10
Then take Lady Judith, and walk a fine boree,
Then take a glass of good claret *ex more*,
Then take as long as you can, *ab uxore*;
And then if friend Dick will but ope your back-door,
      he
Will quickly dispel the black clouds that hang o'er ye,
And make you so bright, that you'll sing tory rory,
And make a new ballad worth ten of John Dory:
(Tho' I work your cure, yet he'll get the glory.)
I'm now in the back school-house, high up one story,
Quite weary with teaching, and ready to *mori*.   20
My candle's just out too, no longer I'll pore ye,
But away to Clem Barry's,—there's an end of my
      story.

                                              1718/1808

Reply, by Sheridan

My pedagogue dear, I read with surprise
Your long sorry rhymes, which you made on my eyes;
As the Dean of St. Patrick's says, earth, seas, and
      skies!
I cannot lie down, but immediately rise,
To answer your stuff and the Doctor's likewise.
Like a horse with a gall, I'm pester'd with flies,
But his head and his tail new succour supplies,
To beat off the vermin from back, rump, and thighs.
The wing of a goose before me now lies,

Which is both shield and sword for such weak
    enemies.   10
Whoever opposes me, certainly dies,
Tho' he were as valiant as Condé or Guise.
The women disturb me a crying of pies,
With a voice twice as loud as a horse when he neighs.
By this, Sir, you find, should we rhyme for a prize,
That I'd gain cloth of gold when you'd scarce merit
    frize.

                        1718/1808

To Thomas Sheridan

DEAR Tom, I'm surpris'd that your verse did not
    jingle;
But your rhyme was not double, 'cause your sight was
    but single.
For as Helsham observes, there's nothing can chime,
Or fit more exact than one eye and one rhyme.
If you had not took physic, I'd pay off your bacon,
But now I'll write short, for fear you're short-taken.
Besides, Dick forbid me, and call'd me a fool;
For he says, short as 'tis, it will give you a stool.
    In libris bellis, tu parum precis ocellis;
Dum nimium scribis, vel talpâ cæcior ibis,   10
Aut ad vina redis, nam sic tua lumina lædis:
Sed tibi cœnanti sunt collyria tanti?
Nunquid eges visu, dum comples omnia risu?
Heu Sheridan cœcus, heu eris nunc cercopithecus.
Nunc bene nasutus mittet tibi carmina tutus:
Nunc ope Burgundi, malus Helsham ridet abunde,
Nec Phœbi fili versum quis mittere Ryly.
    Quid tibi cum libris? relavet tua lumina Tybris
Mixtus Saturno; penso sed parcè diurno
Observes hoc tu, nec scriptis utere noctu.   20

Nonnulli mingunt et palpebras sibi tingunt.
Quidam purgantes, libros in stercore nantes
Lingunt; sic vinces videndo, mi bone, lynces.
Culum oculum tergis, dum scripta hoc flumine mergis;
Tunc oculi et nates, ni fallor, agent tibi grates.
Vim fuge Decani, nec sit tibi cura Delani:
Heu tibi si scribant, aut si tibi fercula libant,
Pone loco mortis, rapis fera pocula fortis.
Hæc tibi pauca dedi, sed consule Betty my Lady,
Huic te des solæ, nec egebis pharmacopolæ.   30
     Hæc somnians cecini,
       JON. SWIFT.

Oct. 23, 1718.

         1718/1808

An Answer, by Sheridan

PERLEGI versus versos, Jonathan bone, tersos;
Perlepidos quidèm; scribendo semper es idem.
Laudibus extollo te, tu mihi magnus Apollo;
Tu frater Phœbus, oculis collyria præbes,
Ne minus insanæ reparas quoque damna Dianæ,
Quæ me percussit radiis (nec dixeris ussit)
Frigore collecto; medicus moderamine tecto
Lodicum binum permit, et negatis mihi vinum.
O terra et cœlum! quàm redit pectus anhelum.
Os mihi jam siccum, liceat mihi bibere dic cum?   10
Ex vestro grato poculo, tam sæpe prolato,
Vina crepant: sales ostendet quis mihi tales?
Lumina, vos sperno, dum cuppæ guadia cerno:
Perdere etenim pellem nostram, quoque crura
  mavellem.
 Amphora, quàm dulces risus queis pectora mulces,
Pangitur a Flacco, cum pectus turget Iaccho:

Clarius evohe ingeminans geminatur et ohe;
Nempe jocosa propago, hesit sic vocis imago.

1718/1808

Sheridan, a Goose

TOM, for a goose you keep but base quills,
They're fit for nothing else but pasquills.
I've often heard it from the wise,
That inflammations in the eyes
Will quickly fall upon the tongue,
And thence, as fam'd John Bunyan sung,
From out the pen will presently
On paper dribble daintily.
Suppose I call'd you goose, it is hard
One word should stick thus in your gizzard.   10
You're my goose, and no other man's;
And you know, all my geese are swans:
Only one scurvy thing I find,
Swans sing when dying, geese when blind.
But now I smoke where lies the slander,—
I call'd you goose, instead of gander;
For that, dear Tom, ne'er fret and vex,
I'm sure you cackle like the sex.
I know the gander always goes
With a quill stuck across his nose;   20
So your eternal pen is still
Or in your claw, or in your bill.
But whether you can tread or hatch,
I've something else to do than watch.
As for you're writing I am dead,
I leave it for the second head.

Deanry-House, Oct. 27, 1718.

1718/1808

302

Sheridan's Reply

A HIGHLANDER once fought with a Frenchman at
    Margate,
The weapons a rapier, a backsword, and target;
Brisk Monsieur advanc'd as fast as he could,
But all his fine pushes were caught in the wood;
While Sawney with backsword did slash him and nick
    him,
While t'other, enraged that he could not once prick
    him,
Cry'd 'Sirrah, you rascal, you son of a whore,
Me'll fight you, begar, if you'll come from your door!'
    Our case is the same; if you'll fight like a man,
Don't fly from my weapon, and sculk behind Dan; 10
For he's not to be pierc'd; his leather's so tough,
The devil himself can't get through his buff.
Besides, I cannot but say that it is hard,
Not only to make him your shield, but your vizard;
And like a tragedian, you rant and you roar,
Thro' the horrible grin of your *larva*'s wide bore.
Nay, further, which makes me complain much, and
    frump it,
You make his long nose your loud speaking-trumpet;
With the din of which tube my head you so bother,
That I scarce can distinguish my right ear from
    t'other.   20

    You made me in your last a goose;
        I lay my life on't you are wrong,
    To raise me by such foul abuse;
        My quill you'll find's a woman's tongue;

    And slit, just like a bird will chatter,
        And like a bird do something more;
    When I let fly, 'twill so bespatter,
        I'll change you to a black-a-moor.

I'll write while I have half an eye in my head;
I'll write while I live, and I'll write when you're dead.
Tho' you call me a goose, you pitiful slave,   31
I'll feed on the grass that grows on your grave.
                              1718/1808

Mary the Cook-Maid's Letter to Dr. Sheridan

WELL; if ever I saw such another Man since my
      Mother bound my Head,
You a Gentleman! marry come up, I wonder where
      you were bred?
I am sure such Words does not become a Man of
      your Cloth,
I would not give such Language to a Dog, faith and
      troth,
Yes; you call'd my Master a Knave: Fie, Mr.
      Sheridan, 'tis a Shame
For a Parson, who shou'd know better Things, to
      come out with such a Name.
Knave in your Teeth, Mr. *Sheridan*, 'tis both a Shame
      and a Sin,
And the Dean, my Master, is an honester Man than
      you and all your Kin:
He has more Goodness in his little Finger, than you
      have in your whole Body,
My Master is a personable Man, and not a spindle-
      shank'd Hoddy-doddy.   10
And now whereby I find you would fain make an
      Excuse,
Because my Master one Day in Anger, call'd you
      Goose.
Which, and I am sure, I have been his Servant four
      Years since *October*,

And he never call'd me worse than *Sweet-heart*, drunk
    or sober:
Not that I know his Reverence was ever concern'd to
    my Knowledge,
Tho' you and your Come-rogues keep him out so late
    in your wicked College.

You say you will eat Grass on his Grave; a Chris-
    tian eat Grass!
Whereby you now confess your self to be a Goose or
    an Ass:
But that's as much as to say, that my Master should
    die before ye;
Well, well, that's as God pleases, and I don't believe
    that's a true Story,   20
And so say I told you so, and you may go tell my
    Master; what care I?
And I don't care who knows it, 'tis all one to *Mary*.
Every Body knows, that I love to tell Truth, and
    shame the Devil;
I am but a poor Servant, but I think gentle Folks
    should be civil.
Besides, you found Fault with our Vittles one Day
    that you was here,
I remember it was upon a *Tuesday*, of all Days in the
    Year.
And *Saunders* the Man says, you are always jesting
    and mocking,
Mary, said he, (one Day, as I was mending my
    Master's Stocking,)
My Master is so fond of that Minister, that keeps the
    School;
I thought my Master a wise Man, but that Man
    makes him a Fool.   30
Saunders, said I, I would rather than a Quart of Ale,
He would come into our Kitchen, and I would pin a
    Dish-clout to his Tail.

And now I must go, and get *Saunders* to direct this
     Letter,
For I write but a sad Scrawl, but my Sister *Marget*
     she writes better.
Well, but I must run and make the Bed before my
     Master come's from Pray'rs,
And see now, it strikes Ten, and I hear him coming
     up Stairs:
Whereof I could say more to your Verses, if I could
     write written Hand;
And so I remain in a civil Way, your Servant to
     command,

                        MARY.
                        1718/1732

A Letter to the Reverend Dr. Sheridan

SIR,

    Whate'er your Predecessors taught us,
I have a great Esteem for *Plautus*;
And think your Boys may gather there-hence,
More Wit and Humour than from *Terence*.
But as to Comic *Aristophanes*,
The Rogue's too Bawdy and too Prophane is.
I went in vain to look for *Eupolis*,
Down in the ¹*Strand* just where the new Pole is,
For I can tell you one Thing, that I can,
You will not find it in the *Vatican*.   10
He and *Cratinus* used, as *Horace* says,
To take his greatest Grandees for Asses.
Poets, in those Days, us'd to venture high,
But these are lost full many a Century.

---

¹ N.B.   *The* Strand *in* LONDON. *The Fact may be false, but the
Rhyme cost me some Trouble.*

Thus you may see, dear Friend, *ex pede* hence
My Judgment of the old Comedians.

Proceed to Tragicks, first *Euripides*
(An Author, where I sometimes dip a-Days)
Is rightly censur'd by the Stagirite,
Who says, his Numbers do not fadge a-right.   20
A Friend of mine, that Author despises ⎫
So much, he swears the very best Piece is ⎬
For ought he knows, as bad as *Thespis*'s. ⎭
And that a Woman, in those Tragedies
Commonly speaking, but a sad Jade is.
At least, I'm well assured, that no Folk lays
The Weight on him, they do on *Sophocles.*
But above all I prefer *Æschylus*,
Whose moving Touches, when they please, kill us.

And now I find my Muse but ill able   30
To hold out longer in Trysyllable.
I chose these Rhymes out, for their Difficulty.
Will you return as hard ones, if I call t'ye?
                                    1718/1735

The Answer

BY DR. SHERIDAN

SIR,
    I thank you for your comedies.
I'll stay and read 'em now at home a-days,
Because Pareus wrote but sorrily
Thy notes, I'll read Lambinus thoroughly;
And then I shall be stoutly set a-gog
To challenge every Irish Pedagogue.
I like your nice epistle critical,

Which does in threefold rhymes so witty fall;
Upon the comic dram' and tragedy
Your notion's right, but verses maggotty;   10
'Tis but an hour since I heard a man swear it,
The Devil himself could hardly answer it.
As for your friend the sage Euripides,
[1]I believe you give him now the slip o'days;
But mum for that——pray come a Saturday
And dine with me, you can't a better day:
I'll give you nothing but a mutton chop,
Some nappy mellow'd ale with rotten hop,
A pint of wine as good as Falern',
Which we poor masters, God knows, all earn; 20
We'll have a friend or two, sir, at table,
Right honest men, for few're comeatable;
Then when our liquor makes us talkative,
We'll to the fields, and take a walk at eve.

    Because I'm troubled much with laziness.
    These rhymes I've chosen for their easiness.

                    1718/1735

From Dr. Swift to Dr. Sheridan

Dec. 14, 1719, 9 *at Night.*

SIR,

It is impossible to know by your Letter whether the Wine is to be bottled To-morrow, or no.

[If it be, or be not, why did not you in plain *English* tell us so?]

For my part, it was by meer Chance I came to sit with the Ladies this Night.

And, if they had not told me there was a Letter from you, and your Man *Alexander* had not gone, and

---

[1] N.B.   You told me you forgot your Greek.

come back from the Deanry, and the Boy here had not been sent to let *Alexander* know I was here, I should have missed the Letter outright.

Truly I don't know who's bound to be sending for Corks to stop your Bottles, with a Vengeance.

Make a Page of your own Age, and send your Man *Alexander* to buy Corks, for *Saunders* already hath got above ten Jaunts.

Mrs. *Dingley* and Mrs. *Johnson* say, truly they don't care for your Wife's Company, although they like your Wine; but they had rather have it at their own House, to drink in quiet.

However, they own it is very civil in Mr. *Sheridan*, to make the Offer; and they cannot deny it.

I wish *Alexander* safe at St. *Catherine*'s To-night, with all my Heart and Soul, upon my Word and Honour.

But I think it base in you to send a poor Fellow out so late at this Time of Year, when one would not turn out a Dog that one valued; I appeal to your Friend Mr. *Conna*.   10

I would present my humble Service to my Lady *Mountcashell:* but, truly, I thought she would have made Advances to have been acquainted with me, as she pretended.

But now I can write no more, for you see plainly my Paper is ended.

> P. S.   *I wish when you prated,*
> *Your Letter you'd dated,*
> *Much Plague it created,*
> *I scolded and rated;*
> *My Soul it much grated,*
> *For your Man, I long waited.*
> *I think you are fated,*
> *Like a Bear to be baited:*   20
> *Your Man is belated,*

The Case, I have stated,
And me you have cheated.
My Stable's unslated,
Come back t'us well freighted;
I remember my late-head
And wish you Translated,
          For teazing me.

2 P. S.   Mrs. Dingley
    Desires me singly   30
    Her Service to present you,
    Hopes that will content you;
    But Johnson Madam
    Is grown a Sad Dame,
    For want of your Converse,
    And cannot send one Verse.

3 P. S.   You keep such a twattling   [VIDA,
    With you and your bottling,   [Rule 34
    But I see the Sum Total,
    We shall ne'er have one Bottle;   40
    The long and the short,
    We shall not have a Quart.
    I wish you would sign't,
    That we may have a Pint.
    For all your colloguing,
    I'd be glad of a Knogging:
    But I doubt 'tis a Sham,
    You won't give us a Dram.
    'Tis of Shine, a Mouth Moon-full,
    You won't part with a Spoon-full,   50
    And I must be nimble,
    If I can fill my Thimble,
    You see I won't stop,
    Till I come to a Drop;
    But I doubt the Oraculum,
    Is a poor Supernaculum;

Tho' perhaps you may tell it
For a Grace, if we smell it.   STELLA.
                                1719/1745

A Letter
from Dr. Sheridan to Dr. Swift

I'D have you to know, as sure as you're Dean,
On Thursday my cask of Obrien I'll drain:
If my wife is not willing, I say she's a quean,
And my right to the cellar, I Gad I'll maintain
As bravely as any that fought at Dunblain:
Go tell her it over and over again.
I hope, as I ride to the town, it won't rain;
For, should it, I fear it will cool my hot brain,
Intirely extinguish my poetic vein;
And then I should be as stupid as Kain,   10
Who preach'd on three heads, tho' he mention'd but
       twain.
Now Wardel's in haste, and begins to complain;
Your most humble servant, Dear Sir, I remain,
                                T. S——N.

  Get Helsham, Walmsley, Delany,
  And some Grattans, if there be any,
  Take care you do not bid too many.

                                1719/1765

Dr. Swift's Answer to Dr. Sheridan

THE verses you sent on the bottling your wine
Were, in ev'ry one's judgment, exceedingly fine;
And I must confess, as a Dean and divine,
I think you inspir'd by the Muses all nine.

I nicely examin'd them ev'ry line,
And the worst of them all, like a barn-door, did shine,
Oh, that Jove would give me such a talent as thine!
With Delany or Dan I would scorn to combine:
I know they have many a wicked design;
And, give Satan his due, Dan begins to refine.   10
However, I wish, honest comrade of mine,
You would really on Thursday leave St. Catherine
Where I hear you are cramm'd ev'ry day like a swine.
With me you'll no more have a stomach to dine,
Nor, after your vittles, lie sleeping supine:
So I wish you were toothless like Lord Masserine.
But, were you as wicked as lewd Aretine,
I wish you would tell me which way you incline.
If, when you return, your road you don't line,
On Thursday I'll pay my respects at your shrine,   20
Wherever you bend, wherever you twine,
In square or in opposite circle, or trine.
Your beef will on Thursday be salter than brine:
I hope you have swill'd, with new milk from the kine,
As much as the Liffee's outdone by the Rhine;
And Dan shall be with us, with nose aquiline.
If you do not come back, we shall weep out our eyn,
Or may your gown never be good Lutherine.
The beef you have got, I hear, is a chine:
But, if too many come, your Madam will whine;   30
And then you may kiss the low end of her spine.
But enough of this Poetry Alexandrine:
I hope you will not think this a Pasquine.

                                      1719/1765

Upon Stealing a Crown when the Dean was Asleep

BY DR. SHERIDAN

DEAR Dean, since you in sleepy wise
Have op'd your Mouth, and clos'd your Eyes,
Like Ghost I glide along your Floor,
And softly shut the Parlour Door;
For should I break your sweet Repose,
Who knows what Money you might lose?
Since oftentimes it has been found,
A Dream has giv'n ten thousand Pound.
Then sleep, my Friend, dear Dean, sleep on,
And all you get shall be your own.   10
Provided you to this agree,
That all you lose belongs to me.

The Dean's Answer

So about twelve at Night, the Punk
Steals from the Cully when he's drunk;
Nor is contented with a Treat,
Without her Privilege to cheat.
Nor can I the least Diff'rence find,
But that you left no Clap behind.
But Jest apart, restore, you Capon ye,
My twelve [1]Thirteens and Six-pence ha'penny.
To eat my Meat, and drink my Medlicot,
And then to give me such a deadly Cut—   10
But 'tis observ'd, that Men in Gowns
Are most inclin'd to plunder *Crowns*.
Could you but *change* a Crown as easy
As you can steal one, how 'twould please ye!

[1] An *English* Shilling passeth for thirteen Pence in *Ireland*.

I thought the ¹Lady at St. *Cath'rines*
Knew how to set you better Patterns;
For this I will not dine with ²*Agmondisham*,
And for his Victuals let a Ragman dish 'em.
    Saturday Night.

1719/1745

A Copy of Verses from Thomas Sheridan, Clerk, to George Nim-Dan-Dean, Esq;

Written July 15th, 1721, at Night.

I'D have you t'know *George*, *Dan*, *Dean*, 'nd *Nim*,
That I've learned how Verse t' compose trim,
Much better b'half th'n you, n'r you, n'r him
And th't I'd rid'cule their, 'nd your Flam Flim,
Ay' b't them, p'rhaps, says you, 't's a m'rry Whim
With 'bundance of mark't Notes i' th' Rim,
So th't I ought n't for t' be morose 'nd t' look grim,
Think n't your 'p'stle put m' in a Meagrim;
Though, 'n Rep't't'on Day, I'appear ver' slim,
Th' last Bowl't *Helsham*'s did m' Head t' swim,   10
So th't I h'd man' Aches 'n'v'ry scrubb'd Limb,
Cause th' Top of th' Bowl I'h'd oft us'd t'skim;
And b'sides *D'lan*' swears th't I h'd swall'w'd s'v'r'l Brim-
mers, 'nd that my Vis'ge's cov'r'd o'r with r'd Pim-
ples: M'r'o'er though m'Scull were (s'tis n't) 's strong's Tim-
ber, 't must have ak'd. Th' Clans of th' C'lledge Sanh'drim,

pres'nt th'r humbl' and 'fect'nate Respects; that's
t'say, *D'lan'*, *'chlin*,

P. Ludl', *Dic' St'wart*, *H'lsham*, Capt'n *P'rr'*
Walmsl'nd, Longsh'nks *Tlmm.*

1721/1762

George Nim-Dan-Dean, Esq; to Mr. Sheridan

DEAR *Sheridan!* a gentle Pair
Of *Gallstown* Lads (for such they are)
Beside a Brace of grave Divines
Adore the Smoothness of thy Lines;
Smooth as our Bason's Silver Flood,
'Ere *George* had robb'd it of its Mud;
Smoother than *Pegasus*' old Shoe,
'Ere *Vulcan* comes to make him new.
The Board on which we set our A——s
Is not so smooth as are thy Verses,   10
Compar'd with which (and that's enuff)
A Smoothing-Ir'n itself is ruff.
Nor praise I less that Circumcision,
By modern Poets call'd Elision,
Which in its proper Stations plac't
Makes thy Verse smooth, and makes them last.
Thus, a wise Taylor is not pinching;
But turns at ev'ry Seam an Inch in,
Or else, be sure, your Broad-cloth Breeches
Will ne'er be smooth, nor hold the Stitches.   20
Thy Verse, like Bricks, defy the Weather,
When smooth'd by rubbing them together;
Thy Words so closely wedg'd and short, are
Like Walls, more lasting without Mortar;
By leaving out the needless Vowels
You save the Charge of Lime and Trowels.

One Letter still another locks
Each groov'd, and dove-tail'd like a Box.
Thy Muse is tuckt up and succinct,
In Chains thy Syllables are linkt,   30
Thy Words together ty'd in small Hanks
Close as the *Macedonian* Phalanx;
Or like the Umbo of the *Romans*
Which fiercest Foes could break by no Means.
The Critick to his Grief will find
How firmly these Indentures bind:
So, in the kindred Painter's Art
The short'ning is the nicest Part.
    Philologers of future Ages
How will they pore upon thy Pages!   40
Nor will they dare to break the Joints,
But help thee to be read with Points:
Or else, to shew their learned Labour, you
May backward be perus'd like *Hebrew*,
Wherein they need not lose a Bit,
Or, of thy Harmony or Wit,
To make a Work compleatly fine,
Number and Weight and Measure join.
Then all must grant your Lines are weighty,
Where thirty weigh as much as eighty.   50
All must allow your Numbers more,
Where twenty Lines exceed fourscore;
Nor can we think your Measure short
Where less than forty fill a Quart,
With *Alexandrian* in the Close
Long, long, long, long, like *Dan*'s long Nose.
                                    1721/1746

316

George Nim-Dan-Dean's
Invitation to Mr. Thomas Sheridan

Gallstown, August 2d, 1721

DEAR Tom, this verse, which however the begin-
ning may appear, yet in the *end's good metre*,
Is sent to desire that, when your August vacation
comes, your *friends you'd meet here.*
For why should you stay in that filthy hole, I mean
the *city so smoaky,*
When you have not one friend left in town, or at least
one that's *witty, to joke w'ye?*
For, as for honest John, tho' I am not sure on't, yet
I'll be *hang'd, less he*
Be gone down to the county of Wexford with that
great peer the Lord *Anglesey.*
Oh! but I forgot, perhaps, by this time, you may have
one come to town, but I don't know whether he
be friend or *foe, Delany:*
But, however, if he be come, bring him down, and
you shall go back in a fortnight, for I know
there's *no delaying ye.*
Oh! I forgot too, I believe there may be one more, I
mean that great fat joker, *friend Helsham, he*
That wrote the Prologue, and if you stay with him,
depend on't, in the *end, he'll sham ye.*   10
Bring down Long Shanks Jim too, but now I think
on't, he's not come yet from *Courtown, I fancy;*
For I heard, a month ago, that he was down there a
courting Sly Nancy.
However, bring down yourself, and you bring down
all; for, to say it *we may venture,*
In thee Delany's spleen, John's mirth, and Helsham's
jokes, and the soft soul of amorous *Jemmy center.*

POSTSCRIPT

I had forgot to desire you to bring down what I say
    you have, and you'll believe me as sure as a *gun,*
    and own it;
I mean, what no other mortal in the universe can
    boast of, your own spirit of *pun, and own wit.*
And now I hope you'll excuse this rhyming, which I
    must say is (tho' written somewhat at *large*) *trim*
    and clean;
And so I conclude, with humble respects as usual,
    Your most dutiful and obedient
                    George Nim-Dan-Dean.
                         1721/1765

To George Nim-Dan-Dean, Esq; Upon his incomparable Verses, &c. of August 2d, M DCC XXI[1]

    HAIL, human compound quadrifarious!
Invincible as Wight Briareus!
Hail! doubly doubled mighty merry one,
Stronger than triple-body'd Geryon!
O may your vastness deign t'excuse
The Praises of a puny Muse,
Unable, in her utmost flight,
To reach thy huge Colossian height.
T'attempt to write like thee were frantic,
Whose lines are, like thyself, gigantic.   10

    Yet let me bless, in humbler strain,
Thy vast, thy bold Cambysian vein,

---

[1] These verses were all written in circles, one within another,
as appears from the observations in the following poem by Dr.
Swift.—Deane Swift.

Pour'd out t'inrich thy native isle,
As Egypt wont to be with Nile.
Oh how I joy to see thee wander,
In many a winding loose meander,
In circling mazes, smooth and supple,
And ending in a clink quadruple;
Loud, yet agreeable withal,
Like rivers rattling in their fall.   20
Thine, sure is poetry divine,
Where wit and majesty combine;
Where ev'ry line, as huge as seven,
If stretch'd in length, would reach to Heaven:
Here all comparing would be sland'ring,
The least is more than Alexandrine.

    Against thy verse Time sees with pain,
He whets his envious scithe in vain;
For, tho' from thee he much may pare,
Yet much thou still wilt have to spare.   30

        Thou hast alone the skill to feast
With Roman elegance of taste,
Who hast of rhymes as vast resources
As Pompey's caterer of courses.

    O thou, of all the Nine inspir'd!
My languid soul, with teaching tir'd,
How is it raptur'd, when it thinks,
On thy harmonious set of clinks;
Each answ'ring each in various rhymes,
Like Echo to St. Patrick's chimes?   40

    Thy Muse, majestic in her rage,
Moves like Satira on the stage,
And scarcely can one page sustain
The length of such a flowing train:

Her train, of variegated dye,
Shews like Thaumantia's in the sky;
Alike they glow, alike they please,
Alike imprest by Phœbus' rays.

Thy verse—(Ye Gods! I cannot bear it)
To what, to what shall I compare it?   50
'Tis like, what I have oft heard spoke on,
The famous statue of Laocoon.
'Tis like——O yes, 'tis very like it,
The long long string with which you fly kite.
'Tis like what you, and one or two more,
Roar to your Echo in good-humour;
And ev'ry couplet thou hast writ
Concludes like Rattah-whittah-whit.

                                        1721/1765

To Mr. Thomas Sheridan
upon his Verses written in Circles

IT never was known that circular letters,
By humble companions were sent to their betters:
And, as to the subject, our judgment mehercle
Is this, that you argue like fools in a circle.
But now for your verses; we tell you, *imprimis*,
The segment so large 'twixt your reason and rhyme is,
That we walk all about, like a horse in a pound,
And, before we find either, our noddles turn round.
Sufficient it were, one would think, in your mad rant,
To give us your measures of lines by a quadrant.   10
But we took our dividers, and found your d—n'd
     metre,
In each single verse, took up a diameter.
But how, Mr. Sheridan, came you to venture

320

George, Dan, Dean, and Nim to place in the center[1]?
'Twill appear, to your cost, you are fairly trepann'd,
For the cord of your circle is now in their hand;
The cord, or the radius, it matters not whether,
By which your jade Pegasus fixt in a tether,
As his betters are us'd, shall be lash'd round the ring,
Three fellows with whips, and the Dean holds the
    string.   20
Will Hancock declares you are out of your compass,
To encroach on his art by writing of bombas';
And has taken just now a firm resolution
To answer your style without circumlocution.

Lady Betty presents you her service most humble,
And is not afraid your Worship will grumble,
That she makes of your verses a hoop for Miss Tam,
Which is all at present; and so I remain—
                   1721/1765

Sheridan to Swift

I CAN'T but wonder, Mr. Dean,
To see you live, so often slain.
My arrows fly and fly in vain,
But still I try and try again.
I'm now, Sir, in a writing vein;
Don't think, like you, I squeeze and strain.
Perhaps you'll ask me what I mean;
I will not tell, because it's plain.
Your Muse, I am told, is in the wane;
If so, from pen and ink refrain.   10
Indeed, believe me, I'm in pain
For her and you; your life's a scene

---

[1] There were four human figures in the centre of the circular
verses.—Deane Swift.

Of verse, and rhymes, and hurricane,
Enough to crack the strongest brain.
Now to conclude, I do remain,
Your honest friend,   TOM SHERIDAN.
1721?/1808

Swift to Sheridan

POOR Tom, wilt thou never accept a defiance,
Tho' I dare you to more than quadruple alliance.
You're so retrograde, sure you were born under
        Cancer;
Must I make myself hoarse with demanding an answer?
If this be your practice, mean scrub, I assure ye,
And swear by each Fate, and your new friends, each
        Fury,
I'll drive you to Cavan, from Cavan to Dundalk;
I'll tear all your rules, and demolish your pun-talk:
Nay, further, the moment you're free from your
        scalding,
I'll chew you to bullets, and puff you at Baldwin.   10
1721?/1808

Poetical Epistle to Dr. Sheridan

SOME ancient authors wisely write,
That he who drinks will wake at night,
Will never fail to lose his rest,
And feel a streightness in his chest;
A streightness in a double sense,
A streightness both of breath and pence:
Physicians say, it is but reasonable,
He that comes home at hour unseasonable,

322

(Besides a fall and broken shins,
Those smaller judgments for his sins;)   10
If, when he goes to bed, he meets
A teazing wife between the sheets,
'Tis six to five he'll never sleep,
But rave and toss till morning-peep.
Yet harmless Betty must be blamed
Because you feel your lungs inflamed;
But if you would not get a fever,
You never must one moment leave her.
This comes of all your drunken tricks,
Your Parry's and your brace of Dicks;   20
Your hunting Helsham in his laboratory
Too, was the time you saw that Drab lae a Pery.
But like the prelate who lives yonder-a
And always cries he is like Cassandra;
I always told you, Mr. Sheridan,
If once this company you were rid on,
Frequented honest folk, and very few,
You'd live till all your friends were weary of you.
But if rack punch you still would swallow,
I then forewarned you what would follow.   30
Are the Deanery sober hours?
Be witness for me all ye powers.
The cloth is laid at eight, and then
We sit till half an hour past ten;
One bottle well might serve for three
If Mrs. Robinson drank like me.
Ask how I fret when she has beckon'd
To Robert to bring up a second;
I hate to have it in my sight,
And drink my share in perfect spite.   40
If Robin brings the ladies word,
The coach is come, I 'scape a third;
If not, why then I fall a talking
How sweet a night it is for walking;
For in all conscience, were my treasure able,

I'd think a quart a piece unreasonable;
It strikes eleven,—get out of doors.—
This is my constant farewell.

Yours,

J. S.

Oct. 18th 1724, nine in the morning.

You had best hap yourself up in a chair, and dine
with me than with the provost.

1724/1814

On the Five Ladies at Sots-Hole, with the Doctor at their Head

THE LADIES TREATED THE DOCTOR

Sent as from an Officer in the Army

FAIR Ladies, Number five,
   Who in your merry Freaks,
With little *Tom* contrive
   To feast on Ale and Steaks.
While he sits by a Grinning,
   To see you safe in [1]*Sots-Hole*,
Set up with greasy Linnen,
   And neither Muggs nor Pots whole.
Alas! I never thought
   A Priest would please your Palate;   10
Besides, I'll hold a Groat,
   He'll put you in a Ballad:
Where I shall see your Faces
   On Paper daub'd so foul,
They'll be no more like Graces,
   Than *Venus* like an Owl.
And we shall take you rather

[1] *A famous Ale-house in Dublin for Beef-stakes.*

To be a Midnight Pack
Of Witches met together,
   With *Belzebub* in Black.   20
It fills my Heart with Woe,
   To think such Ladies fine,
Should be reduc'd so low,
   To treat a dull Divine:
Be by a Parson cheated!
   Had you been cunning Stagers,
You might yourselves be treated
   By Captains and by Majors.
See how Corruption grows,
   While Mothers, Daughters, Aunts,   30
Instead of powder'd Beaus,
   From Pulpits chuse Gallants.
If we, who wear our Wiggs
   With Fan-Tail and with Snake,
Are bubbled thus by Prigs;
   Z——ds who wou'd be a Rake?
Had I a Heart to fight,
   I'd knock the Doctor down;
Or could I read and write,
   I'gad I'd wear a Gown.   40
Then leave him to his Birch;
   And at the *Rose* on *Sunday*,
The Parson safe at Church,
   I'll treat you with *Burgundy*.

                 1728/1735

The Five Ladies Answer to the Beau with the Wig and Wings at his Head

BY SHERIDAN

You little scribbling Beau,
    What Dæmon made you write?
Because to write you know
    As much as you can fight.

For compliment so scurvy,
    I wish we had you here;
We'd turn you topsy-turvy
    Into a mug of beer.

You thought to make a farce on
    The man and place we chose;   10
We're sure a single Parson
    Is worth a hundred Beaux.

And you would make us vassals,
    Good Mr. Wig and Wings,
To silver-clocks and tassels;
    You wou'd, you Thing of Things!

Because around your cane
    A ring of diamonds is set;
And you, in some bye-lane,
    Have gain'd a paultry grizette: 20

Shall we, of sense refin'd,
    Your trifling nonsense bear,
As noisy as the wind,
    As empty as the air?

We hate your empty prattle,
    And vow and swear 'tis true;

There's more in one child's rattle
Than twenty fops like you.

1728/1765

The Beau's Reply
to the Five Ladies Answer

WHY, how now, dapper Black,
   I smell your gown and cassock,
As strong upon your back,
   As Tisdal smells of a sock.

To write such scurvy stuff!
   Fine Ladies never do't;
I know you well enough,
   And eke your cloven foot.

Fine Ladies, when they write,
   Nor scold, nor keep a splutter: 10
Their verses give delight,
   As soft and sweet as butter.

But Satan never saw
   Such haggard lines as these:
They stick athwart my maw,
   As bad as Suffolk-cheese.

1728/1765

Ballyspellin

BY DR. SHERIDAN

ALL you that would refine your Blood,
   As pure as fam'd *Llewellyn*,

327

By Waters clear, come ev'ry Year,
   To drink at *Ballyspellin*.

Tho' Pox or Itch your Skins enrich
   With Rubies past the telling,
'Twill clear your Skin before you've been
   A Month at *Ballyspellin*.

If Ladies Cheek be green as Leek
   When she comes from her Dwelling,   10
The kindling Rose within it glows
   When she's at *Ballyspellin*.

The sooty Brown, who comes from Town,
   Grows here as fair as *Helen*,
Then back she goes to kill the Beaux
   By Dint of *Ballyspellin*.

Our Ladies are as fresh and fair
   As *Ross*, or bright *Dunkelling*:
And *Mars* might make a fair Mistake
   Were he at *Ballyspellin*.   20

We Men submit as they think fit,
   And here is no rebelling;
The Reason's plain, the Ladies reign;
   They're Queens at *Ballyspellin*.

By matchless Charms, unconquer'd Arms,
   They have the Pow'r of quelling,
Such desperate Foes as dare oppose
   Their Power at *Ballyspellin*.

Cold Water turns to Fire and burns,
   I know because I fell in   30
A Stream which came from one bright Dame,
   Who drank at *Ballyspellin*.

Fine Beaux advance, equipt for Dance,
    And bring their *Anne* or *Nell* in
With so much Grace, I'm sure no Place
    Can vie with *Ballyspellin.*

No Politicks, no subtle Tricks,
    No Man his Country selling,
We eat, we drink, we never think
    Of these at *Ballyspellin.*   40

The troubled Mind, the puft with Wind,
    Do all come here *Pell-Mell* in;
And, they are sure, to work their Cure
    By drinking *Ballyspellin.*

If Dropsy fills you to the Gills,
    From Chin to Toe, tho' swelling,
Pour in, pour out, you cannot doubt
    A Cure at *Ballyspellin.*

Death throws no Darts through all these Parts,
    No Sextons here are knelling;   50
Come judge and try, you'll never *die,*
    But *live* at *Ballyspellin.*

Except you feel Darts tipt in Steel,
    Which here are ev'ry Belle in;
When from their Eyes sweet Ruin flies,
    We die at *Ballyspellin.*

Good Chear, sweet Air, much Joy, no Care,
    Your Sight, your Taste, your Smelling,
Your Ears, your Touch, transporteth much
    Each Day at *Ballyspellin.*   60

Within this Ground we all sleep sound,
    No noisy Dogs a yelling;

Except you wake, for *Cælia*'s Sake,
    All Night at *Ballyspellin*.

Here all you see, both he and she,
    No Lady keeps her Cell in;
But all partake the Mirth we make
    Who drinks at *Ballyspellin*.

My Rhimes are gone, I think I've none,
    Unless I should bring Hell in: 70
But since I am here to Heav'n so near,
    I can't at *Ballyspellin*.

The Answer

DARE you dispute, you sawcy Brute?
    And think there's no rebelling,
Your scurvy Lays, and senseless Praise,
    You give to *Ballyspellin?*

Howe'er you bounce, I here pronounce,
    Your Med'cine is repelling;
Your Water's Mud, and sours the Blood,
    When drank at *Ballyspellin*.

Those pocky Drabs, to cure their Scabs,
    You thither are compelling;   10
Will back be sent, worse than they went,
    From nasty *Ballyspellin*.

Llewellyn why, as well may I
    Name honest Doctor *Pellin*;
So hard sometimes you tug for Rhimes,
    To bring in *Ballyspellin*.

No Subject fit to try your Wit,
   When you went colonelling;
But dull Intrigues 'twixt Jades and Teagues,
   That met at *Ballyspellin*.   20

Our Lasses fair, say what you dare,
   Who Sowings make with Shelling,
At *Market-Hill* more Beaux can kill,
   Than yours at *Ballyspellin*.

Wou'd I was whipt when *Sheela* stript,
   To wash herself our Well in;
A Bum so white, ne'er came in Sight,
   At paultry *Ballyspellin*.

Your Mawkins there, Smocks *Hempen* wear,
   Of *Holland*, not an Ell in,   30
No, not a Rag, whate'er you brag,
   Is found at *Ballyspellin*.

But, *Tom* will prate at any Rate,
   All other Nymphs expelling:
Because he gets a few *Grisets*,
   At lousy *Ballyspellin*.

There's bonny *Jane* in yonder Lane,
   Just o'er against the *Bell Inn*;
Where can you meet a Lass so sweet,
   Round all your *Ballyspellin*.   40

We have a Girl, deserves an Earl,
   She came from *Enniskillin*;
So fair so young, no such among
   The Belles at *Ballyspellin*.

How wou'd you stare to see her there,
   The foggy Mist dispelling;

That cloud the Brows, of ev'ry Blowse
　　Who lives at *Ballyspellin*.

Now, as I live, I would not give
　　A *Stiver* for a *Skellin*,　　　　　　　　50
To towse, and kiss, the fairest Miss
　　That leaks at *Ballyspellin*.

Who e'er will raise such Lies as these,
　　Deserves a good Cudgeling:
Who falsly boasts of Belles and Toasts,
　　At dirty *Ballyspellin*.

My Rhimes are gone, to all but one,
　　Which is our Trees are felling.
As proper quite, as those you write,
　　To force in *Ballyspellin*.　　　　　　　60
　　　　　　　　　　　1728/1728?

To Dr. Helsham

Sir,
　　When I left you, I found myself of the Grape's
　　　　Juice sick:
I'm so full of Pity, I never abuse Sick;
And the patientest Patient that ever you knew sick;
Both when I am Purge-sick, and when I am Spew-
　　sick.
I pitied my Cat, whom I knew by her Mew sick;
She mended at first, but now she's anew sick.
Captain *Butler* made some in the Church black and
　　blue sick;
Dean *Cross*, had he preach'd, would have made us all
　　Pew-sick;

332

Are not you, in a Crowd, when you sweat and you
    stew, sick?

Lady *Santry* got out of the ¹Church when she grew
    sick,   10

And, as fast as she could, to the Deanery flew sick.

Miss *Morice* was (I can assure you 'tis true) sick:

For, who would not be in that numerous Crew sick?

Such Musick would made a Fanatick or Jew sick:

Yet, Ladies are seldom at *Ombre*, or *Lue*, sick;

Nor is old ²*Nanny Shales*, whene'er she does brew,
    sick.

My Footman came home from the Church, of a
    Bruise sick,

And look'd like a Rake, who was made in the Stews
    sick;

But you learned Doctors can make whom you chuse
    sick.

Poor I myself I was, when I withdrew, sick,   20

For the Smell of them made me like Garlick and Rue
    sick.

And I got thro' the Crowd, tho' not led by a Clew,
    sick.

You hop'd to find many (for that was your Cue)
    sick;

But, there were not a Dozen (to give 'em their Due)
    sick,

And those to be sure, stuck together like Glew, sick.

So are Ladies in Crowds, when they squeeze and they
    screw, sick.

You may find they are all, by their yellow pale Hue,
    sick;

So am I, when Tobacco, like *Robin*, I chew, sick.

Nov. 23. at Night,
    1731.   1731/1746

¹ St. *Patrick*'s Cathedral, where the Musick on St. *Cæcilia*'s
Day was usually performed.
   ² Vide *Grattan, inter Belchamp et Clonshogh.*

To Dr. Sheridan

Nov. 23, at Night.

IF I write any more, it will make my poor Muse
    sick.
This Night I came home with a very cold Dew sick,
And I wish I may soon be not of an A-gue sick;
But, I hope I shall ne'er be, like you, of a Shrew sick,
Who often has made me, by looking ascue, sick.

1731/1746

Addenda Quædam

To Dr. Sheridan at Cavan

MY Wife a rattling,
My Children tattling.
My Money spent is,
And due my Rent is.
My School decreasing,
My Income ceasing.
All People tease me,
But no Man pays me.
My Worship is bit,
By that Rogue *Nisbit*.   10
To take the right Way,
Consult Friend *Whiteway*.
Would you get still more?
Go flatter *Kilmore*.
Your Geese are old,
Your W[ife] a Scold.
You live among ill
Folks in a Dunghill,
You never have an
Old Friend at *Cavan*.   20

1736/1746

A Satyr on an inconstant Lover

You are as faithless as a Carthaginian,
To love at once Kate, Nell, Doll, Martha, Jenny, Ann.
1737/1746

Anglo-Latin Verses

A LOVE SONG

Apud in is almi des ire,
Mimis tres I ne ver re qui re.
Alo veri findit a gestis,
His miseri ne ver at restis.

AN EPIGRAM

Dic, heris agro at, an da quarto fine ale,
Fora ringat ure nos, an da stringat ure tale.
?/1746

TO SAMUEL BINDON, ESQ.

Mollis abuti
Has an accuti
No lasso finis
Molli divinis
Omi de armis tres
Imi na dîs tres
Cantu disco ver
Meas alo ver.

CLUB VERSES

Be mi sol ab ride lis as fit formis as fora mare,
Amat i, a ruas apto prata se ver.
 Do es ure de an ab usu
Heris abrato fine Patri gesto
At nite. Cani prognostick
Arrogavit me.

?/1767

A Cantata

338

Riddles

About nine or ten Years ago, some ingenious Gentlemen,
  Friends to the Author, used to entertain themselves
  with writing Riddles, and send them to him and their
  other Acquaintance, Copies of which ran about, and
  some of them were printed both here and in England.
  The Author, at his leisure Hours, fell into the same
  Amusement; although it be said, that he thought them
  of no great Merit, Entertainment, or Use. However,
  by the Advice of some Persons, for whom the Author
  hath a great Esteem, and who were pleased to send us
  the Copies, we have ventured to print the few follow-
  ing, as we have done two or three before, and which
  are allowed to be genuine; because, we are informed,
  that several good Judges have a Taste for such Kind of
  Compositions. [1735]

A RIDDLE

IN Youth exalted high in Air,
Or bathing in the Waters fair,
Nature to form me took Delight,
And clad my Body all in white:
My Person tall, and slender Waist,
On either Side with Fringes grac'd;
Till me that Tyrant Man espy'd,
And dragg'd me from my Mother's Side:
No Wonder now I look so thin;
The Tyrant stript me to the Skin: 10
My Skin he flay'd, my Hair he cropt;
At Head and Foot my Body lopt:
And then, with Heart more hard than Stone,
He pick't my Marrow from the Bone.
To vex me more he took a Freak,
To slit my Tongue, and made me speak:

But, that which wonderful appears,
I speak to Eyes and not to Ears.
He oft employs me in Disguise,
And makes me tell a thousand Lyes: 20
To me he chiefly gives in Trust
To please his Malice, or his Lust.
From me no Secret he can hide;
I see his Vanity and Pride:
And my Delight is to expose
His Follies to his greatest Foes.

    All Languages I can command,
Yet not a Word I understand.
Without my Aid, the best Divine
In Learning would not know a Line: 30
The Lawyer must forget his Pleading,
The Scholar could not shew his Reading.
Nay; Man, my Master, is my Slave:
I give Command to kill or save.
Can grant ten thousand Pounds a Year,
And make a Beggar's Brat a Peer.

    But, while I thus my Life relate,
I only hasten on my Fate.
My Tongue is black, my Mouth is furr'd,
I hardly now can force a Word.   40
I die unpity'd and forgot;
And on some Dunghill left to rot.

               1724/1726

ANOTHER

    ALL-RULING Tyrant of the Earth
To vilest Slaves I owe my Birth.
How is the greatest Monarch blest,
When in my gaudy Liv'ry drest!

No haughty Nymph has Pow'r to run
From me; or my Embraces shun.
Stabb'd to the Heart, condemn'd to Flame,
My Constancy is still the same.
The fav'rite Messenger of *Jove*,
And [1]*Lemnian* God consulting strove,   10
To make me glorious to the Sight
Of Mortals, and the Gods Delight.
Soon would their Altars Flame expire,
If I refus'd to lend them Fire.

                                        ?/1735

ANOTHER

By Fate *exalted high* in Place;
Lo, here I stand with *double Face*;
Superior none on Earth I find;
But see *below me* all Mankind.
Yet, as it oft' attends the Great,
I almost *sink* with my own *Weight*;
At every *Motion* undertook,
The Vulgar all consult my *Look*.
I sometimes give Advice in *Writing*,
But never of my own *Inditing*.   10

I am a Courtier in my Way;
For those who *rais'd* me, I *betray*;
And some give out, that I entice
To Lust, and Luxury, and Dice:
Who Punishments on me inflict,
Because they find their Pockets pick't.

By riding *Post* I lose my Health;
And only to get others Wealth.

                                        ?/1735

[1] VULCAN.

343

ANOTHER

BECAUSE I am by Nature *blind*,
I wisely chuse to walk *behind*;
However, to avoid Disgrace,
I let no Creature see my *Face*.
My *Words* are few, but spoke with *Sense*:
And yet my *speaking* gives Offence.
Or, if to *whisper* I presume,
The Company will fly the Room,
By all the World I am *oppress't*,
And my *Oppression* gives them *Rest*.   10

Through me, though sore against my Will
Instructors ev'ry Art instill,
By Thousands I am *sold* and *bought*,
Who neither get, nor lose a Groat;
For none, alas, by me can gain,
But those who give me *greatest Pain*.
Shall Man presume to be my Master,
Who's but my *Caterer* and *Taster?*
Yet, though I always have my Will
I'm but a meer *Depender* still: 20
An humble *Hanger-on* at best;
Of whom all People *make a Jest*.

In me, Detractors seek to find
Two Vices of a diff'rent Kind:
I'm too *profuse* some Cens'rers cry,
And all I get, I *let it fly*:
While others give me many a Curse,
Because too *close* I hold my *Purse*.
But this I know, in either Case
They dare not *charge* me to my *Face*.   30
'Tis true, indeed, sometimes I *save*,
Sometimes *run out* of all I have;
But when the Year is at an End,

344

Computing what I *get* and *spend*,
My *Goings out*, and *Comings in*,
I cannot find I lose, or win,
And therefore, all that know me, say,
I justly keep the *middle Way*.
I'm always by my Betters led;
I last *get up*, am first *a-bed*.   40
Though, if I rise *before my Time*,
The Learn'd in Sciences sublime,
Consult the Stars and thence foretel
Good Luck to those, with whom I dwell.
                                    ?/1735

ANOTHER

THE Joy of Man, the Pride of Brutes,
Domestick Subject for Disputes,
Of Plenty, thou the Emblem fair,
Adorn'd by Nymphs with all their Care:
I saw thee rais'd to high Renown,
Supporting half the *British* Crown;
And often have I seen thee grace
The chaste *Diana*'s infant Face;
And whensoe'er you please to shine,
Less useful is her Light than thine;   10
Thy num'rous Fingers know their Way,
And oft in *Celia*'s Tresses play.

To place thee in another View,
I'll shew the World strange Things and true;
What Lords and Dames of high Degree,
May justly claim their Birth from thee;
The Soul of Man with Spleen you vex;
Of Spleen you cure the Female Sex.
Thee, for a Gift, the Courtier sends
With Pleasure to his special Friends;   20
He gives; and with a gen'rous Pride,

Contrives all Means the Gift to hide:
Nor oft can the Receiver know
Whether he has the Gift or no.
On Airy Wings you take your Flight,
And fly unseen both Day and Night;
Conceal your Form with various Tricks;
And few know how and where you fix.
Yet some, who ne'er bestow'd thee, boast
That they to others give thee most: 30
Mean Time, the Wise a Question start,
If thou a real Being art;
Or, but a Creature of the Brain,
That gives imaginary Pain:
But the sly Giver better knows thee;
Who feels true Joys, when he bestows thee.
                                        ?/1735

ANOTHER

THOUGH I, alas! a Pris'ner be,
My Trade is, Pris'ners to set free.
No Slave his Lord's Commands obeys,
With such *insinuating* Ways.
My Genius *piercing*, *sharp* and *bright*,
Wherein the Men of Wit delight.
The Clergy keep me for their Ease,
And *turn* and *wind* me, as they please.
A new and wond'rous Art I show
Of raising Spirits from below;   10
In *Scarlet* some, and some in *White*;
They rise, walk round, yet never fright.
In at each *Mouth* the *Spirits* pass,
Distinctly seen as through a Glass:
O'er *Head* and *Body* make a Rout,
And drive at last all *Secrets* out:
And still, the more I shew my Art,
The more they *open every Heart*.

A greater Chymist none, than I,
Who from *Materials hard and dry*,   20
Have taught Men to *extract* with Skill,
More precious Juice than from a Still.

Although I'm often *out of Case*,
I'm not asham'd to shew my *Face*.
Though at the Tables of the Great,
I near the Side-board take my Seat;
Yet, the plain 'Squire, when Dinner's done,
Is never pleas'd, 'till I make one.
He kindly bids me near him stand;
And often takes me by the *Hand*.   30

I twice a Day a *hunting* go;
Nor ever fail to *seize my Foe*;
And, when I have him by the *Pole*,
I drag him upwards from his *Hole*.
Though some are of so stubborn Kind,
I'm forc'd to leave a *Limb* behind.

I hourly wait some fatal End;
For, I can *break*, but scorn to *bend*.

?/1735

ANOTHER

The Gulph of all Human Possession

COME hither and behold the Fruits,
Vain Man, of all thy vain Pursuits,
Take wise Advice and *look behind*,
Bring all *past* Actions to thy Mind.
Here you may see, as in a Glass,
How soon all human Pleasures pass.
How will it mortify thy Pride,
To turn the true impartial Side!

How will your Eyes contain their Tears,
When all the sad *Reverse* appears!   10

    This Cave within its Womb confines
The last Result of all Designs:
Here lye deposited the Spoils
Of busy Mortals endless Toils:
Here, with an easy Search we find
The *foul Corruptions* of Mankind.
The wretched Purchase here behold
Of Traytors who their Country sold.

    This Gulph insatiable imbibes
The Lawyer's Fees, the Statesman's Bribes. 20
Here, in their proper Shape and Mien,
Fraud, Perjury, and Guilt are seen.

    Necessity, the Tyrant's Law,
All human Race must hither draw:
All prompted by the same *Desire*,
The vig'rous Youth, and aged Sire:
Behold, the Coward, and the Brave,
The haughty Prince, the humble Slave,
Physician, Lawyer, and Divine,
All make *Oblations* at this Shrine.   30
Some enter boldly, some by Stealth,
And leave *behind* their fruitless Wealth.
For, while the bashful Sylvan Maid,
As half asham'd, and half afraid,
Approaching, finds it hard to part
With that, which dwelt so *near her Heart*;
The courtly Dame, unmov'd by Fear,
Profusely pours her *Off'rings* here.

    A Treasure here of *Learning* lurks,
Huge Heaps of never-dying Works;   40

Labours of many an ancient Sage,
And Millions of the present Age.

In at this Gulph all Off'rings pass,
And lye an undistinguish'd Mass.
Deucalion, to restore Mankind
Was bid to throw the Stones *behind*;
So, those who here their Gifts convey,
Are forc't to *look another Way*:
For, few, a chosen few, must know,
The Mysteries that lye below.   50

Sad Charnel-house! a dismal Dome,
For which all Mortals leave their Home;
The Young, the Beautiful, and Brave,
Here bury'd in one common Grave,
Where each Supply of *Dead* renews
Unwholesome *Damps, offensive Dews*:
And lo! the *Writing on the Walls*
Points out where each new *Victim* falls;
The *Food of Worms*, and Beasts obscene,
Who round the Vault luxuriant reign.   60

See where those mangled Corpses lye,
Condemn'd by Female Hands to dye;
A comely Dame once clad in white,
Lyes there confin'd to endless Night;
By cruel Hands her Blood was spilt,
And yet her *Wealth* was all her Guilt.

And here six Virgins in a Tomb,
All beauteous Offspring of one Womb,
Oft in the Train of *Venus* seen,
As fair and lovely as their Queen: 70
In Royal Garments each was drest,
Each with a Gold and Purple Vest;

I saw them of their Garments stript,
Their Throats were cut, their Bellies ript,
Twice were they bury'd, *twice* were born,
Twice from their Sepulchres were torn;
But, now dismember'd here are cast,
And find a resting Place at last.

Here, oft the curious Trav'ler finds,
The Combat of *opposing Winds*:   80
And seeks to learn the secret Cause,
Which alien seems from Nature's Laws:
Why at this *Cave*'s tremendous *Mouth*,
He feels at once both *North* and *South*:
Whether the Winds in Cavern pent
Through *Clifts* oppugnant force a Vent;
Or, whether, *op'ning all his Stores*,
Fierce *Æolus* in Tempests roars.

Yet, from this *mingled Mass* of Things,
In Time a new Creation springs.   90
These *crude* Materials once shall rise,
To fill the Earth, and Air, and Skies:
In various Forms appear agen
Of Vegetables, Brutes, and Men,
So *Jove* pronounc'd among the Gods,
Olympus trembling as he nods.

1724/1735

ANOTHER

Louisa to Strephon

AH, *Strephon*, how can you despise
Her, who, without thy Pity, dies?
To *Strephon* I have still been true,
And of as noble Blood as you;

Fair Issue of the genial Bed,
A Virgin in thy Bosom bred;
Embrac'd thee closer than a Wife;
When thee I leave, I leave my Life.
Why should my Shepherd take amiss
That oft I wake thee with a Kiss? 10
Yet you of ev'ry Kiss complain;
Ah, is not Love a pleasing Pain?
A Pain which ev'ry happy Night
You cure with Ease and with Delight;
With Pleasure as the Poet sings,
Too great for Mortals less than Kings.

Chloe, when on thy Breast I lye,
Observes me with revengeful Eye:
If *Chloe* o'er thy Heart prevails,
She'll tear me with her desp'rate Nails; 20
And with relentless Hands destroy
The tender Pledges of our Joy,
Nor have I bred a spurious Race;
They all were born from thy Embrace.

Consider, *Strephon*, what you do;
For, should I dye for Love of you,
I'll haunt thy Dreams, a bloodless Ghost;
And all my Kin, a num'rous Host,
Who down direct our Lineage bring
From Victors o'er the *Memphian* King; 30
Renown'd in Sieges and Campaigns,
Who never fled the bloody Plains;
Who in tempestuous Seas can sport,
And scorn the Pleasures of a Court;
From whom great *Sylla* found his Doom;
Who scourg'd to Death that Scourge of *Rome*,
Shall on thee take a Vengeance dire;
Thou, like *Alcides*, shalt expire,

When his envenom'd Shirt he wore,
And Skin and Flesh in Pieces tore,   40
Nor less than Shirt, my Rival's Gift,
Cut from the Piece that made her Shift,
Shall in thy dearest Blood be dy'd,
And make thee tear thy tainted Hyde.

1730/1735

ANOTHER

Depriv'd of Root, and Branch, and Rind,
Yet Flow'rs I bear of ev'ry Kind;
And such is my prolifik Pow'r,
They bloom in less than half an Hour:
Yet Standers-by may plainly see
They get no Nourishment from me.
My Head, with Giddiness, goes round;
And yet I firmly stand my Ground:
All over naked I am seen,
And painted like an *Indian* Queen.   10
No Couple-Beggar in the Land
E'er join'd such Numbers Hand in Hand;
I join them fairly with a *Ring*;
Nor can our Parson blame the Thing;
And tho' no Marriage Words are spoke,
They part not till the *Ring* is broke.
Yet hypocrite Fanaticks cry,
I'm but an Idol rais'd on high;
And once a Weaver in our Town,
A damn'd *Cromwellian*, knock'd me down.   20
I lay a Pris'ner twenty Years;
And then the Jovial Cavaliers,
To their old Post restor'd all Three,
I mean the Church, the King, and Me.

1725/1735

More Riddles

The Author and his Friends used to divert themselves for Amusement in making Riddles, some of which have been printed in the second Volume of his Works, and were well received; as we hope, the following will be, although we cannot tell the Authors of each. [1746]

A RIDDLE

    I WITH borrow'd Silver shine,
What you see is none of mine,
First I shew you but a Quarter,
Like the Bow that guards the *Tartar*,
Then the Half, and then the Whole,
Ever dancing round a Pole.
And what will raise your Admiration,
I am not one of GOD's Creation,
But sprung (and I this Truth maintain)
Like *Pallas* from my Father's Brain.   10
And after all, I chiefly owe
My Beauty to the Shades below.
Most wondrous Forms you see me wear
A Man, a Woman, Lion, Bear,
A Fish, a Fowl, a Cloud, a Field,
All Figures Heav'n or Earth can yield,
Like *Daphne* sometimes in a Tree,
Yet am not one of all you see.

ANOTHER

BEGOTTEN, and Born, and dying with Noise,
The Terror of Women, and pleasure of Boys,
Like the Fiction of Poets concerning the Wind,
I'm chiefly unruly, when strongest confin'd.
For Silver and Gold I don't trouble my Head,

But all I delight in is Pieces of Lead;
Except when I trade with a Ship or a Town,
Why then I make Pieces of Iron go down.
One Property more I would have you remark,
No Lady was ever more fond of a Spark;　　10
The Moment I get one my Soul's all a-fire,
And I roar out my Joy, and in Transport expire.

ANOTHER

THERE is a Gate, we know full well,
That stands 'twixt Heav'n, and Earth, and Hell,
Where many for a Passage venture,
But very few are found to enter;
Altho' 'tis open Night and Day,
They for that Reason shun this Way:
Both Dukes and Lords abhor its Wood,
They can't come near it for their Blood.
What other Way they take to go,
Another Time I'll let you know.　　10
Yet Commoners with greatest Ease,
Can find an Entrance when they please.
The poorest hither march in State,
(Or they can never pass the Gate)
Like *Roman* Generals triumphant,
And then they take a Turn and jump on't.
If gravest Parsons here advance,
They cannot pass before they dance;
There's not a Soul, that does resort here,
But strips himself to pay the Porter.　　20

ANOTHER

FROM Heav'n I fall, tho' from Earth I begin,
No Lady alive can shew such a Skin.
I am bright as an Angel, and light as a Feather,
But heavy, and dark, when you squeeze me together.

354

Tho' Candor and Truth in my Aspect I bear,
Yet many poor Creatures I help to ensnare.
Tho' so much of Heav'n appears in my Make,
The foulest Impressions I easily take.
My Parent and I produce one another,   9
The Mother the Daughter, the Daughter the Mother.

ANOTHER

I'M up, and down, and round about,
Yet all the World can't find me out,
Tho' Hundreds have employ'd their Leisure,
They never yet cou'd find my Measure.
I'm found almost in ev'ry Garden,
Nay, in the Compass of a Farthing.
There's neither Chariot, Coach, or Mill,
Can move an Inch except I will.

ANOTHER

I AM jet-Black, as you may see,
    The Son of Pitch, and gloomy Night;
Yet all that know me will agree,
    I'm dead except I live in **Light.**

Sometimes in Panegyrick high,
    Like lofty *Pindar* I can soar,
And raise a Virgin to the Sky,
    Or sink her to a pocky Whore.

My Blood this Day is very sweet,
    To-morrow of a bitter Juice,   10
Like Milk 'tis cry'd about the Street,
    And so apply'd to diff'rent Use.

Most wond'rous is my Magick Power;
    For with one Colour I can paint;

I'll make the Dev'l a Saint this Hour,
  Next make a Devil of a Saint.

Thro' distant Regions I can fly,
  Provide me but with Paper Wings,
And fairly shew a Reason, why
  There shou'd be Quarrels among Kings. 20

And after all you'll think it odd,
  When learned Doctors will dispute,
That I shou'd point the Word of GOD,
  And shew where they can best confute.

Let Lawyers bawl and strain their Throats,
  'Tis I that must the Lands convey
And strip the Clients to their Coats;
  Nay give their very Souls away.

ANOTHER

  EVER eating, never cloying,
  All devouring, all destroying,
  Never finding full Repast,
  Till I eat the World at last.

ANOTHER

  WE are little airy Creatures,
  All of diff'rent Voice and Features,
  One of us in Glass is set,
  One of us you'll find in Jet,
  T'other you may see in Tin,
  And the fourth a Box within,
  If the fifth you shou'd pursue,
  It can never fly from you.

ANOTHER

ALL of us in one you'll find,
Brethren of a wond'rous Kind,
Yet among us all no Brother
Knows one Tittle of the other;
We in frequent Councils are,
And our Marks of Things declare,
Where, to us unknown, a Clerk
Sits, and takes them in the Dark.
He's the Register of All
In our Ken, both great and small;   10
By us forms his Laws, and Rules,
He's our Master, we his Tools;
Yet we can, with greatest Ease,
Turn and wind him where we please.

One of us alone can sleep,
Yet no Watch the rest will keep,
But the Moment that he closes,
Ev'ry Brother else reposes.

If Wine's bought, or Victuals drest
One enjoys them for the Rest.   20

Pierce us all with wounding Steel,
One for all of us will feel.

Tho' ten thousand Canons roar,
Add to them ten thousand more,
Yet but one of us is found
Who regards the dreadful Sound.

Do what is not fit to tell,
There's but one of us can smell.

ANOTHER

Fontinella to Florinda

WHEN on my Bosom thy bright Eyes,
   Florinda, dart their Heav'nly Beams,
I feel not the least Love Surprize,
   Yet endless Tears flow down in Streams.
There's nought so beautiful in thee,
But you may find the same in me.

The Lillies of thy Skin compare;
   In me you see them full as white,
The Roses of your Cheeks, I dare
   Affirm, can't glow to more Delight.   10
Then, since I shew as fine a Face,
Can you refuse a soft Embrace.

Ah lovely Nymph, thou'rt in thy Prime!
   And so am I whilst thou art here;
But soon will come the fatal Time,
   When all we see shall disappear.
'Tis mine to make a just Reflection,
And yours to follow my Direction.

Then catch Admirers while you may;
   Treat not your Lovers with Disdain;   20
For Time with Beauty flies away,
   And there is no Return again.
To you the sad Account I bring,
Life's Autumn has no second Spring.

ANOTHER

NEVER speaking, still awake,
Pleasing most when most I speak,
The Delight of old and young,

Tho' I speak without a Tongue.
Nought but one Thing can confound me,
Many Voices joining round me;
Then I fret, and rave and gabble,
Like the Labourers of *Babel*.
Now I am a Dog, or Cow,
I can bark, or I can low,　　　　　　　　　10
I can bleat, or I can sing,
Like the Warblers of the Spring.
Let the Love-sick Bard complain,
And I mourn the cruel Pain;
Let the happy Swain rejoice,
And I join my helping Voice;
Both are welcome, Grief or Joy,
I with either sport and toy.
Tho' a Lady, I am stout,
Drums and Trumpets bring me out;　　　　20
Then I clash and roar, and rattle,
Join in all the Din of Battle.
Jove, with all his loudest Thunder,
When I'm vext, can't keep me under;
Yet so tender is my Ear,
That the lowest Voice I fear;
Much I dread the Courtier's Fate,
When his Merit's out of Date,
For I hate a silent Breath,
And a Whisper is my Death.　　　　　　　30

ANOTHER

Most Things by me do rise and fall,
And as I please they're great and small;
Invading Foes, without Resistance,
With Ease I make to keep their Distance;
Again, as I'm dispos'd, the Foe
Will come, tho' not a Foot they go.
Both Mountains, Woods, and Hills, and Rocks,

And gaming Goats, and fleecy Flocks,
And lowing Herds, and piping Swains,
Come dancing to me o'er the Plains.   10
The greatest Whale, that swims the Sea
Does instantly my Pow'r obey.
In vain from me the Sailor flies,
The quickest Ship I can surprize,
And turn it as I have a Mind,
And move it against Tyde and Wind.
Nay, bring me here the tallest Man,
I'll squeeze him to a little Span,
Or bring a tender Child and pliant,
You'll see me stretch him to a Giant;   20
Nor shall they in the least complain,
Because my Magick gives no Pain.

ANOTHER

WE are little Brethren twain,
Arbiters of Loss and Gain,
Many to our Counters run,
Some are made, and some undone.
But, Men find it to their Cost,
Few are made, but Numbers lost.
Tho' we play them Tricks for ever,
Yet, they always hope, our Favour.
                                        ?/1746

A Riddle by Dr. Delany

Inscribed to the Lady Carteret

I REACH all Things near me, and far off to boot,
Without stretching a Finger, or stirring a Foot,
I take them all in too, to add to your Wonder,

Tho' many and various, and large and asunder,
Without jostling or crowding they pass Side by Side,
Thro' a wonderful Wicket, not Half an Inch wide.
Then I lodge them at Ease in a very large Store,
Of no Breadth, or Length, with a thousand Things
    more.
All this I can do without Witchcraft or Charm,
Tho' sometimes they say I bewitch, and do Harm;   10
Tho' cold I inflame, and tho' quiet invade,
And nothing can shield from my Spell but a Shade.
A Thief that has robb'd you, or done you Disgrace,
In magical Mirror I'll shew you his Face:
Nay, if you'll believe what the Poets have said,
They'll tell you I kill, and can call back the Dead.
Like Conjurers safe in my Circle I dwell,
I love to look black too, it heightens my Spell;
Tho' my Magick is mighty in every Hue,
Who see all my Power must see it in YOU.   20

The Same Answered by Dr. Swift

> WITH Half an Eye
> Your *Riddle* I spy.
> I observe your Wicket
> Hemm'd in by a Thicket,
> And whatever passes
> Is strained thro' Glasses.
> You say it is quiet,
> I flatly deny it;
> It wanders about,
> Without stirring out,   10
> No Passion so weak
> But gives it a Tweak;
> Love, Joy, and Devotion
> Set it always in Motion.

And, as for the Tragick
Effects of its Magick,
Which you say it can kill,
Or, revive at its Will,
The Dead are all sound
And revive above Ground,   20
After all you have writ,
It cannot be Wit,
Which plainly does follow,
Since it flies from *Apollo*.
Its Cowardice such,
It cries at a Touch,
'Tis a perfect Milksop,
Grows drunk with a Drop.
Another great Fault,
It cannot bear Salt;   30
And a Hair can disarm
It of every Charm.

                                    1726?/1726

To Dr. Sheridan

SIR,
Pray discruciate what follows:

  The dullest Beast, and Gentleman's Liquor,
When young is often due to the Vicar.
  The dullest Beast, and Swine's Delight
Make up a Bird very swift of Flight.
  The dullest Beast when high in Stature,
Add another of royal Nature,
For breeding is a useful Creature.
  The dullest Beast, and a Party distrest,
When too long, is bad at best.
  The dullest Beast, and the Saddle it wears,   10

Is good for Partridge, not for Hares,
    The dullest Beast and kind Voice of a Cat,
Will make a Horse go, though he be not fat.
    The dullest of Beasts and of Birds in the Air,
Is that by which all *Irishmen* swear.
    The dullest Beast and fam'd College for *Teagues*
Is a Person very unfit for Intrigues.
    The dullest Beast and a Cobler's Tool,
With a Boy that is only fit for School,
In Summer is very pleasant and cool.   20
    The dullest Beast, and that which you kiss,
May break a Limb of Master or Miss.
    Of Serpent-Kind, and what at distance kills,
Poor Miss *Dingley* oft hath felt its Bills.
    The dullest Beast and Eggs unsound,
Without it I rather would walk on the Ground.
    The dullest Beast and what covers a House,
Without it a Writer is not worth a Louse.
    The dullest Beast, and scandalous Vermin
Of roast or boil'd, to the Hungry is charming.   30
    The dullest Beast, and what's cover'd with Crust,
There's nobody but a Fool that would trust.
    The dullest Beast mending Highways,
Is to a Horse an evil Disease.
    The dullest Beast and a Hole in the Ground,
Will dress a Dinner worth five Pound.
    The dullest Beast, and what Doctors pretend
The Cook-maid often hath by the End.
    The dullest Beast and Fish for Lent
May give you a Blow you'll for ever repent.   40
    The dullest Beast and a shameful Jeer,
Without it a Lady should never appear.

                   ?/1746

Probatur Aliter

A LONG-EAR'D Beast, and a Field-house for Cattle,
Among the Coals does often rattle.

A long-ear'd Beast, a Bird that prates,
The Bridegroom's first Gift to their Mates,
Is by all pious Christians thought,
In Clergymen the greatest Fault.

A long-ear'd Beast, and Women of Endor,
If your Wife be a Scold, that will mend her.

With a long-ear'd Beast, and Med'cines Use,
Cooks make their Fowl look tight and spruce.   10

A long-ear'd Beast and holy Fable,
Strengthens thè Shoes of half the Rabble.

A long-ear'd Beast, and Rhenish Wine,
Lies in the Lap of Ladies fine.

A long-ear'd Beast and *Flanders* College,
Is Dr. *T[isdal]l* to my Knowledge.

A long-ear'd Beast, and Building Knight;
Censorious People do in spight.

A long-ear'd Beast, and Bird of Night,
We Sinners are too apt to slight.   20

A long-ear'd Beast, and shameful Vermin,
A Judge will eat, tho' clad in Ermin.

A long-ear'd Beast, and *Irish* Cart,
Can leave a Mark and give a Smart.

A long-ear'd Beast, in Mud to lye,
No Bird in Air so swift can fly.

A long-ear'd Beast, and a sputt'ring old Whig,
I wish he were in it a dancing a Jig.

A long-ear'd Beast, and Liquor to write,
Is a damnable Smell both Morning and Night.   30

A long-ear'd Beast, and the Child of a Sheep,
At Whist they will make a desperate Sweep.

A Beast long-ear'd, and till Midnight you stay,
Will cover a House much better than Clay.

A long-ear'd Beast, and the Drink you love best

You call him a Sloven in earnest or jest.
  A long-ear'd Beast, and the sixteenth Letter,
I'd not look at all, unless I look't better.
  A long-ear'd Beast give me, and Eggs unsound,
Or else I will not ride one Inch of Ground.   40
  A long-ear'd Beast, another Name for Jeer,
To Ladies Skins there's nothing comes so near.
  A long-ear'd Beast, and kind Noise of a Cat,
Is useful in Journies, take Notice of that.
  A long-ear'd Beast, and what seasons your Beef,
On such an Occasion the Law gives Relief.
  A long-ear'd Beast, a Thing that Force must drive
    in,
Bears up his House, that's of his own contriving.
                        ?/1746

LATIN POEMS

Ad Amicum Eruditum Thomam Sheridan

DELICIÆ *Sheridan* Musarum, dulcis amice,
Sic tibi propitius Permessi ad flumen *Apollo*
Occurrat, seu te mimum convivia rident;
Æquivocosve sales spargis, seu ludere versu
Malles; dic, *Sheridan*, quisnam fuit ille Deorum,
Quæ melior natura orto tibi tradidit artem
Rimandi genium puerorum, atq; ima cerebri
Scrutandi? Tibi nascenti ad cunabula *Pallas*
Astitit; & dixit, mentis præsaga futuræ,
Heu puer infelix! nostro sub sydere natus; 10
Nam tu pectus eris sine corpore, corporis umbra;
Sed levitate umbram superabis, voce cicadam:
Musca femur, palmas tibi Mus dedit, ardea crura.
Corpore sed tenui tibi quod natura negavit;
Hoc animi dotes supplebunt; teq; docente,
Nec longum Tempus, surget tibi docta juventus,
Artibus egregiis animas instructa novellas.
Grex hinc Pœnius venit, ecce, *salutifer* orbi.
Ast, illi causas orant; his insula visa est
Divinam capiti nodo constringere mitram. 20

Natalis te horæ non fallunt signa; sed usq;
Conscius, expedias puero seu lætus *Apollo*
Nascenti arrisit; sive illum frigidus horror
Saturni premit, aut septem inflavere triones.

Quin tu altè penitusq; latentia semina cernis,
Quæq; diu obtundendo olim sub liminis auras
Erumpent, promis; quo ritu sæpè puella
Sub cinere hesterno sopitos suscitat ignes.

Te Dominum agnoscit quocunq; sub aere natis;
Quos indulgentis nimium custodia matris   30
Pessundat: Nam sæpè vides in stipite matrem.

Aureus at ramus venerandæ dona Sibyllæ,
Æneæ sedes tantùm patefecit Avernas:
Sæpè puer, tua quem tetigit semel aurea virga,
Cœlumq; terrasq; videt, noctemq; profundam.

1717/1735

Carberiæ Rupes in Comitatu Corgagensi apud Hibernicos

ECCE! ingens fragmen scopuli quod vertice summo
Desuper impendet, nullo fundamine nixum
Decidit in fluctus: maria undiq; & undiq; saxa
Horrisono Stridore tonant, & ad æthera murmur
Erigitur; trepidatq; suis *Neptunus* in undis.
Nam longâ venti rabie, atq; aspergine crebrâ
Æquorei laticis, specus imâ rupe cavatur:
Jam fultura ruit, jam summa cacumina nutant;
Jam cadit in præceps moles, & verberat undas.
Attonitus credas, hinc dejecisse Tonantem   10
Montibus impositos montes, & *Pelion* altum
In capita anguipedum cœlo jaculâsse gigantum.

Sæpe etiam spelunca immani apperitur hiatu
Exesa è scopulis, & utrinq; foramina pandit,
Hinc atq; hinc a ponto ad pontum pervia Phœbo:
Cautibus enormè junctis laquearia tecti
Formantur; moles olim ruitura supernè.
Fornice sublimi nidos posuere palumbes,
Inq; imo stagni posuere cubilia phocæ.

Sed, cum sævit hyems, & venti carcere rupto   20
Immensos volvunt fluctus ad culmina montis;
Non obsessæ arces, non fulmina vindice dextrâ
Missa Jovis, quoties inimicas sævit in urbes,
Exæquant sonitum undarum, veniente procellâ:
Littora littoribus reboant; vicinia latè,
Gens assueta mari, & pedibus percurrere rupes,
Terretur tamen, & longè fugit, arva reliquens.

Gramina dum carpunt, pendentes rupe capellæ
Vi salientis aquæ de summo præcipitantur,
Et dulces animas imo sub gurgite linquunt.   30

Piscatur terrâ non audet vellere funem;
Sed latet in portu tremebundus, & aera sudum
Haud sperans, Nereum precibus votisq; fatigat.
                                        1723/1735

*We have added a Translation of the preceding Poem,
for the Benefit of our English Readers. It is done by
Mr. W. Dunkin, M.A. for whom our supposed Author
hath expressed a great Regard, on Account of his
ingenious Performances, although unacquainted with
him.*

Carbery Rocks in the County of Cork, Ireland

Lo! from the Top of yonder Cliff, that shrouds
Its airy Head amidst the azure Clouds,
Hangs a huge Fragment; destitute of Props,
Prone on the Waves the rocky Ruin drops.
With hoarse Rebuff the swelling Seas rebound,
From Shore to Shore the Rocks return the Sound:
The dreadful Murmur Hea'vn's high Convex cleaves,
And *Neptune* shrinks beneath his Subject Waves;

371

For long the whirling Winds and beating Tides
Had scoop'd a Vault into its nether Sides.   10
Now yields the Base, the Summits nod, now urge
Their headlong Course, and lash the sounding Surge.
Not louder Noise could shake the guilty World,
When *Jove* heap'd Mountains upon Mountains hurl'd,
Retorting *Pelion* from his dread Abode,
To crush Earth's rebel Sons beneath the Load.

    Oft too with hideous Yawn the Cavern wide
Presents an Orifice on either Side,
A dismal Orifice from Sea to Sea
Extended, pervious to the God of Day: 20
Uncouthly join'd, the Rocks stupendous form
An Arch, the Ruin of a future Storm:
High on the Cliff their Nests the *Woodquests* make,
And Sea-Calves stable in the oozy Lake.

    But when bleak Winter with her sullen Train
Awakes the Winds, to vex the watry Plain;
When o'er the craggy Steep without Controul,
Big with the Blast, the raging Billows rowl;
Not Towns beleaguer'd, not the flaming Brand
Darted from Heav'n by *Jove's* avenging Hand,   30
Oft as on impious Men his Wrath he pours,
Humbles their Pride, and blasts their gilded Tow'rs,
Equal the Tumult of this wild Uproar:
Waves rush o'er Waves, rebellows Shore to Shore.
The neighb'ring Race, tho' wont to brave the Shocks,
Of angry Seas, and run along the Rocks,
Now pale with Terror, while the Ocean foams,
Fly far and wide, nor trust their native Homes.

    The Goats, while pendent from the Mountain-Top
The wither'd Herb improvident they crop,   40
Wash'd down the Precipice with sudden Sweep,
Leave their sweet Lives beneath th' unfathom'd Deep.

The frighted Fisher with desponding Eyes,
Tho' safe, yet trembling in the Harbour lies,
Nor hoping to behold the Skies serene,
Wearies with Vows the Monarch of the Main.

Fabula
Canis et Umbræ

ORE cibum portans catulus dum spectat in undis,
Apparet liquido prædæ melioris imago:
Dum speciosa diu damna admiratur, et alte
Ad latices inhiat, cadit imo vortice præceps
Ore cibus, nec non simulachrum corripit unà.
Occupat ille avidus deceptis faucibus umbram;
Illudit species, ac dentibus aëra mordet.

?/1765

NOTES

NOTES

ABBREVIATIONS or short titles of sources of texts are given immediately following titles of poems. 'F' refers to the Faulkner edition cited as a general source in Canon and Text, p. xl. ('F.xi' is the volume dated 1763.) The Nichols and Scott editions are those of 1803 and 1814, respectively. Other short titles are clear in themselves or by reference to the Bibliography.

p. 1. Pindaric Odes and Heroic Verse. Swift never collected any of these poems, evidently desiring their suppression. The only one published at the time it was written is the *Ode to the Athenian Society.* References in his early letters and in these poems point to other verse compositions that have not come to light: 'The Poet', 'The Ramble', and a partial translation of the *Aeneid.*

p. 3. Ode to the King. Miscellanies, Fairbrother, 1735, iv. 1 (verse section). Williams identifies this as Swift's 'missing' Pindaric ode (see *Poems*, p. 4). He cites the Fairbrother volume as its first publication, though it should be noted that John Dunton quotes the first two stanzas, without identifying author or poem, in *The Dublin Scuffle*, 1699, p. 379.

l. 139. Rapt in the Vortex of the Brittish Star. Cf. *Tale of a Tub*, Sect. ix: '*Cartesius* reckoned to see before he died, the Sentiments of all Philosophers, like so many lesser Stars in his *Romantick* System, rapt and drawn within his own *Vortex.*' Cf. similar usage in *Ode to Sancroft, ll.* 62–3 (p. 20).

l. 145. Vile Disease. Louis XIV's disease is also identified as *fistula in ano* in the *Tale of a Tub*, Sect. ix.

p. 8. Ode to the Athenian Society. Miscellanies,

Dodsley, 1750, x. 178. With the publication of this poem in a bound volume of John Dunton's periodical *The Athenian Gazette* (1692), Swift appeared in print for the first time. Pons says he took his cue from Cowley, whose poem 'To the Royal Society' appeared in Sprat's *History of the Royal Society*. The situations are analogous, though the poems resemble each other too little to justify Pons in calling Swift's an 'imitation'. Defoe, Motteux, Tate, and Richardson also contributed panegyrical odes to Dunton's periodical. In a letter of May 3, 1692, Swift says that Sir William Temple enlisted his interest in the Athenian Society, and that the poem 'was all rough drawn in a week, and finished in two days after'. He confesses, 'I cannot write anything easy to be understood though it were but in the praise of an old shoe.' The remark is apt. This is his worst poem by odds.

ll. 180–5. Pons finds in these lines the 'germ' of the 'Æolism' of the *Tale of a Tub*, Sect. viii.

l. 278. *There is a Noon-tide in our Lives*. A possible allusion to the speech of Brutus, *Julius Caesar*, IV. iii.

l. 298. Swift's image of '*Gothick* Swarms' probably reflects a passage in Temple's 'Of Poetry'. Cf. *Paradise Lost*, I. 351.

p. 18. *Ode to Dr. William Sancroft. Works*, ed. Nichols, x. 1. In a letter of May 3, 1692, Swift says he has been at work on an ode to Sancroft for five months, but 'I cannot finish it for my life, and I have done nine stanzas and do not like half of them, nor am nigh finished, but there it lies'. The additions he mentions probably account for stanzas x, xi, and xii, though even with them the poem is incomplete. Sancroft was deprived of Canterbury as a non-juror.

l. 1. *Truth is eternal*. Swift's subject is Truth, which he equates with Virtue as our 'weak knowledge' sees it:

Sancroft's virtue is the 'brightest pattern' of truth that Earth can show (stanza iii). The lukewarm Platonism of stanza ii, with its characteristic scorn of the Cartesians, reveals the mistrust of sense that is a philosophical burden in the odes. Prior is assailed by a similar Pyrrhonism in the ode he wrote at St. John's.

l. 2. *Bright effluence.* Swift probably has in mind Milton's 'Bright effluence of bright essence increate' in the invocation to Bk. III, *Paradise Lost.*

ll. 62–3. Cf. note to *Ode to the King*, *l.* 139 (p. 377).

p. 27. *Ode to Sir William Temple. Miscellanies,* Dodsley, 1750, x. 194. Swift's letter of May 3, 1692, contains flattering references to Temple that would have occasioned some mention of this poem if it had been written by then. Hence its position here after the ode to Sancroft, which the letter does mention. Temple has been traditionally blamed for Swift's 'pindaric infatuation'; but it would appear that Swift was far gone with Cowley before he settled down at Moor Park in 1692 (his earlier visit does not have equal significance). Temple's influence is probably at work in this and later poems, which are toned down to descriptive treatment of local themes in heroic verse. His own verse supports this view. His essays reveal many tastes that became Swift's own, including the Renaissance preference for history over philosophy as the measure of wisdom. His essay 'Upon the Gardens of Epicurus' projects the rural, utopian scene in which, under the guise of Epicurus, he liked to imagine himself. Swift's panegyric places Temple in the scene and echoes phrases of the essay.

l. 1. *Virtue, the greatest of all Monarchies.* Cf. Temple's essay 'Of Heroic Virtue', which is defined as 'the deserving well of Mankind'. Much as in the ode to Sancroft, Swift approaches his subject the long way around, abstractly, argumentatively, and with occasional lapses into satire.

l. 28. Yeats found this highly personal stanza one of the brighter spots in the early poems, revealing Swift's rebellion against school and preference for the way of poetry. Stanza xi bears out this view. Swift attacks the 'schools' and pedantry in the spirit of Temple's 'Essay upon the Ancient and Modern Learning', though he could have found similar views in Bacon and Hobbes.

l. 29. *Plato's Paradox.* The doctrine of 'remembrance' in the *Phaedo* and *Meno*; but Swift is also arguing, via Locke and somewhat satirically, that we inscribe our *tabula rasa* only with 'rules' and bookish learning, until we can remember nothing else. Thus 'odly' we make good Plato's paradox.

l. 97. *Methinks, when you expose the Scene.* Referring to Temple's memoirs, which Swift copied for the press. They take a disillusioned view of 'The Thoughts of Monarchs, and Designs of States'.

l. 135. *Sing (belov'd Muse) the Pleasures of Retreat.* On this theme, which runs through the rest of his early poems, Swift achieves a lyrical note counter to the high intellectual tone of the odes.

ll. 192–5. *In vain I strive to cross this spacious Main.* An echo of Cowley's 'The Complaint' in *The Mistress*: 'To all the Ports of Honour and of Gain, | I often steer my course in vain, | Thy Gale comes cross, and drives me back again.' The remonstrances of Cowley and the Muse are often heard in these poems. Swift proclaims his dedication to poetry (an 'incurable disease'), but confesses unabashedly his feeling of enslavement to the Muse, who is usually portrayed as hectoring him. Most of the poems betray an inner struggle, a polarization of opposing forces: poetry and philosophy, learning and pedantry, ancients and moderns, truth and opinion, retirement and courts, religion and zeal. Swift tends toward satire when his side begins to lose, or when he feels himself incapable of lending it sufficient strength to win.

ll. 208–9. *In vain all wholesome Herbs I sow.* Another echo of Cowley's poem: 'There is a sort of stubborn Weeds, | Which, if the Earth but once, it ever breeds. | No wholsom Herb can near them thrice, | No useful Plant can keep alive.'

ll. 210–12. *Whate'er I plant ... Seeds and runs up to Poetry.* This sounds remarkably like young Keats, though Swift claims to lament the decree of Nature that he shall be a poet. His extremely sensitive nature comes out quite clearly in lines like these.

p. 34. *A Description of Mother Ludwell's Cave.* Moore Smith, *Early Essays and Romances of Sir William Temple*, 1930, p. 186. Collected here for the first time. Moore Smith pointed out verbal resemblances of this poem, discovered among papers formerly at Moor Park, to other early poems; but Williams (*Poems*, p. 1068) was not convinced and excluded it. J. M. Murry has recently marshalled the evidence favouring Swift's authorship. The verbal resemblances will appear in a close reading, and are not noted here. The *Description* anticipates the style, themes, and subject-matter of Swift's heroic verse. As a species of 'local poetry' it is indebted to *Cooper's Hill*, which saves Denham's bacon in the *Battle of the Books*. Mother Ludwell's Cave, one of the natural wonders of Surrey, was adjacent to Moor Park. See note to *To Mr. Congreve*, *l.* 1 (p. 382). *Hæ latebræ dulces, et si mihi credis, amœnæ.* This, from Horace, Epistle XVI, Book I, should read: 'Hæ latebræ dulces, etiam, si credis, amœnæ.' Murry points to a similar misquotation by Swift in a letter of August 3, 1713, as virtually putting his 'signature' to this poem.

p. 36. *To Mr. Congreve. Works*, ed. Nichols, x. 29.

Swift was with Congreve, two years his junior, at Kilkenny School and Trinity College, Dublin. They were lifelong friends. In a letter dated December 6, 1693, Swift says he intends to send this poem ('almost two hundred and fifty lines not Pindaric') to Congreve to be printed in front of *The Double Dealer*, then being acted, if the play proves successful. It did not, and there is no evidence that the poem was sent. Congreve had scored a brilliant success the preceding January with his first play, *The Old Batchelor*.

l. 1. *Thrice, with a prophet's voice and prophet's pow'r.* The opening lines allude to a local tradition of Mother Ludwell to the effect that this 'white witch' supplied her neighbours 'whatever they might require, from a yoke of oxen to a caldron, provided the petitioner went to the cave at midnight, turned thrice round, and thrice repeated aloud the name of the article desired, with a promise to return within two days. The next morning it was ready at the entrance of the cave'. From Murray's *Handbook for Surrey* (5th edn., 1898), which notes that the cave is 'said to have been frequently the scene of Swift's meditations'. Later references in the poem (*l.* 187, 'Here by a mountain side, a reverend cave') identify Swift's Muse with Mother Ludwell, who in primitive times inspired the local druid: this is the same identification made in *A Description of Mother Ludwell's Cave* (*l.* 5, 'I that of Ludwell sing, to Ludwell run, Her self my muse, her spring my Helicon'). Swift's recusancy from the 'town' tradition (which he is naturally conscious of in writing to Congreve), his pride in (as his Muse says) 'truth, retreat, and innocence', has a certain charm; but the veneer may have owed more to circumstances than to inclination.

ll. 191–4. *Here, on a better day, some druid dwelt.* The

'prophet's voice' of the opening line, and 'we the high priesthood' of the next, are evidence of Swift's fanciful conception of himself in the native druidic tradition.

p. 43. *Occasioned by Sir William Temple's Late Illness &c.* Works, ed. Nichols, x. 36. Again Swift's 'private muse' is a principal speaker, in her usual hectoring style.

ll. 17–22. After his fling with Cowley, Swift was settling down with Denham and Waller, when in this poem he abruptly renounced the 'whole delusion'. These lines show his progress in mastering a fashionable style and one Temple was fond of.

l. 41. *Dorothea.* Lady Temple, *née* Dorothy Osborne, mourning the death three years earlier of the last of seven children, a son who committed suicide.

l. 52. *Dorinda.* Martha Lady Giffard, Temple's sister, who was widowed within three weeks of her marriage.

ll. 81–112. This brief, self-revelatory analysis of delusion—and the unhappiness it has brought him —is perhaps the 'personal' background of the digression on madness in the *Tale of a Tub*, Sect. ix.

ll. 113–30. This little allegory of Time and Hope vividly portrays the 'unhappy restless thoughts' that possessed Swift at twenty-six, as he strove to repress his 'scorn of fools'. This poem marks the end of the struggle, and his next utterances are satirical and in prose.

p. 49. *Miscellany Poems.* All these except *A Ballad on the Game of Traffick* Swift collected in his *Miscellanies*, 1711.

p. 51. *Verses &c.* F.ii.9. This society verse announces the change in Swift's style, subject, and inspiration. The occasion was well established: cf. Waller's 'Written in my Lady Speke's Singing-Book', Walsh's 'Written in a Lady's Table-Book'. The difference is that Swift writes satirically.

p. 52. *The Humble Petition &c.* F.ii.1. The scene is the household of the Earl of Berkeley, Lord Justice of Ireland, to whom Swift was chaplain (1699–1701). Frances Harris was one of Lady Berkeley's gentle-women.

l. 1. *Lady Betty.* Berkeley's daughter, later Lady Betty Germaine, who remained Swift's loyal friend. She figures in the next two poems.

p. 56. *A Ballad on the Game of Traffick.* F.viii.312. The scene is again the Berkeley household, but in England.

l. 17. *Herries.* Frances Harris of the preceding poem.

p. 57. *A Ballad to the Tune of 'The Cut-purse'.* F.ii.7. This tune, apparently popular in Swift's day, is sung by Cutpurse in Jonson's *Bartholomew Fair.*

p. 59. *The Description of a Salamander.* F.ii.10. Lord Cutts won the name 'salamander' for his bravery under fire at Namur; but Swift, as Scott notes, 'has employed his wit in deducing from his vices and follies, the name bestowed on him for his intrepid bravery'. The motive of Swift's vicious attack on Cutts, who was commander-in-chief in Ireland at the time the poem was written, is not known. Like later poems on Vanbrugh and Partridge, this is a species of sheer wit in the manner of the 'metaphysical conjectures' of the *Tale of a Tub.*

p. 61. *The History of Vanbrug's House.* F.ii.29. Williams (*Poems,* p. 85) prints this poem from Swift's MS. Swift ridicules the playwright Vanbrugh by way of describing the miniscule origins of his architectural designs at Whitehall and Blenheim. The theme is that of *The Beasts Confession* (p. 443): how men mistake their talents. Vanbrugh 'had a long quarrel with me about those Verses on his House', he says in the *Journal to Stella,* November 7, 1710; 'Lady Marlborough used to teaze him with them'.

'I was forty-seven years old when I began to think of death,' he writes in a letter of October 31, 1729.

p. 91. *The Author's Manner of Living.* F.viii.320. This undated poem undoubtedly belongs to the early years of exile. Swift writes to Pope on June 28, 1715: 'When I do not dine abroad, or make an entertainment, which last is very rare, I eat a mutton-pie, and drink half a pint of wine'; and to Ford on December 20, 1718, 'I have been just dining in my Closet alone on a Bief Stake and Pint of wine.'

p. 91. *On Censure.* F.ii.246.

p. 92. *Poems from the Holyhead Journal.* Craik, *Life*, p. 538. These poems are interspersed in the journal Swift kept during a week's delay at Holyhead *en route* to Ireland in 1727, following his last visit to England. 'I want to see the journals of your travels from Holyhead, which Mr. Sheridan seems highly delighted with,' Pope wrote in January, 1728, while soliciting contributions for their *Miscellanies*. But it was not published until 1882.

p. 97. *The Dean to Himself &c.* F.xiii.294. Williams (*Poems*, p. 521) prints this poem from Swift's MS., which is endorsed 'imperfect'. Ball (*Swift's Verse*, p. 255) finds the occasion in the criticism of Swift for the music festival held in his cathedral by the Dublin Musical Society on St. Cecilia's Day, November 23, 1730, and the sermon by Dr. Sheridan, chaplain of the society, extolling the use of music in divine worship.

p. 97. *The Day of Judgement.* *Works*, ed. Nichols, xi. 228. The futility of life had become an obsession. He writes to Pope on April 20, 1731: 'The common saying of life being a farce is true in every sense but the most important one, for it is a ridiculous tragedy, which is the worst kind of composition.' Cf. with this poem *The Place of the Damn'd*, p. 566.

p. 98. *Midnight Memorandum.* *Correspondence*, ed.

Ball, v. 453. Collected here for the first time, this epigram has a rightful place in Swift's poetry. Dr. John Lyon, Swift's vicar, transcribed the memorandum in his copy of Hawkesworth's *Life of Swift* (Forster Collection), where the two lines read: 'I walk before no Man, a Hawk in his Fist; | Nor, am I a Brillant [*sic*], whenever I list.'

p. 99. *On his own Deafness.* F.viii.366.

p. 101. *Poems to Vanessa.* From 1718 society verse and trifles are almost invariably a by-product of Swift's social intercourse, and the contagious nature of his versifying is evidenced in poems by more than a dozen of his friends, including Vanessa and Stella, which have survived. It will be seen in the following notes that I place the exchange of verses between Swift and Vanessa in the same period.

p. 103. *Cadenus and Vanessa.* F.ii.42. Swift's longest poem, a chilling contrast to the passion of her letters, is addressed to Esther Vanhomrigh (1688–1723). After her death it circulated in several manuscript copies. The earliest of many unauthorized editions appeared in April or May, 1726, in Dublin and London. Swift published it in the Pope–Swift *Miscellanies*, 1727, and his *Works*, 1735, but without the lines given here in square brackets, which leave no doubt of Vanessa's passion. The poem has generally been dated 1713 (the probable time of the scene it portrays) with revisions in 1719 (see *Poems*, p. 684). My reasons for believing 1719–1720 to be the actual time of composition must be summarized:

(i) There is no certainly dated use of the names Cadenus and Vanessa earlier than 1720, when they begin to be used in letters of Swift and Esther. The poems to Stella begin in 1719, and there is no earlier use of this pseudonym.

(ii) There is no evidence of the existence of the poem—or of any other verses to or from Vanessa—

earlier than 1719. Swift's letter in French of May 12, 1719, refers to this or some other poem. Letters of 1720 clearly refer to it. Several poems that Vanessa and Stella addressed to Swift are generally thought to belong to this, rather than an earlier, period.

(iii) There are parallels between *Cadenus and Vanessa* and poems of 1719–1720, notably the Stella poems. There are less striking parallels with an unfinished poem of 1713, *To Lord Harley on his Marriage* (see p. 583), which came to Swift's mind in 1720 (see his letter to Prior on January 25).

(iv) The parallels that have been pointed out between the poem and the correspondence before 1719–1720 appear to be allusions to Vanessa's letters, which were in Swift's possession. He liked to remind her of past incidents in their friendship.

(v) Swift had a strong motive for backdating the fresh revelations contained in the poem because of the strain in his relationship with Stella that had been created three years earlier by the revelations following Vanessa's death. In a letter of April 19, 1726, replying to a warning that the poem was to be printed, Swift wrote: 'It was written at Windsor near fourteen years ago, and dated. It was a task performed on a frolic among some ladies ... I forget what is in it, but believe it to be only a cavalier business ... I never saw it since I writ it.' In a letter to another correspondent on July 7, after its printing, he wrote: 'The thing you mention, which no friend would publish, was written fourteen years ago, at Windsor.' It is curious that Swift should remember so little about the poem except that it was 'dated'—no time (or place) of composition is assigned in the early editions, and he omits the remark in writing to his second correspondent, who would have seen these. There is a difficulty in 'Cadenus' (= *decanus*), since Swift was not made

dean until 1713. The poem in its authorized publication in the *Miscellanies*, 1727, first bears the date
1713. Swift was given to making unreliable statements about his writings, and the two letters just
mentioned, as well as others on different subjects to
the same correspondents, contain statements known
to be deceptive.

(vi) The questionable evidence that Swift provides
is reason to seek other evidence for dating the poem.
This evidence points to the latter part of 1719 and
the early part of 1720.

l. 53. *Collected in that Infant's Mind*. Cf. Venus's
ambition that Vanessa possess every virtue with the
action of Pallas, who 'Fixt *Honour* in her Infant
Mind', in *To Stella, Visiting Me in my Sickness*,
1720, *l.* 6 (p. 136).

l. 167. *Less modest than the Speech of Prudes*. For
Swift's portrait of a prude see *Phyllis; or, the Progress of Love*, 1719, *ll.* 1–18 (p. 213).

ll. 201–10. *Mistakes Vanessa for a Boy*. This motif of
mistaken sex to account for manly virtues also
appears in *To Stella, Visiting Me in my Sickness*,
ll. 85–92 (p. 138).

ll. 306–7. *Advanc'd like Atalanta's Star*. Cf. 'Take
Pattern by your *Sister* Star ... When you are seen,
be seen from far,' in *The Progress of Beauty*, 1719,
ll. 57–9 (p. 218).

ll. 346–51. A possible allusion to Vanessa's remark in
her letter of June 6, 1713: 'Lord! how much do we
differ from the ancients, who used to sacrifice everything for the good of their commonwealth.' This
theme of ancient virtue appears in *To Stella, Visiting
Me in my Sickness*, *ll.* 51–4 (p. 137).

ll. 386–92. *Mopsa ... Corinna ... Phyllis*. Swift
praises Vanessa and Stella by contrasting them with
the generality of women. Cf. for worse examples his
Chloe, Sylvia, Phillis, and Iris in *To Stella, Who*

Collected and Transcribed his Poems, 1720, *ll.* 39–52 (p. 140).

ll. 444–61. Stella's social gifts are praised in similar language in *On the Death of Mrs. Johnson*. Cf. the admiration of Stella's listeners in *To Stella, Visiting Me in my Sickness*, *ll.* 79–84 (p. 138).

ll. 464–5. The story as told to this point does not support these two lines. They may refer to a design in which Pallas was to give formal instruction to Vanessa rather than just endow the infant's mind. Cf. *Verses to Vanessa*, p. 130, and note.

l. 529. *Declin'd in Health, advanc'd in Years.* Despite their humour, these and other lines (*ll.* 501, 503, 537, 549, 636, 778) refer to Cadenus's state of health and years much as Swift describes himself in letters, particularly those to Ford, of 1718–1719, when he seems preoccupied with his 'late time of life', his 'turn of blood at 50', the 'sang-froid of fifty'. At this time we also hear the first of many complaints about his eyes (see *l.* 527), which 'begin to grudge me reading'.

ll. 532–9. A similar figure of youth and age, good health and poor, appears in the last lines of *To Stella, Visiting Me in my Sickness*, *ll.* 117–24 (p. 139).

ll. 606–13. A possible allusion to Vanessa's description of a similar situation in an undated letter of 1714: 'You once had a maxim, which was to act what was right and not mind what the world said. I wish you would keep to it now.'

l. 660. *She rally'd well, he always knew.* Cf. Swift's letter to Vanessa, September 3, 1712: 'You railly very well: Mr. Lewis allows you to do so.' For Swift's rules of raillery see *To Mr. Delany*, p. 585.

ll. 768–9. *Love, hitherto a transient Guest.* Cf. the similar couplet in *To Stella, Who Collected and Transcribed his Poems*, *ll.* 13–14 (p. 140).

ll. 780–5. *But Friendship in its greatest Height.* Friendship rather than love is also what Swift offers Stella: cf. *To Stella, Who Collected and Transcribed his Poems, ll.* 9–14 (p. 140).

p. 129. *A Rebus.* F.viii.353. In the absence of any date, Vanessa's rebus and Swift's answer must be assigned to 1718–1720. His trifles for 1718 furnish examples of this type of amusement. His answer suggests an earlier date than 1720, when he resumed his political pamphlets.

p. 130. *Verses to Vanessa. Works*, ed. Scott, xix. 426. These pieces are from letters of Swift to Vanessa of July, 1720 (the first two) and August 12, 1720 (the third). The couplets may well be rejected lines of *Cadenus and Vanessa*, possibly a speech by Pallas.

p. 133. *Poems to Stella.* Unlike her lonely rival, Esther Johnson (1681–1728) was a central figure among intimates of the deanery circle: Sheridan, Delany, Ford, the Jacks (John Rochfort and the Rev. John Grattan, a brother), and Robin (the Rev. Robert Grattan, a third brother), who followed Swift's lead in verse-making (see *Trifles*, p. 265). The profusion of trifles to which they contributed had already enjoyed a year's growth when, in 1719, Swift established his custom of writing polite verses commemorating her birthday, apparently adopting the name Stella at the same time. Less regularly other anniversaries were celebrated: Stella wrote on Swift's, Delany and Ford on Stella's, Swift on Ford's (see p. 602) and Rebecca Dingley's (see p. 628).

p. 135. *Stella's Birth-Day*, 1719. F.ii.100.

l. 1. *Stella this Day is Thirty-four.* Poetic licence of a charitable kind, for she was thirty-eight. When he speaks of her beauty 'at Sixteen', he is suggesting what is explicitly stated in her birthday poem for 1725—that Beauty and Wit are confined to youth:

'The God of Wit, and Beauty's Queen, He Twenty-one, and she Fifteen.' In *Cadenus and Vanessa* 'For Sixteen Years the Cause was spun', *i.e.*, while Vanessa grew up. But he does not commence writing verses to his friends until he and they are a safe distance from the age of gallantry.

p. 135. *To Stella, Visiting Me &c.* F.ii.230. Swift was ill during the early months of 1720, and this tribute apparently takes the place of the birthday poem.

l. 1. *Pallas.* She rather than Venus endows Stella and Vanessa as infants with the qualities he finds admirable.

ll. 51. *Heroes and Heroines of old.* Cf. *Cadenus and Vanessa, ll.* 346–51 (p. 113).

ll. 85–92. Cf. *Cadenus and Vanessa, ll.* 201–10 (p. 108).

ll. 121–4. Cf. *Cadenus and Vanessa, ll.* 532–9 (p. 118).

p. 139. *To Stella, Who Collected &c.* F.ii.111. Referring to Stella's transcripts (now preserved at Woburn Abbey) of eighteen of his poems: *The Fable of Midas*, 1712, *Atlas; or, the Minister of State*, 1712, *Toland's Invitation to Dismal*, 1712, *Imitation of Horace Epistle VII Book I*, 1713, *Imitation of Horace Satire VI Book II*, 1714, *A Quiet Life and a Good Name*, 1719, *Phyllis; or, the Progress of Love*, 1719, *The Progress of Beauty*, 1719, *The Run upon the Bankers*, 1720, *The Bubble*, 1720, *Apollo to Dean Swift*, 1721, *Epilogue to a Play*, 1721, *Epigrams* (3), 1723? *Stella's Birth-Day*, 1721, and *To Stella, on her Birthday*, 1722. Stella's work on these poems that followed his *Miscellanies*, 1711, suggests that he was preparing another collection of his verses, which Pope levied on for their joint *Miscellanies*, 1727.

ll. 13–14. Cf. *Cadenus and Vanessa, ll.* 768–9 (p. 125).

ll. 30–8. Cf. *The Progress of Poetry, ll.* 17–46 (p. 440).

l. 40. *For Chloe, Sylvia, Phillis, Iris.* These 'Goddesses enroll'd in *Curll's* Collections' come to mind as contrasts to his treatment of Stella, and are the subject of a series of poems begun in 1719 (see *Impersonal Satires*, p. 209).

p. 144. *Stella's Birth-Day*, 1721. F.ii.101.

p. 146. *To Stella, on her Birthday*, 1722. *Works*, ed. Nichols, x. 265.

p. 146. *Stella's Birth-Day, a Great Bottle of Wine &c.* F.ii.202.

ll. 18–20. *Jacks . . . Robin . . . Ford . . . Jim . . . Sheridan*. See note to p. 133.

l. 30. *Eusden*. Laurence Eusden, poet laureate 1718–1730.

l. 60. *Rebecca*. Rebecca Dingley, Stella's companion. See *A New Year's Gift for Bec*, p. 607, and *Bec's Birthday*, p. 628.

p. 149. *Stella at Wood-Park*. F.ii.152. This poem is made up of two draft poems, one entitled 'Stella's Distress on the 3rd fatal day of October 1723', commencing 'The Winter now begins to frown'; the other untitled, commencing 'Don Carlos in a merry Spight'. Both exist in Ford's MS. and are printed by Williams (*Poems*, p. 744). The quotation is from Horace, Epistle XVIII, Book I. In the far background of this charming, light-hearted poem is Swift's strained relationship with Stella. During Vanessa's last days he appears to have sequestered Stella at Wood Park, the Irish estate of Charles Ford, in the hope of shielding her from rumour; while he, immediately following Vanessa's death on June 2, 1723, departed on his 'summer expedition of four months'. The composition of the poem probably belongs to his visits at Wood Park in September and October, and the following weeks. The last lines, an awkward codicil, show that he could not take for granted Stella's response to his raillery.

p. 152. *To Stella*, 1724. F.xiii.295.

p. 153. *Stella's Birth-Day*, 1725. F.ii.176.

ll. 23–5. *At fifty-six.* Swift was fifty-eight. *Forty-three.* Stella was forty-four.

p. 155. *A Receipt to Restore Stella's Youth.* F.ii.206. Swift's letters of 1725 reveal his concern for Stella's health, which had begun to fail. She refused his entreaties to visit England, but went in the spring to Sheridan's summer house at Quilca, where Swift joined her. This poem deals with the Quilca visit. For other verses on Quilca see Epigrams, p. 409.

p. 157. *Stella's Birth-Day*, 1727. F.ii.227. Swift writes 'while Time is running fast', with the premonition that she will not see another birthday. She died on January 28, 1728, towards the end of her forty-sixth year. The poem is similar to the 'Three Prayers for Stella', composed late in 1727, in assisting 'her preparation for a better life'. The naked sincerity of Swift's grief lifts his poem above the conventions of birthday raillery. Only in a poem in this quiet, restrained tone could a simple image like Swift's 'radiant Dart' be so striking and effective.

p. 161. *Poems at Market Hill.* The society verse of which Stella was the central figure found a new stimulus after her death in Swift's three visits to Market Hill (now Gosford Castle): June 1728 to February 1729, June to October 1729, and June to September 1730. His hosts were Sir Arthur and Lady Acheson, but his subject is the place as well as the inhabitants, and humorous glances at Cooper's Hill and Penshurst show his awareness of the component of 'local poetry' in this society verse.

p. 163. *Lady Acheson Weary of the Dean.* F.xi.418. I have adopted the title of the poem as originally published in preference to Faulkner's 'Dean Swift at Sir Arthur Acheson's in the North of Ireland'.

p. 164. *My Lady's Lamentation.* F.xiii.309.

ll. 203–24. Henry Jenney, Archdeacon of Dromore, John Walmsley, Rector of Clonfeacle, and

Nathaniel Whaley, Rector of Armagh, all neighbouring clergymen and eligible guests at Market Hill. Not eligible was Richard Daniel, Dean of Armagh, who claimed possession of Whaley's living.

p. 171. *On Cutting Down &c.* F.ii.235. A transcript in the Welbeck MSS. is dated September 14, 1728.

p. 174. *Upon a Very Old Glass.* F.viii.194.

p. 175. *To Janus &c.* F.ii.289. In this poem Swift shortens his line to seven syllables: a verse form he uses in half a dozen poems preceding *The Legion Club*, its chief example.

p. 176. *The Grand Question Debated.* F.ii.266. I have not reprinted Faulkner's introductory note, called 'The Preface to the English Edition', which mentions the 'North of Ireland' background of the poem, the incorrect manuscripts that run about, and the annotation that has been added to explain 'some expressions peculiar to Ireland'.

p. 182. *Drapier's Hill.* F.ii.290.

p. 183. *To Dean Swift.* F.xiii.317. By Swift.

p. 184. *Robin and Harry.* F.xiii.325. Williams (*Poems*, p. 877) prints from Swift's MS., which is dated August 4, 1729. The subjects are Robert and Henry Leslie, sons of Charles, the non-juror; Swift visited them at Market Hill. Henry, who had seen service in the Spanish army, was married to a Spanish woman.

p. 186. *A Pastoral Dialogue.* F.ii.252. A transcript in the Welbeck MSS. is dated September 20, 1729.

p. 189. *The Revolution &c.* F.ii.296.

p. 192. *A Panegyric &c.* F.ii.304.

p. 203. *The Dean's Reasons &c.* F.xiii.318. A transcript in the Forster Collection is dated September, 1730.

p. 207. *Daphne.* F.xiii.323. The subject is Lady Acheson.

p. 209. *Impersonal Satires.* Many of the poems brought together under this heading deal with the kind of women that Stella and Vanessa according to the poems addressed to them, are not. Swift's pre-occupation with these opposite numbers while writing to women he admired is remarkable. The first three are among the poems Stella copied (see p. 393). After her death the satire becomes increasingly offensive and remote from reality.

p. 211. *A Quiet Life &c.* F.ii.178.

p. 213. *Phyllis &c.* F.ii.96.

p. 216. *The Progress of Beauty.* F.ii.105.

p. 219. *The Progress of Marriage.* F.xiii.346. Williams (*Poems*, p. 289) prints from Swift's MS., which is dated January 1721–2. Swift confides to this unpublished poem his opinion of the marriage late in life of Benjamin Pratt, Dean of Down and former Provost of Trinity College, Dublin, to a young heiress who in little more than twelve months was a widow. Pratt was acquainted with Vanessa and served as executor to her brother, Bartholomew, who died in 1715. Swift had known him since their college days.

p. 224. *Pethox the Great.* F.ii.148.

ll. 73–80. *The Britons, once a savage Kind.* Cf. *Gulliver's Travels*, Book iii, Chapter viii (written at about this time): 'How the pox under all its Consequences and Denominations had altered every Lineament of an *English* Countenance; shortened the Size of Bodies, unbraced the Nerves, relaxed the Sinews and Muscles, introduced a sallow Complexion, and rendered the Flesh loose and *rancid.*'

p. 228. *The Furniture of a Woman's Mind.* F.ii.248. Elrington Ball (*Swift's Verse*, p. 224) describes this poem as a 'study' for the next, which 'superseded' it; but the differences are considerable. This is a character; whereas the *Journal* is what it describes itself to be, 'The Annals of a Female Day'.

p. 230. *The Journal of a Modern Lady.* F.ii.255. This poem does not reveal the fact that it was written at

Market Hill with Lady Acheson as subject. Hence its position here.

p. 238. *Death and Daphne.* F.ii.324. Like *The Journal*, this poem is known to portray Lady Acheson of Market Hill, but has no recognizable connection with the place. It was long supposed to have Mrs. Laetitia Pilkington, the Dublin poetess, as its subject.

p. 242. *To Betty the Grizette.* F.ii.328.

l. 13. *Sets of Phrases, cut and dry.* Cf. the opening lines of *The Furniture of a Woman's Mind*, p. 228.

p. 243. *The Lady's Dressing-Room.* F.ii.318.

p. 247. *A Beautiful Young Nymph &c.* F.ii.342.

p. 250. *Strephon and Chloe.* F.ii.345.

p. 259. *Cassinus and Peter.* F.ii.356.

p. 263. *Apollo &c.* F.ii.330.

p. 265. *Trifles.* The light-hearted pieces that testify to Swift's renewed interest in versifying around 1718 are the work, often barely distinguishable, of himself and his Irish friends. The Vice in this verse warfare was the young Dublin schoolmaster, the Rev. Thomas Sheridan, 'the David of the clerical Saul', who not only versified tirelessly himself but was the cause of verse in others. Less energetic and occasionally serious was the Rev. Patrick Delany, a fellow of Trinity College, Dublin, like Sheridan twenty years younger than Swift. George and John ('Nimrod') Rochfort were hosts to the circle at Gaulstown House (see *The Part of a Summer*, p. 596). The Rev. Daniel Jackson acquired a measure of fame because of his nose, which is the subject of more than a dozen poems. Others, including Stella, occasionally took a hand in the trifles, but most were written by Sheridan on the one hand and the 'human compound quadrifarious' George Nim-Dan-Dean Esq., usually Swift alone, on the other. I have suppressed poems not by Swift except where their inclusion adds to the interest or continuity of what was a serial and manifold outflow, in good company, of sheer high spirits.

pp. 267–84. *On Dan Jackson's Picture* ... *The Last Speech &c.* Of this group of fifteen poems, all are from F.xi.373–89, except *On the Same*, p. 267, *The Pardon*, p. 281, and *The Last Speech &c.*, p. 284, from *Works*, ed. Scott, xv. 81–95.

pp. 286–7. *The Reverend Dr. Sheridan* ... *Dean Swift's Answer &c.* The source of these two poems is F.vi.192–3.

pp. 288–93. *Dr. Sheridan's Reply &c.* ... *The Dean to Thomas Sheridan.* The source of these five poems is *Works*, ed. Scott, xv. 57–63.

p. 294. *A Left-Handed Letter &c.* F.xi.436.

pp. 296–303. *To the Dean of St. Patrick's* ... *Sheridan's Reply.* The source of these eight poems is *Works*, ed. Scott, xv. 43–54, 100–1. Williams does not print the three poems on pp. 298–9. The first of these, by Sheridan, introduces the 'eyes' theme, which Swift plays upon in *To Thomas Sheridan*, p. 300, and *Sheridan, A Goose*, p. 302. *Sheridan's Reply*, p. 303, closes the 'eyes' group.

p. 304. *Mary the Cook-Maid's Letter &c.* F.ii.164.

p. 306. *A Letter to the Reverend Dr. Sheridan.* F.vi.190.

p. 307. *The Answer. Works*, ed. Scott, 1824, xv. 59.

p. 308. *From Dr. Swift to Dr. Sheridan.* F.viii.384. Faulkner accidentally omitted *l.* 2, which appears in other editions.

p. 311. *A Letter from Dr. Sheridan to Dr. Swift.* F.xiii.329.

p. 311. *Dr. Swift's Answer to Dr. Sheridan.* F.xiii.330.

p. 313. *Upon Stealing a Crown &c.* F.viii.336.

p. 313. *The Dean's Answer.* F.viii.337.

p. 314. *A Copy of Verses &c.* F.xi.392.

p. 315. *George Nim-Dan-Dean, Esq; to Mr. Sheridan.* F.viii.351. Faulkner's title is 'To Dr. Sheridan'. But

he printed the poem again, xi. 393, with the preceding poem, which it answers, this time giving the title
adopted here for use with the earlier text. Williams
apparently overlooked the earlier text, printing this
and the preceding poem from F.xi.392–3. These are
the verbal variants: *l.* 1 gentle] loving *l.* 2 such] so
l. 5 Silver] gentle *ll.* 9–10] *omitted l.* 13 I] we *l.* 15
Stations] Station *l.* 35 *Grief*] Cost *l.* 52 twenty Lines
exceed fourscore;] forty Lines, exceed fourscore.

p. 317. *George Nim-Dan-Dean's Invitation to Mr.
Thomas Sheridan.* F.xiii.362.

p. 318. *To George Nim-Dan-Dean, Esq.* F.xiii.366.

p. 320. *To Mr. Thomas Sheridan &c.* F.xiii.369.

p. 321. *Sheridan to Swift. Works*, ed. Scott, xv. 102.

p. 322. *Swift to Sheridan. Works*, ed. Scott, xv. 102.

p. 322. *Poetical Epistle to Dr. Sheridan. Works*, ed.
Scott, x. 573. Not collected by Williams. Scott
notes: 'From the original manuscript in possession
of Leonard Macnally, Esq. Barrister at Law,
Dublin.'

p. 324. *On the Five Ladies &c.* F.ii.250. The trifles
revive only fitfully after Stella's death, which broke
the deanery circle. The 'doctor' in the title is
Sheridan.

p. 326. *The Five Ladies Answer &c.* F.xiii.327.

p. 327. *The Beau's Reply &c.* F.xiii.328.

p. 327. *Ballyspellin.* F.xi.420.

p. 330. *The Answer.* F.xi.423.

p. 332. *To Dr. Helsham.* F.viii.453. Helsham was for
many years Swift's physician. He wrote verses, of
course.

p. 334. *To Dr. Sheridan.* F.viii.453.

p. 334. *Addenda Quædam.* F.viii.443. From Swift's
letter to Sheridan, June 5, 1736, in which these
'*addenda quædam*' to Sheridan's description of life at
Cavan are set as prose.

p. 335. *A Satyr &c.* F.viii.451. This distich, from

Swift's letter to Sheridan, April 9, 1737, is collected here for the first time.

p. 335. *Anglo-Latin Verses.* F.viii.460; xvi.13–14 (App.).

p. 337. *A Cantata.* F.viii.467. Swift's words, ridiculing musical imitations of sounds, were set by Dr. John Echlin, who was his consultant on matters affecting the cathedral choir.

p. 341. *Riddles.* F.ii.181–97. The answers to these nine riddles are: a pen, gold, gold, the posteriors, a horn, a corkscrew, a privy, louse to his patron (anagram of 'Louisa to Strephon'), and a maypole.

p. 353. *More Riddles.* F.viii.341–51. The answers to these thirteen riddles are: the moon, a cannon, the gallows, snow, a circle, ink, time, the vowels, the five senses, a fountain, an echo, reflection in a mirror, and a pair of dice.

p. 360. *A Riddle ... Answered.* F.xi.426–8.

p. 362. *To Dr. Sheridan.* F.viii.456. A string of riddles with these answers: *l.* 2, a swine; *l.* 4, a swallow; *l.* 7, a stallion; *l.* 9, a sail; *l.* 11, a spaniel; *l.* 13, a spur; *l.* 15, a soul; *l.* 17, a sloven; *l.* 20, a salad; *l.* 22, a slip; *l.* 24, a sparrow; *l.* 26, a saddle; *l.* 28, a style; *l.* 30, a slice; *l.* 32, a spy; *l.* 34, a spavin; *l.* 36, a spit; *l.* 38, a skewer; *l.* 40, assault; *l.* 42, a smock.

p. 364. *Probatur Aliter.* F.viii.458. Another string, with these answers: *l.* 2, a shovel; *l.* 6, aspiring; *l.* 8, a switch; *l.* 10, a skewer; *l.* 12, a sparable; *l.* 14, a shock; *l.* 16, a sloven (Ass-Louvain); *l.* 18, asperse; *l.* 20, a soul; *l.* 22, a slice; *l.* 24, a scar; *l.* 26, a swallow; *l.* 28, a sty; *l.* 30, a sink; *l.* 32, a slam; *l.* 34, a slate; *l.* 36, a swine; *l.* 38, askew; *l.* 40, a saddle; *l.* 42, a smock; *l.* 44, a spur; *l.* 46, assault; *l.* 48, a snail.

p. 369. *Ad Amicum &c.* F.ii.387.

p. 370. *Carberiæ Rupes.* F.ii.389.

p. 371. *Carbery Rocks.* F.ii.390.

p. 373. *Fabula Canis et Umbræ.* F.xiii.352.